Once in Golconda

Wiley Investment Classics

Once in Golconda

A True Drama of Wall Street
1920–1938

John Brooks

John Wiley & Sons, Inc.

New York • Chichester • Weinheim • Brisbane • Singapore • Toronto

Library of Congress Cataloging-in-Publication Data:

Brooks, John, 1920–
    Once in Golconda : a true drama of Wall Street, 1920–1938 / John
Brooks.
        p.   cm.
    Includes bibliographical references and index.
    ISBN 0-471-35753-7 (cloth : alk. paper)—ISBN 0-471-35752-9
(pbk. : alk. paper)
        1. New York Stock Exchange—History. 2. Wall Street—History.
    3. Stock exchanges—United States—History.   I. Title.
HG4572.B7   1999
332.64'273—dc21   99-33868

Foreword

"Golconda, now a ruin, was a city in Southeastern India where, according to legend, everyone who passed through got rich." Its riches faded, its fine buildings collapsed, and its glories disappeared, never to return.

That tends to be the way with legendary sources of unimaginable wealth. They flourish for a time, and then they go forever. There's one exception. It's called Wall Street, a name that strictly speaking applies only to a narrow gully in the south of Manhattan, but that can be taken as a proxy for Tokyo, London, and other financial markets everywhere.

Unlike Golconda, Wall Street can come back from the dead. Although slumps follow booms, the grass never quite gets to grow over its pavements. It's a concrete tribute to the human spirit—to ingenuity, to dynamism, to creativity, and, from time to time, to the willing suspension of disbelief. In the high wild times that occur every generation or so, when everyone makes money and it seems like a crime not to be rich, investors forget the lessons that their predecessors learned so painfully. They know, with *absolute* certainty, that this time it is going to be different.

In this book, John Brooks—who was one of the most elegant of all business writers—perfectly catches the flavor of one of history's best-known financial dramas: the 1929 crash and its aftershocks. It's packed with parallels and parables for the modern reader.

The great bull market of the 1920s was built on the growth of a completely new industry, based in Detroit as opposed to the Silicon Valley. It created a breed of business heroes, who passed easily from the top of big investment banks into the upper ranks of government. The most successful investments were to be found in a relatively small number of big companies. And it promised a new economic paradigm.

As President Coolidge explained at the end of 1927, America was "entering upon a new era of prosperity." Speculation became respectable, and Wall Streeters generated the kind of glamour that goes with being an insider on the subject that everyone wants to talk about. In the perceptive words of an English journalist who arrived on the scene just before everything went wrong, "If the attitude of Americans to the stock market proved anything, it proved that they believed in miracles. That if you try hard enough, you can make wonderful things happen." Then came the crash of 1929. Share prices recovered a bit the following year, before reaching a point that they were not to see again for nearly a quarter of a century.

The central character in Brooks's story is Richard H. Whitney, who starts out at the top of the Wall Street establishment and ends up in Sing Sing. His story is an extreme example of another recurring feature of financial cycles: Bull markets create heroes and have a wonderful way of covering up mistakes, and worse.

Heroes can all too often come to believe that the rules don't apply to them, especially if they live and work in a narrow community securely cordoned off from the little people. That's when the temptations start.

Richard Whitney didn't start out to be a criminal—the very notion of robbing a bank would have horrified this lofty and fastidious figure. Instead, he bent the rules, little by little, in the fond belief that the rising tide of the stock market would put everything right. When it didn't, he bent the rules some more. Even when he was exposed, his friends were unwilling to admit the truth.

In the words of a top man at J. P. Morgan, "It never occurred to me that Richard Whitney was a thief. What occurred to me was that he had gotten into a terrible jam."

I first read *Once in Golconda* back in the 1970s, during those long dull years when the Dow was struggling to break decisively through the 1,000 mark and when Wall Street was a place where you went to get your bonds underwritten. It seemed at the time like a wonderful fairy story, peopled by characters out of Scott Fitzgerald. Brooks's stories—the bomb outrage of 1920, the marvelous story of the bear raid on the Stutz Motor Car Company of America—stayed in my memory.

But I regarded those tales as artifacts from a distant age, with as much relevance to anything that was ever likely to happen again as the story of Golconda.

Rereading it in 1999, though, I'm not so sure.

RICHARD LAMBERT
The Financial Times

Contents

ONCE IN GOLCONDA

Golconda, now a ruin, was a city
in southeastern India where,
according to legend, everyone who
passed through got rich. A similar
legend attached to Wall Street
between the wars.

Chapter One

Overture:
The Outrage

I

On Thursday, September 16, 1920, a few seconds after the Trinity Church bell had finished tolling noon, the pleasant fall air of downtown Manhattan (weather clear, temperature sixty-nine degrees, market up slightly) was rent by an enormous and devastating explosion. Emanating from a point on Wall Street a few yards east of the intersection of Wall and Broad, and directly between the marble edifice of J. P. Morgan & Company and the barred front of the brand-new United States Assay Office—that is to say, from the precise center, geographical as well as metaphorical, of financial America and even of the financial world—the explosion darkened the area for several minutes with a huge cloud of greenish smoke, set fire to awnings twelve stories above the street, broke virtually every window in the immediate vicinity and some as much as a half-mile away, and spattered a wide area with hundreds of small, shrapnel-like iron slugs that, on later examination, appeared to be

1

fragments of cut-up window sash weights. It pock-marked the austere façade of the Morgan building, at 23 Wall Street, on the southeast corner of the intersection, and blew in all of its north windows, causing a hail of glass fragments to fall on persons on the banking floor below. It bent the heavy bars protecting the Assay Office, on the north side of Wall next to the Sub-Treasury; this building largely escaped interior damage precisely because it had been designed to be a fortress. It shook to the foundations, but by miracle or chance did not materially damage, Wall Street's own church, Trinity, which stood, flanked by its famous old grave-yard containing the bones of Alexander Hamilton, only a short block from the point of explosion. The toppling of Trinity's Gothic Revival spire, had it occurred, would have symbolized the disruption of things as they were as much as the defacing of Morgan's itself.

At the New York Stock Exchange, on Broad Street near the southwest corner of the intersection with Wall, the blast sent hundreds of brokers and traders surging to the center of the trading floor in an effort to avoid glass falling from the room's huge windows; there, driven from Scylla to Charybdis, they were confronted with the prospect of mass extinction by the great glass dome overhead, which threatened to fall but didn't. At the Bankers Trust Company, on the northwest corner, broken glass flew like leaves in a gale, and one of the iron slugs whizzed through the office window of Seward Prosser, the bank's president, missing his head by a few inches.

Others were less fortunate than Prosser. Thirty persons were killed instantly or nearly so by the explosion, and injuries befell some three hundred more, of whom ten died later. But none of the dead were the kings and generals of finance, all of whose lives seemed to be as charmed with good fortune as Prosser's. J. P. Morgan, the most famous man in Wall Street and the public symbol of its power, was on holiday in an English country house; of the five of his partners who were in the building when it was hit, all escaped injury except Morgan's son Junius, who suffered a minor cut. Of the thirty who died at once, none were brokerage partners or senior bank executives, and only one was identified as a broker. Most of the others were Wall Street's attendants and privates, young or old—the stenographers, clerks, bookkeepers, messengers, and porters who with untimely appetite had stepped out of their buildings a minute or two before noon on their way to an early lunch. Three were women, four were teen-age clerks or messengers, one was a young banker of twenty-five, another was a retired businessman of sixty-eight. The value of the securities lost in the confusion was negligible, and as to property damage, which amounted to two or three million dollars, the owners of the buildings or their insurance companies could easily enough absorb that. Whatever the meaning of the explosion, it left Wall Street's power unscathed.

II

Wall Street in 1920 had been the world's principal money center for just about six years. Its triumph had been accomplished under the most humiliating circumstances imaginable—that is, by default, and at a moment when it was flat on its back and gasping for breath. For a century before the First World War, the City of London had been the world's banker and had called the tune in the world's money matters; financing for large American enterprises had usually come in whole or in part from London or from continental Europe via London, and Wall Street, while significant enough domestically, had in international matters served chiefly as a mere broker between American enterprise and transatlantic capital. Then in August, 1914, in the first weeks of the war, Britain appalled the financial world by suspending gold payments against pounds sterling—an action which, in that heyday of the international gold standard, was as if the most feared, respected, and trusted player in a poker game had suddenly announced that he found it necessary to quit the game and refuse to redeem his markers. Along with the Exchequer's subsequent decision to forbid all British investments outside the Empire, the action meant, as the London *Times* admitted, "temporary abandonment of our historic claim as an international money centre," and made it inevitable that "much of the international business we have been accustomed to do should pass to . . . the United States"—which nation, the *Times* declared grimly, "is capable of doing it."

3

If so, just barely. So great was British financial influence in the United States that London's abdication was as paralyzing to Wall Street as if the fighting had broken out in Philadelphia or Detroit. The day war began, stocks crashed sickeningly on the New York Stock Exchange; the following day the Exchange, which had never in its long history been closed for more than ten consecutive days, suspended trading for what was to be a period of nearly nine months. Moreover, there was near-panic in New York banking circles. United States businessmen in their international dealings were net debtors to the extent of more than three billion dollars, almost all of the creditors being from European countries that had become belligerents; these creditors now not only demanded their money but, in the time-honored tradition of creditors in wartime, demanded it in gold. Meanwhile, alarmed bank depositors at home made matters worse by rushing to withdraw their balances. In the first two weeks of the war enough money was taken out of New York banks to bring them to a condition almost as precarious as at the height of the great Panic of 1907. All that autumn, gold drained out of the Treasury, most of it to Canada for London's account, at a frightening rate. With domestic business in shock and foreign trade at a standstill because German destroyers were thought to be watching the ocean highways, Wall Street was almost a ghost town—its banks teetering, its Stock Exchange and brokerage offices closed, and only a handful of "outlaw brokers" defying the Exchange by informally maintaining an "outlaw" stock market outdoors on New Street, where they traded a few issues at panic prices. Thus, the new champion of world finance.

But Wall Street, thanks largely to the circumstance that it was the United States' role to finance and supply the war rather than be bankrupted or devastated by it, quickly grew into its new role. In November, 1914, the gold outflow slackened, in December it ceased, and in January, 1915, a reverse flow began. The Stock Exchange resumed normal operations that April. American loans to the Allies were increasing, and would soon amount to billions; the American export trade, consisting largely of war supplies, but also including huge amounts of food, feed, and cotton, was beginning an expansion that would continue until 1917 at a rate unparalleled in the commercial history of nations; and along with all that, European countries were sending their gold to New York for safekeeping even when they were not sending it in payment for guns. What began as a westward trickle of gold in early 1915 within a year or so became a torrent; for the single month of March, 1916, the United States imported almost as much gold as in any previous entire year. Overnight, as such things go, the world had taken its money out of one bank and put it into another—and not temporarily, since by the time Britain was finally able to resume gold payments in 1925, it was far too late to regain her status.

By 1920 Wall Street had the power to do London's old job, with plenty to spare. The United States, having financed a year and a half of participation in the war largely by selling bonds internally, had changed from a three-billion-dollar international debtor to a three-billion-dollar creditor. The Treasury was sitting on something like one-third of the world's monetary gold supply. The predicted postwar national depression had arrived, but was mild compared to the time of bankruptcies and bread lines that had been predicted. Wall Street even had an inadvertent benefit of the war in a horde of new customers—citizens whose purchases of Liberty Bonds seemed to have given them an enduring taste for investing. Wall Street was sitting pretty, but was still wholly lacking in the imperial self-assurance of its fallen predecessor.

Its lack of self-assurance was to be dramatically shown in its response to the event of noon, September 16.

III

The first local reactions, naturally enough, were individual rather than social or political. Survivors on the street first fled the scene in wild confusion, filling the air with their screams and stumbling over the bodies of the dead and injured; then, in a matter of minutes, their curiosity overcame their fear of a second explosion and they surged tidally back, joined by thousands of others pouring out of the surrounding buildings. Within five minutes there were ten thousand persons milling around the area. Underfoot, the injured cried out for self-protection if not for first aid. A badly hurt boy runner, as foolishly dutiful as Casabianca, pleaded for someone to

5

take charge of the bundle of securities he was carrying so that he could die with his job performed—as he did. A clerk in Schulte's cigar store, at 36 Wall Street, reacting according to habit acquired when he had been in the Army in France, clapped his felt hat on his head in lieu of a steel helmet. The president of the Stock Exchange walked calmly but rapidly (running was forbidden on the Exchange floor) from where he was standing to the rostrum overlooking the floor and rang the gong there, suspending trading for the day within one minute after the explosion. The New York Curb Exchange, which at the time still operated outdoors on Broad Street a couple of hundred feet from the site of the explosion, needed no gong to announce its closing, since its place of business had suddenly been transformed into a mob scene and many of its brokers, stunned or injured, were fighting for their physical rather than their financial hides. Platoons of policemen and doctors from nearby hospitals struggled to get to the fallen victims; a few minutes later came federal troops from Governors Island, who soon succeeded in clearing the immediate area and roping it off.

The cavernous interior of J. P. Morgan & Company, the office most seriously affected, was a shambles of broken glass, knocked-over desks, scattered papers, and the twisted remains of some steel-wire screens that the firm had providentially installed over its windows not long before, and that undoubtedly prevented far worse carnage than actually took place. One Morgan employee was dead, another would die of his wounds the next day, and dozens more were seriously injured. Junius Morgan, sitting at his desk near the north windows on the ground floor, had been pitched forward by the blast and then nicked by falling glass. The press reported that his cut was on the hand, but this was probably an example of the kind of genteel euphemism characteristic of the press in 1920; his surviving former partners later insisted the cut was on the backside. In any case, he himself, after being treated at Broad Street Hospital, announced gallantly that he had "escaped injury." Another young Morgan man, William Ewing, was knocked unconscious, and awoke a few minutes later to find his head wedged into a wastebasket.

The firm's senior partner after J. P. Morgan himself, Henry P. Davison, happened to be out of the building at the time. The other four partners present were fortunate in their situation. They were

Thomas W. Lamont, soon to succeed Davison as Morgan's right hand; Dwight W. Morrow, later to be Ambassador to Mexico and a leading national political figure; Elliott Bacon, member of another Morgan family powerful in national affairs; and Bacon's relative by marriage, George Whitney—a fast-rising young member of the firm, and the brother of another fast-rising young man of Wall Street, the bond broker Richard Whitney. These four were in conference in the elder Morgan's room on the building's second floor, directly on the corner of Broad and Wall; since the room's windows face west and it presents only a fortress-like, windowless wall to the north, they were safe. In view of the unexpectedness of the explosion they can hardly be accused of huddling like cowardly generals in a safe bunker during an attack; nonetheless, such may have been the assumption of an actual general who was among them—a visiting French military dignitary who was Morrow's guest, and who, as the echo of the blast died away, smoke billowed up outside, and glass could be heard tinkling down everywhere, inquired of the partners, "Does this happen often?"

All that afternoon, the police and the federal troops, assisted by some five hundred ex-service men who volunteered their efforts, worked at giving the wounded first aid and getting them into ambulances, and at controlling the crowd, which soon grew to something like forty thousand. Much of the crowd remained into the night—or perhaps it was renewed by new arrivals after the closing of offices uptown—to watch the work of cleaning up debris and boarding up broken windows being carried out in a blaze of arc lights. A grim, exultantly embattled spirit pervaded the leaders of New York finance that night, and was communicated to the mob in the street; the essence of the spirit was: "Back to work tomorrow. The Reds will be defied."

Few seem to have doubted for a moment that the explosion had been a bomb planted by radicals of one stripe or another, although in fact the evidence that was immediately available was equivocal. Witnesses to the events immediately preceding it could agree on hardly anything, but there did seem to be a consensus among them that at about 11:55 an old single-top wagon—red, yellow, or green in different versions—drawn by an even more antiquated dark bay horse, had proceeded along Wall Street and come to a stop in front

7

of the Assay Office. Some went further and said that they had seen kegs or boxes, presumably containing dynamite, in the wagon, but none who immediately came forward could describe the driver or drivers, nor say what he or they had done after the wagon had stopped. Some of this evidence was corroborated by the remains found at the site—parts of a dismembered horse, including two hooves with shoes on them, and fragments of the axles and wheel hubs of the wagon. But none of this established or even suggested whether the blast had been a bomb or an accident. On one side of the question, a casualty said in his dying breaths that he had seen a wagon clearly labeled "Du Pont" overturn in the street; his testimony was supported after a fashion, although not a reassuring one, by others who said they had seen a wagon marked with the names of various other well-known manufacturers of explosives—Hercules Powder Company in one case, Dittmar Powder Company in another, Aetna Explosives Company in a third. Assuming that the wagon had belonged to *some* powder company, it was logical to suppose that the explosion had resulted from an accident to a shipment intended for a demolition project, of which there were several under way in the downtown area and one directly on the southwest corner of Broad and Wall, where the Stock Exchange was building an extension. Unfortunately for this thesis, though, all of the companies mentioned were able to show that they had had no horse-drawn wagons in the area that day, and Du Pont's spokesman went on to offer a possible basis for the witnesses' garbled testimony in the fact that a Du Pont motor truck, duly marked, and carrying not explosives but pigments, had passed a few blocks from Wall Street late that morning.

The evidence of a bomb consisted principally of the cut-up pieces of sash weights that had rained on the surroundings and caused much of the damage and many of the casualties; the police eventually collected over five hundred pounds of these destructive fragments, and it seemed beyond reason that a conveyance transporting explosives for innocent purposes might also have happened to be carrying such an eccentric load. But even more persuasive to many people, in the charged atmosphere of the time, were the implications of the precise location of the blast. The implications were more than symbolic. On the day in question, nine-tenths of a billion dollars in gold, in the form of small bars each weighing about twenty-five pounds and neatly packed in a wooden box, were being moved under armed guard from their old repository in the Sub-Treasury Building to a new one in the Assay Office next door. The workmen were carrying the gold along a wooden ramp crossing the narrow alleyway between the two buildings, and the spot in the street where the explosion occurred was almost directly opposite this alleyway. As it happened, at noon the porters of the treasure and their guards had just quit for lunch and withdrawn into the buildings, clanging shut the well-barred side entrances after them. They thus had escaped almost certain death and, it is possible to speculate, prevented a spectacular raid on the United States Treasury. The loss of all or most of the gold might have created the kind of instant world financial chaos more common in wild-eyed fiction than in life.

Such chaos bred of violence, many Americans were convinced, was just what the forces of radicalism were bent on bringing about; for more than a year the country had been in the grip of a Red scare in some ways comparable to that of the later era of McCarthy. In 1920 "bomb" meant "Red"—more often than not, "foreign Red"—and vice versa. But one way in which the period differed from the McCarthy era was that so many of the bombs of 1919 had been real. That April, bombs intended to explode when the packages containing them were opened were mailed to eighteen prominent persons, among them the mayor of Seattle, who had an antilabor record; the United States Commissioner General of Immigration; a judge famous for having sentenced two radical leaders; the Attorney General of the United States, A. Mitchell Palmer; the Secretary of Labor, William B. Wilson; and the owners of the two most familiar names in finance, John D. Rockefeller and J. P. Morgan. (Most of the bombs failed to reach their destinations for the wonderfully humdrum reason that they were delayed in the New York City Post Office, and therefore discovered, on account of insufficient postage.) A few days later, thrown or planted bombs exploded in Cleveland, Philadelphia, Pittsburgh, New York, and other places, and the anonymous enemies of Palmer—a stubborn

9

Quaker driven by political ambition and a fanatic's zeal, who was bent on making himself the nation's leading radical-fighter—took another shot at him, this time not relying on the Post Office; his house in Washington was heavily damaged by a bomb, but no one was hurt except its thrower, who was killed. Having appointed William J. Flynn and Francis P. Garvan, two of the country's most celebrated detectives, to his department's two key police posts—head of the Bureau of Investigation and assistant in charge of Red-hunting—Palmer that autumn launched a terror campaign against radicals that reached its apogee on the night of January 2, 1920, when, in an elaborately planned system of simultaneous raids, more than four thousand persons suspected of being radicals were summarily arrested in thirty-three different cities. For the most part, the public cheered and hailed Palmer as the nation's savior, even after most of the suspects had been released for lack of evidence.

On the night of September 16, "federal, state, and city authorities were agreed that the devastating blast signaled the long-threatened Red outrages," reported the *Times,* and the conclusion was apparently the same from coast to coast. Police cordons had quickly been thrown around the financial districts of Chicago, Boston, and Philadelphia; police buildings, storehouses of wealth, and prominent men had been put under guard in various cities; thirty detectives encircled J. P. Morgan's residence on Madison Avenue, even though he wasn't there; and Flynn, the FBI chief, had already arrived in New York by express train from Washington and was directing the operations of a staff of investigators. Moreover, the news from Washington was that Palmer and Garvan were on their way.

The following day, September 17, the federal men let it be known that they had come up with—or rather, had had fall into their laps—a classic clue to the nature of the crime, though not to the identity of the criminals. The New York Post Office turned over to them five sheets of paper that had been found loose and with no address in a mailbox at the corner of Cedar Street and Broadway, a two-minute walk from Broad and Wall. On them was crudely printed by means of rubber stamps, with smudges and misspellings that varied from one to another, the incoherent but still lucid message:

Remember
We will not tolerate
any longer
Free the political
prisoners or it will be
sure death for all of you

American Anarchist Fighters

These circulars, the postal authorities told the Justice Department men, had been put in the mailbox on the day of the explosion some time between the 11:30 collection and the next one at 11:58. Since they had been deposited there immediately before the explosion rather than after it and therefore could not represent an effort of anarchists to claim credit for someone else's work, and since, moreover, they were almost identical to some circulars that had been found after some of the 1919 bombings, the papers, unless they had been planted as a red herring, would seem to have represented all but clinching evidence that the explosion had been of an anarchist bomb. But, as other events before and since 1920 have shown, acts of public violence may engage many people's emotions in such a way as to make them incapable of accepting facts that are irrefutable or explanations that are logically obvious—may compel them, in effect, to reject the actual crime and create in their imaginations another one nearer to their hearts' desire. In this case Wall Street, and a good deal of the rest of the country, seems to have wanted the blast to be proved an anarchist bomb, all right, but not to have the question closed so quickly and unceremoniously; instead, it wanted with word and act to argue heatedly the case for an un-American plot, and that is what it did.

IV

The arc lights finally went out at dawn on the seventeenth, and Wall Street prepared to go back to work, not in a mood of "business as usual" but in one of defiance and patriotism. At Morgan's, epitome of the Anglophile, stiff-upper-lip Wall Street style, as opposed to the more flamboyant manner characteristic of the Stock

11

Exchange across the street, great sheets of canvas had been stretched over the shattered windows, a scaffolding buttressed the weakened dome over the banking floor, and what with executives sporting bandaged arms, legs, and heads, and clerks operating typewriters and adding machines with one good hand, the place had the air of an accident ward quietly undergoing occupational therapy. The Stock Exchange, assured by its engineers that the building was safe for occupancy, opened at its usual time, but without the usual heavy-handed joking among the floor brokers and traders, who, according to the *Sun*, had grim expressions and firmly set jaws. Brokerage houses wired their customers reassuring bulletins during the hour before the opening, to allay any panic. But no panic materialized; during the first hour of trading prices rose on the heaviest turnover in more than a month, some issues advancing as much as ten points. As the day proceeded and the firm tone remained, confidence grew, and a leading brokerage house changed the burden of its telegraphed messages from bulletins of reassurance to Fourth-of-July fulminations with pronounced political overtones. "Six years of continuous warfare; millions of dead and crippled," came ticking into the branch offices of this firm.

> Upon this ghastly foundation stand men and women of distorted mind, who have been preaching radicalism and appealing to every debauched mind. These have received courteous attention instead of deserved punishment. . . . Each found many defenders in high places. . . . What more natural result than an effort on the part of these radicals to destroy lives and property in America's financial center? . . . Young men and women working for a living have been the victims of this foul conspiracy. And as for the effect on the stock market, I believe that the market will be stronger than it was. Law and order will prevail and business will continue to make progress.

That evening the *Sun* wrote: "The consensus of Wall Street might well be summed up in this wire."

By coincidence the Sons of the American Revolution had previously scheduled for that day a celebration of the hundred and thirty-third anniversary of the adoption of the Constitution, and so precisely at noon—"the murder hour," as the *Times* put it—a crowd of thousands gathered at the base of the George Washington statue in front of the Sub-Treasury Building, a few feet from a shallow indentation in the pavement of Wall Street made by the explosion. After all had sung "America," boaters held over hearts, a brigadier general of the 79th Division declaimed, "Yesterday one of the greatest outrages ever committed against society was perpetrated on the very spot on which we stand. Are we, as American citizens, going to close our eyes to things like that? I say no, a thousand times no!"

"No!" roared back the crowd.

The general went on, "Those who would do such a thing should be killed every time they show their heads. They should be killed like a snake!"

"Yes!" roared the crowd, whereupon a member of it sprang forward and led everybody in the National Anthem, which hadn't been on the program. Noticing, as the gathering broke up, that the Washington statue was untouched except for a nick or two on its base, some spoke of a miraculous portent. All in all, it was a great day in the Street.

V

For days following the blast, the press, the clergy, and an assortment of political voices viewed "the outrage," as it became known by common consent, as the responsibility of everyone from the "blood-crazed proletariat" to the Wilson Administration. New York City offered a bounty of $10,500 for information leading to the arrest of the perpetrators, and the Burns Detective Agency, believed to be acting for J. P. Morgan & Company, upped the ante by $50,000. Preaching to an unexpectedly huge congregation at Trinity on Sunday morning, the Reverend Dr. William T. Manning, Rector, took occasion to get several things off his chest. Besides the plotters themselves, he said, "there is another class which needs to be rightly dealt with—those who call themselves intellectuals and make themselves safe by declaring that they do not advocate force." It may be safely presumed that the congregation nodded in grim assent.

The spokesmen for the American radical movement seemed to find the whole affair a source of considerable amusement. The

13

secretary of the New York Defense Committee of the most powerful and most feared radical organization, the Industrial Workers of the World, issued a prompt statement in which he expressed his organization's regret that so many people had been killed or injured, and added that, no matter what anyone might say, the IWW "has other things to do than to mix in such stuff." The Russian-language *Russky Golos* said a couple of days after the explosion, "People of the eighteenth century used to say that if there was no God it would be necessary to invent one. In the twentieth century, it is believed that if there are no bomb plots they must be invented. And they are being invented."

No one of any political persuasion seemed to be doing himself any particular credit in reacting to the explosion, and that included the police, local and federal, whose accomplishments in the first few days after it consisted principally of the production of numerous suspects, most of them with foreign names and airtight alibis. The police questioned Carlo Tresca—the well-known Socialist leader, later to be tragically assassinated—but got nowhere. They also questioned one Alexander J. Brailovsky on the grounds that he was of Russian extraction, that he was "said to be a Trotsky-Lenin agent," and that an anonymous letter had reported him to have been seen standing at the corner of Pine and Nassau streets soon after the explosion, talking to three other men and—even worse—laughing. However, Brailovsky was able to prove that he hadn't been anywhere near Pine and Nassau streets that day, and he was released. A bit later, a Brooklyn man named Florean Zelenska was arrested because he possessed radical literature, had once been an employee of Hercules Powder, and had left his home at about eleven o'clock on the morning of September 16 carrying a reddish-yellow bag; it turned out that his destination had been a tailor shop where he worked and that the bag had contained his lunch. On the twenty-third Palmer's man Flynn summed up the first week's work on the case. "Our unshaken conviction is that talk of the disaster in Wall Street as being an accident is plain bunk," he declared. "We are not being diverted or deterred by rumors and reports of stray powder-wagons in the neighborhood or anything of that sort. It was a criminal outrage." "The government never sleeps and it never quits," he added, after a pause for breath.

VI

Sleepless and persevering, the government over the next few months hauled in suspects named Carusso, Abato, Ferro, Fasulo, Luigio, and De Fillipos. No firm evidence could be found against any of them. A few clues and leads gradually turned up. A farrier with a shop in New Chambers Street, not far from Wall Street, identified the shoes of the dismembered horse as his work, but could not recall anything about the man to whom he had sold them; later another farrier in Elizabeth Street insisted that *he* had made the shoes, and said that the horse's owner had been a young, short, barrel-chested, mustached Sicilian who had evidently been in a great hurry. A witness came forward with the information that he had seen the wagon just before the explosion and that its driver, who appeared to the witness to be a Jew, had dropped the reins, climbed down from the wagon's seat, hurried west to Nassau Street, and disappeared behind the Sub-Treasury just in time. Another witness, a Jewish peddler, countered with testimony that the driver had had a rich Scottish accent. Others who claimed to have seen the wagon assigned to its driver other national origins, religions, and modes of escape. Among those who seemed to be able to conjure up vivid and highly personal versions of the affair was one leader of Wall Street itself—Samuel B. Wellington, the septuagenarian president of the West Indies Trading Company, whose account succinctly epitomized the received view in Wall Street circles. Wellington told the police four days later that he had emerged from 37 Wall Street, on the south side a few doors east of J. P. Morgan & Company, at 11:58 on September 16—conveniently enough, he said, he had glanced at the Trinity Church clock on reaching the sidewalk—and had immediately heard a voice calling "Hurry up! Beat it! Get out of this!" Looking around, he had seen two men who looked to him like "East Side peddlers" near the corner of Wall and William streets, beckoning and calling the warnings to a third man, a "greasy fellow" of about sixty, who was beside a wagon in front of the Assay Office. The little tableau burst into motion as all three men began running toward William Street, and turned northward

15

up it; then the scene ended neatly in an unstaged blackout, because Mr. Wellington was knocked out cold by the explosion. Although nobody could be found to corroborate this story, it served perfectly for the revelation that Wall Street needed, and perhaps gained rather than lost force from the fact that the oracle had lapsed into unconsciousness immediately after experiencing his vision. But it did not help the police find a criminal.

One suspect, and indeed the leading one for a few days, was neither a Sicilian, a Jew, a Scot, an East Side peddler, nor a greasy fellow, but a middle-class professional man of Anglo-Saxon lineage with friends high in Wall Street. He was Edwin P. Fischer, a forty-two-year-old graduate of City College and New York Law School and a leading tennis player who had once ranked ninth nationally and had won the New York metropolitan singles championship three times. He had also twice been in mental hospitals, and had, in the days just before the Wall Street explosion, predicted it with hair-raising precision. About two weeks before it, Fischer had arrived early one morning at the West Side Tennis Club, then at Ninety-third Street and Amsterdam Avenue, and talked with the care-taker, Thomas Delehanty. After inveighing for a while—in a man-ner with which Delehanty was familiar from previous conversations with Fischer—against Wall Street in general and J. P. Morgan & Company in particular, he said in a tone of mystery, "Tom, I want to tell you a secret. We are going to blow up Wall Street on the fifteenth." Or maybe, Delehanty testified later, Fischer had said "*They* are going to blow up Wall Street"; he could not be certain on that point, but he *was* certain that he had thought no more about the matter because he considered that Fischer, while charm-ing, gentlemanly, and intelligent, was "a bit light in the head." A week or so after that, a passenger in a Hudson Tube train had encountered a stranger who was carrying a tennis racquet and whose description tallied with Fischer's, and who abruptly leaned forward and said, "Keep away from Wall Street until after the sixteenth. They have sixty thousand pounds of explosives and are going to blow it up." This seems to have been the only occasion when Fischer picked the right day, but over the next week he kept repeating the forecast—sometimes in writing—and scoring remark-ably near-misses as to the time. On September 11 he sent the follow-

16

ing postcard from Toronto to a Wall Street broker friend of his named George F. Ketledge: "Greetings. Get out of Wall Street as soon as the gong strikes at 3 o'clock Wednesday the fifteenth. Good luck. Ed." On the thirteenth he sent similar postcards to several other people who worked in the Wall Street area, including Léonce Arnaud, chief of the French High Commission, at 65 Broadway, where Fischer had been working until about a month earlier, and Sheppard Homans, a prominent insurance man, former partner of the soon-to-be-startled Mr. Prosser of the Bankers Trust and old friend of Fischer's. In each case he warned of a bomb in Wall Street on the afternoon of September 15, in Arnaud's case adding disarmingly, "It may be all bull," and more ominously, "Have a just grievance or so I think." For reasons similar to Delehanty's, none of the recipients took the warnings seriously.

In the Toronto hotel from which he sent the postcards Fischer was heard muttering about "millionaires who ought to be killed." He left it on September 14 to go to Niagara Falls, where he was overtaken on the evening of the sixteenth—the day of the explosion—by his brother-in-law, Robert A. Pope, who then knew nothing of the bomb warnings but had heard of the hotel threats and had immediately concluded that his relative was undergoing a mental breakdown. By the following morning Pope had learned of the bomb warnings, if not from Fischer himself then from the newspapers, which featured them in banner headlines; whichever the case, he persuaded Fischer to accompany him to Hamilton, Ontario, where they both had friends, and turn himself in to the authorities. On being questioned by them as to how he had predicted the explosion, Fischer replied, "I don't know where the message came from—through the air, I guess. . . . I know when anything awful is going to happen." He also described Wall Street as "the center of evil in the world." Oddly enough, Pope, whose sanity was not in question, unhesitatingly corroborated Fischer's view that he had psychic powers, and noted that the powers seemed to be particularly acute when his brother-in-law was in an abnormal mental condition.

Pending the arrival of United States authorities and the completion of extradition proceedings, Fischer was held in the Hamilton jail, where he was described as being cheerful and a model prisoner.

17

On Monday the twentieth the authorities moved him by train to New York for further questioning. Arriving at Grand Central Station, where a large crowd of reporters and others was on hand to greet him, he lost no time in exhibiting his eccentricity. When asked why his clothes appeared bulky, he replied that it was because he was wearing three costumes—two outer layers of business suits for warmth, and tennis clothes underneath in case the opportunity to play should present itself. Then, walking across the terminal, he picked up three cigars that someone had dropped and pocketed them, saying, "I don't smoke, but I'll keep them." (The cigars were instantly confiscated by his guards and sent to the police laboratory to be examined for concealed messages. None were found.) He was then questioned at great length by the police and examined at Bellevue Hospital. The conclusion reached as a result of these inquisitions was that he was innocent of any connection with the explosion, and that he was mad; on October 2 he was committed to Amityville Sanitarium, and after a two-month stay there he was released, apparently recovered. The last word on the Fischer affair, so far as Wall Street was concerned, was spoken by his friend Homans, who said, "No conspirators, after talking with Fischer for ten minutes, would consider letting him into a plot with them." There remained—and remains—the tortured coincidence that his insistently repeated warnings had been so nearly right, which was considered strange enough at the time, and which latter-day probability analysts might well declare to be unacceptable as an explanation.

Whether or not he was innocent of any sort of complicity, Fischer was certainly mad, although not much more illogical than his friends the powers of Wall Street, who rejected the accident theory of the explosion perhaps because of the mailed anarchist threats but more likely because it called into question, by implication, the perfection of the free-enterprise system; rejected Fischer as a suspect perhaps because the police had rejected him but more likely because they felt that a man of his sort, even though a lunatic, would never have a part in such an act; and eagerly embraced the radical-conspiracy theory because it suited their prejudices. It did more than that; by making them feel embattled, it elevated their interests into principles. For months afterward, important financial men

18

were guarded at announced public appearances, jaws remained set at the Stock Exchange, and brokers at lunch exchanged bomb experiences with the elaborate insouciance of veterans who have risked all in a good cause. Selling paper for money—the basic business of Wall Street—had graduated from a mere way of making a living into a defiance of the country's enemies, a moral act, and Wall Street was well launched into a decade when it could savor the treacherous and comfortable sensation of feeling its activities to be right as well as profitable.

VII

For a decade and more, the local and federal police went on conducting one of the most extensive and prolonged investigations on record. They visited over four thousand stables up and down the Atlantic seaboard in an effort to establish ownership of the horse; every blacksmith east of Chicago, and even the editors of every blacksmith trade journal, in an effort to identify the horseshoes conclusively; and every sash-weight manufacturer and dealer in the country in an effort to trace the source of the iron slugs. These procedures, which were uniformly fruitless, were mocked from time to time by confessions to the crime, each of which caused a momentary stir until it was shown to be implausible. One confessor, a disaffected former Burns detective who subsequently recanted and backed up his recantation with an unbreakable alibi, may simply have been taking a devious revenge on his old employers. A man who came forward in 1924 to assume full responsibility for the explosion turned out to have been confined in San Quentin Prison at the time of it. As late as the end of the 1930s a New York police captain would occasionally assign a bright young detective to the case on the chance that a fresh mind might see it in some new perspective. But the case was hopeless. By then it was far too late for a solution, and, moreover, Wall Street had other problems to occupy it.

Meanwhile, all through the two decades of our story, the explosion had its dramatic and highly visible monument. The monument consisted of the scars that were allowed to remain untouched on the north façade of 23 Wall Street. Ragged and eye-catching, an inch deep in places and suggesting moon craters as seen through a telescope, they were concentrated just under the sill of the second window from the building's east end. No plaque explained them, or was necessary; the passer-by who stopped to stare at them soon came to draw the knowing and superior smile that a native bestows on a tourist anywhere. Exactly why they were not erased was not clear; on this as on so many other subjects, J. P. Morgan & Company kept official silence. In the thirties some took to expressing the view that their survival for so long had come to make the Morgan bank look like a fusty old Blimp flaunting his ribbons from ancient campaigns. But Morgan men, when kidded on the subject, insisted that it was perfectly natural. "There's no particular feeling of martyrdom behind leaving them there," one old partner explained. "It's the practical thing to do. After all, replacing those great blocks would be inordinately and unnecessarily expensive. And besides— it's right and proper that they should stay there."

Right and proper or not, the scars served to remind Wall Street of its heroic martyrdom, and to enhance its sense of being a stage for great events. As, indeed, they still do today.

Chapter Two

Ticker Tyranny

I

"In a sense, the financial conflict is more bitter and ruthless than war itself; in war, friend and foe can be distinguished." So B. F. Winkelman, a shrewd Philadelphia lawyer with Wall Street connections, wrote in 1932 about the stock market in the 1920s. Except for a few newly arrived provincials who were instantly identifiable by outré items of apparel such as wide-brimmed hats and two-color shoes, the warriors of Wall Street wore pretty much the same uniform regardless of which particular army or task force they were enlisted in at any particular time, and never was the fighting so bitter and ruthless as when one foe was a former friend become a secret renegade. It was a time of transition, in Wall Street as in the nation as a whole, from the dominance of individual men to that of institutions. Single powerful bankers like J. P. Morgan or his key partners could still make or break industrial enterprises by granting or withholding capital, and the whole stock market could be moved sharply upward or downward by the mere rumor that a famous bull like W. C. Durant, or a famous bear like Jesse Livermore, was active in it. But institutions were coming up fast, and the Wall Street

21

institution whose power and influence were growing most rapidly, the institution fast on its way to replacing Morgan's as the center of national financial power, was the New York Stock Exchange.

Indeed, the Stock Exchange in 1920, so newly risen to such power that it had not yet mellowed into responsibility, was probably in a more arbitrary and arrogant mood than at any time before or since. Unshackled by any sort of public regulation, and governed by rules of its own devising, it was fully capable of summarily changing those rules to its own advantage, carrying on vindictive vendettas, and explaining itself to the public in terms so patently preposterous as to seem to express contempt. The men who ran the Exchange, like those who were to run the biggest corporations a generation later, were themselves relatively faceless; they drew their strength and courage from the institution, and were perhaps among the first "organization men." Yet they were vastly different, too; they were organization men of an earlier sort, not less tough or aggressive, but more charming, more opinionated, more anxious to please their friends and less so to please everyone else, more frankly selfish and less socially responsible, far more anxious to be thought of, and to think of themselves, as gentlemen. They were out of a single mold. Later in the decade the key committees of the Exchange would include self-made men, intellectuals, Westerners, even Jews; but to a man these were products of old Eastern stock who had grown up in more or less genteel circumstances. They had gone to the best New England preparatory schools primarily to learn manners, participate in sports, and, of course, make the right friends—certainly not primarily to prepare for college, since in those days college was not considered necessary as a preparation for Wall Street and was often simply skipped as a waste of time. They were not overly bright, but they had a kind of stubborn shrewdness. Their lives were inclined to revolve around urban clubs, and they were consummate snobs. They were remarkably ignorant about art, literature, music, history, world affairs apart from business, theoretical economics—just about everything but the matter at hand, and sports. They were unabashedly preoccupied with money and never dreamed of trying to disguise the fact, of which they were not ashamed; they had no ambitions except to become richer and more socially prominent. They were politically conservative or reactionary; they wanted to tell government what it should do but not to serve in it themselves—another sort of Wall Streeter aspired to that. Above all, they were charming when they chose to be, and never discourteous except on purpose. They were looked down on by the Wall Street high-brows, especially lawyers, but idolized as the high-brows never were by the community's striving newcomers—youngsters from the boondocks or the urban Irish slums—who admired from afar their lordly manners and often profited from their paternal patronage. They were just about the last, in America, of something or other, not quite a caste but perhaps a democratic version of one.

The Stock Exchange was the fortress of their popinjay airs and their mutually protective ruthlessness. Yet the fortress was not unassailable. Just as the most dramatic and characteristic financial conflicts of earlier times had been man against man, and those of later times would be business against government, so those of 1920 pitted man against institution.

The lone, rash challenger of the Stock Exchange that year was a member of it, though not a ruling member—Allan A. Ryan, son of one of the last survivors of another dying breed. Ryan *père,* whose impoverished Scotch-Irish parents in upcountry Virginia had given him the prophetic name of Thomas Fortune, started life as a dry-goods clerk in Baltimore, moved to New York to become a brokerage clerk, and in the mid-1880s fell in with William C. Whitney, the transit entrepreneur and founder of a famous dynasty whose protégé and then partner Ryan became, and who described Ryan later as "the most adroit, suave, and noiseless man that American finance has ever known." Starting with horsecars, Thomas Fortune Ryan and Whitney began taking over and consolidating New York City's public transportation, and by the time of Whitney's death in 1904 they had, with the help of such tactics as stock-watering and franchise-buying that a grand jury in 1908 found "dishonest and probably criminal" but still not actionable, not only absorbed the Interborough Rapid Transit Company and gained control of the entire city system but had amassed what the historian Matthew Josephson later called "two of the quickest and largest fortunes of the whole era of frenzied finance." All but penniless in 1886, Ryan was worth fifty million in 1905 by the estimate of his own representative. So suave and noiseless as to be all but inaudible to reporters—he was said to have talked to them only twice in his life, on each occasion merely to make a brief formal statement—he was nevertheless known admiringly in the press as "the great opportunist." Eventually he broadened his business interests to include banking, tobacco, railroads, life insurance, diamonds, oil, rubber, coal, coke, lead, electricity, and typewriters; increased his fortune to more than one hundred million, and in 1924 paid the tenth-largest individual income tax ($791,851) in the country; became the leading benefactor of the Democratic Party and the leading American benefactor of the Catholic Church; and built a Fifth Avenue mansion with a private chapel and an art gallery specializing in busts of himself, three of them by Rodin.

II

The son of this classical capitalist buccaneer was quite a different sort of fellow. He was physically frail, inclined to moral scruple, and talkative to the press; at the same time, though, he had inherited his father's stubborn will, independence, and aptitude for financial manipulation. Unlike his father, he had behind him a good formal education, at various private schools and at Georgetown University; moreover, the elder Ryan undertook to tutor him in the intricacies of finance, and in 1915, when Allan was thirty-five, turned over to him his seat on the Stock Exchange. Three years later the young man acquired another equally formidable mentor—Charles M. Schwab, the celebrated first president of United States Steel and later of Bethlehem Steel. "Thomas F. Ryan and I have been friends for many years," Schwab explained to an acquaintance much later. "When he was retiring from business, he brought his boy Allan to me. Told me Allan was his hope for the future. Would I look after him? I have looked out for Allan ever since." Under such guidance—and with an unknown amount of his father's money as his initial stake—Ryan and his firm, Allan A. Ryan & Company, became forces to be reckoned with in Wall Street. He became known as a powerful and clever bull operator, optimistic

24

about the economy's future, and particularly adept at the delicate yet brutal art of squeezing short sellers, the pessimists who borrow stock and then sell it for future delivery in the hope of later buying it back at a lower price to settle their loans and clear a profit. In the great bull-market year of 1919, in which the rate of turnover of shares (that is, total sales in relation to number of shares listed) on the Stock Exchange exceeded that of any other year before or for many years after, he was generally thought of as the mightiest bull of them all; the very whisper that he was buying was enough to bring about a general rise in prices, and one day, riding uptown with a banker, he let fall that he was now worth thirty million dollars. He operated in many fields—oils, textiles, chemicals, candy, manufacturing tools, and so on—but his biggest investment was thought to be in the Stutz Motor Car Company of America, Inc., makers of the famous Bearcat, of which he had bought a controlling interest and assumed the presidency in 1916.

At the beginning of 1920 Ryan was just under forty, a somewhat formal man with a prominent but not flamboyant mustache and sad, probing eyes; he and his wife and children had a properly grand house in Murray Hill and, apart from an alleged penchant for the racetrack, he was reputed to lead the life of a conservative financier. His Stutz company, despite the keen competition among automobile manufacturers in those days when there were hundreds of makes of car on the market, was in excellent shape. Besides racing models like the Bearcat—so low and sleek of line that some models required the driver to lie all but prostrate at the wheel, and soon to be as much a hallmark of flaming youth as the raccoon coat and the hip flask—the company manufactured a family-sized car, long-hooded and classic in its lines, with a high price tag and a look of quiet authority, which, or so the advertisements for it boasted, "knows no master on the road." Ryan estimated that Stutz's net profit for the year 1920 would amount to around five million dollars. All in all, his life seemed to be one of unmarred success, except for the single blemish of a bitter and continuing quarrel with his father. In October, 1917, Thomas Fortune Ryan had remarried less than two weeks after the death of his first wife, Allan's mother, and gossip both in Wall Street and in the salons uptown attributed the falling-out to this action. The gossip was never confirmed or denied by either the father or the son; what was known early in 1920 was that they were not on speaking terms.

That January, on a trip to Indianapolis to inspect the Stutz factory there, Ryan caught influenza and was hospitalized for two weeks. He had a long history of respiratory illnesses; in his youth his father had once sent him to a sanitarium in Denver in the belief that he had tuberculosis, and was supposed at one time to have despaired of his son's recovery, and, more recently, friends had repeatedly urged Allan to retire from business, or at least from the hectic business of stock speculation, in the interest of his health. Illnesses and entreaties alike only goaded him to harder work. Back in New York, and suffering from pneumonia that had come as a sequel to influenza, Ryan during February learned certain things from his business associates that led him to believe his affairs needed his immediate attention. Stutz stock, which had been selling on the Stock Exchange at around $100 a share at the beginning of the year, had risen steadily throughout January and then, on February 2, had suddenly advanced in a bound from 120 to 134; at this stage, Ryan was told, organized short selling had appeared as speculators who thought the price had risen too high pounced on what they took to be its exposed position. This was a bear raid, and among the raiders, it was revealed later, were some of the leading members of the Stock Exchange—men whom Ryan, as an outsider to the Exchange's ruling clique, could not call friends, but often joked and bantered with from time to time on the floor or in the Stock Exchange Luncheon Club. In the course of making a killing in Stutz they might maim the company and separate Ryan from much of his fortune—or, contrariwise, their maneuver might end up costing them their own shirts—but in either case the antagonists would be supposed to take it all in good part and continue the joking and bantering during the contest and after it. Such was the code.

At all events, a bear raid was precisely the maneuver Ryan was best equipped by experience, temperament, and aptitude to combat and crush. Rising from his sickbed in Murray Hill, he went to Wall Street, at first in the care of a nurse, to do battle. His aim was to buy all the Stutz stock that was offered for sale, on an ascending price scale that would close a vise progressively tighter on the short sellers, who, of course, would eventually have to buy stock themselves in order to cover what they had sold. To conduct his campaign, Ryan needed enormous sums of cash, and it later became clear that to raise it he resorted to enormous loans from persons and banks. Evidently he put up the personal possessions of himself and his family as collateral. "We never loaned him more than $1,500,000 on furs," the president—by that time the ex-president—of the Chase National Bank told the Wall Street reporter Clarence Barron in 1921.

At first, Ryan lost ground. So great was the short-selling pressure that, despite his efforts, by early March the price of Stutz had dropped back to near 100. But then the tide turned decisively. By the morning of March 24 Stutz was up to 245; that day it shot up to 282, and a week later had skyrocketed to 391. In the course of the startling rise, practically all Stutz stockholders except Ryan, his firm, and members of his family decided to take their profits, and sold their stock—which was snapped up in every case by Ryan; meanwhile, the opportunity to get an inflated price for Stutz appealed more and more to the short sellers, whose number and activity increased, and Ryan bought their offerings, too. Toward the end of the month, the stock that they were selling *to* Ryan had first to be borrowed *from* him, since there was no longer anyone else who had any. Confident that he was winning, he gladly went on lending and then buying it, and the wild, uncontrolled rise to 391 on March 31 signaled his victory. The short sellers, it was clear, had disastrously underestimated his strength; they were overpowered, and their remaining choices were to buy back the stock they owed him, at his price, thereby incurring huge losses, or, alternatively, to face professional ruin and perhaps a prison term for breach of contract. Ryan, who was feeling much better by this time, had engineered in Stutz what Wall Street calls a corner.

In the light of this situation, certain events of March 31 appear odd indeed. Ryan was in a position to know who most of the short sellers were, since in recent days it was he and he alone who had loaned the stock; he knew, then, that most of them, like him, were members of the Stock Exchange, and some of them, unlike him, members of its key committees. On the morning of March 31 Ryan was summoned to appear before the Exchange's Business Conduct

Committee to explain the gyrations of Stutz. He might have thrown the question back at certain of his interrogators, whom he knew to be among the short sellers; instead, he explained to the committee that the scarcity of Stutz stock had apparently been brought about by the fact that he and his family now owned it all—and even, because of clerical confusion, had contracts for a few more shares than actually existed. He then named the terms on which he would settle with the short sellers, still diplomatically omitting to mention that some of them were seated in front of him. He would, he said, sell them all the shares they needed to fulfill their contracts at $750 per share.

The short sellers present may well have blanched at this proposition, since it meant a loss to them of from $350 to $650 on each share they were short, and some of them were short hundreds. But Ryan was apparently within his rights, and the sellers' dilemma was of their own making; moreover, since a successful cornerer may theoretically set an infinite price, any finite one is theoretically a bargain. Just as the destruction of a company and its stockholders is the logical end of a successful bear raid, so a corner is the logical end of a successful bull counterattack; the losers' only right was to plead for mercy, since Exchange rules at that time, while they discouraged both denouements, did not forbid either. Previous corners on the Exchange, like the famous one of 1901 in the stock of Northern Pacific Railroad, had sometimes caused vast social harm but had nevertheless always ended with the short sellers paying their conqueror's price rather than with any sort of official intervention; no Geneva Convention existed to mitigate the cruelty of the financial war. But in this case the conquered instantly showed themselves to be in no mood to plead for mercy. Early the same afternoon, the Business Conduct Committee, now buttressed by the Law Committee, had Ryan on the carpet again, as if *he* were the one in trouble. This time the Exchange men seized the offensive by suggesting that they were considering striking Stutz from the trading list, on one pretext or another. Ryan, knowing that such a move might be a grave blow in that it would deprive Stutz of a ready market, boldly replied that if such action were taken his settlement price would be not $750 per share but $1,000. Following this exchange of threats, the meeting broke up and the two Stock Exchange committees went to report its outcome to their ultimate authority, the Governing Committee. During the half-hour between the end of the meeting and the end of the day's trading on the Exchange floor, there was a further extraordinary development. Some of the Exchange members who were trapped short sellers, knowing full well that Ryan had them cornered, nevertheless dug themselves deeper into the corner by borrowing still more stock from him and then selling it short. This apparently suicidal move came to appear less illogical shortly after the close, when the Governing Committee announced that by unanimous vote it had decided forthwith to suspend all dealings in Stutz for an indefinite period. Reminded by a reporter that no precedent or rule of the Exchange appeared to sanction this action, a Stock Exchange spokesman replied airily, "The Stock Exchange can do anything."

III

Thus deprived of a ready market, and with his huge borrowings hanging over his head, Ryan was indeed in trouble. But he still had his corner; the stock he had loaned was returnable on demand, and the short sellers were required to produce it, somehow or other, whenever he might call for it. Furthermore, Stutz Motor Car Company, of which he was now virtually the sole owner, was still profitably turning out Bearcats and cars that knew no master on the road. For a few days Ryan kept his own council, marshaling legal advice and planning tactics, while the Stutz affair became the chief, indeed almost the only, topic in Wall Street. The gossip centered on the identity of the short sellers, a matter of which the public knew nothing. Some could not resist suggesting, without evidence, that Ryan's own father was among those seeking his ruin, to settle their quarrel; others said the villain was Schwab, but at least this calumny was laid to rest a few days later when Ryan was smoothly re-elected to the board of Schwab's company, Bethlehem Steel. (Schwab said later that there *had* been a spell of bad feeling between him and Ryan, stemming from a casually slighting remark about the Stutz company that Schwab had made at a dinner party and that a helpful lady had then repeated to Ryan; but far from selling Stutz short, Schwab had lent Ryan a round million dollars with which to defend it.) Another story was that the whole thing was the result of a trifling fifty-thousand-dollar bet, a bit of blood sport among the financial titans. Stock Exchange spokesmen, apparently confident that Ryan would not dare violate the Wall Street code of secrecy on private contracts by naming the borrowers of stock, circulated as fact what may have been the wildest story of all. Most of the short sellers, said the Exchange men with straight faces, were just investors of modest means in outland towns like Kankakee and Peoria. The idea of the country's Aunt Janes, most of whom had only discovered the existence of the stock market in the two years since the end of the war, as board-room regulars engaging in sophisticated maneuvers like selling short was so dumfounding to all that no one appears to have made any comment on it.

On April 5 the Exchange announced through its Law Committee that it considered Ryan's contracts void. "The Exchange will not treat failure to deliver Stutz Motor stock, due to inability of the contracting party to obtain same, as a failure to comply with contract," declared the committee, repudiating in a single sentence the principle on which all Exchange operations were based, and it went on to top off this astounding ukase with the suggestion that if Ryan was still unsatisfied he resort to "action at law." (To emphasize the futility of this recourse, an Exchange member called the attention of the press to the fact that in the course of its 128-year history the Exchange had had only two of its rulings overthrown by the courts.) Accepting the challenge, though not in the manner proposed to him, Ryan the following day sent to the board of governors an ultimatum of his own that for toploftiness rivaled that of his antagonist. Blithely, or perhaps tactfully, ignoring the Exchange's action of the day before, he simply assumed the validity of his contracts and laid down his terms for their settlement—among others, that the Exchange negotiate a price with him on behalf of all the short sellers who were its members, to save him the trouble of negotiating with them individually, and that Stutz stock be promptly relisted. The Exchange did not deign to reply.

With the impasse at the point where the alternatives seemed to be ruin for Ryan or grave loss of face for the Exchange, lawyers began to appear on the scene. Dos Passos Brothers, the leading experts on

Stock Exchange law, and the firm of the novelist John Dos Passos' father, rendered an opinion holding, on abstruse grounds, that Ryan's contracts were probably unenforceable. A Protective Committee was appointed to represent the short sellers—it delicately avoided saying who its clients were—and for advisory legal counsel it obtained the Olympian Charles Evans Hughes, who four years earlier had missed by a whisker being elected President of the United States. Ryan himself engaged the humbler counsel of the firm of Stanchfield and Levy. "We contend that the outstanding contracts to deliver stock . . . are invalid," said Charles A. Morse, chairman of the Protective Committee, on April 9. "We are going to fight it out on these lines if it takes all summer." "I do not consider that the fight has yet started," Ryan riposted three days later, garbling his military quotation a bit more than Morse had done, but preserving the spirit. By this time the fight had become a public entertainment in financial circles; crowds clustered around the news tickers in brokerage offices watching for the latest statement by Ryan or his enemies, and greeting it with cheers and applause or else boos, according to taste. And, indeed, there was high drama in the Stutz affair. Although probably no more of a reformer or hero than the next stockbroker, Ryan had trapped himself in a reformist and heroic role—that of singlehanded challenger of the integrity of the nation's most powerful financial institution.

On April 13 he began his all-out offensive. Shortly after noon he called on the secretary of the Stock Exchange and tendered his resignation, submitting with it a long statement of explanation in which he said, "So long as your body is responsible only to itself, and so long as you can make your own rules and regulations for their immediate execution . . . so long as you permit men who have personal financial interest at stake to take part in your deliberations, your judgments, and your decisions . . . I cannot with self-respect continue as a member." But besides being an act of conscience, his resignation was a tactical move, since it freed him from the discipline of Exchange rules, and, in his own view, of Wall Street customs as well. That evening he gave a reporter from the *World* the names of nine Stock Exchange members who, he implied without actually saying, owed him Stutz stock and were therefore caught short. The names, although none of them were well known

31

outside of Wall Street even then, were those of some of the Exchange's staunchest pillars, many of them members of the committees that had sat in judgment over Ryan. When the list was printed the following day, most of the men named, as soon as they had recovered from their shock at this flaunting of the code, denied categorically that they or their firms were short of Stutz, except perhaps on behalf of some of their customers—a qualification that made the denials almost laughable, since the circumstance that they had sold short for customers rather than for themselves in no way lessened their responsibility for their contracts.

Besides losing that point, the establishment suffered two other setbacks that day. People outraged by the implications of Ryan's revelations began talking about a legislative investigation to consider the possibility of government regulation, state or even federal, of the Stock Exchange, and this, as one observer put it mildly, was "a development that many earnest friends of the Stock Exchange are extremely anxious to avoid." And meanwhile, the same issue of the *World* in which the list of names appeared also carried a cryptic line or two about Thomas Fortune Ryan, whose name had hitherto been mysteriously missing from newspaper discussions of the Stutz case. Although the elder Ryan remained officially as noiseless as ever, the *World*, without giving the source of its information, declared that he "admired the fighting spirit of his son and would back him in his controversy to the limit of his resources." If this was true—if family quarrels were forgotten and the old man's unfathomed bag of tricks and uncounted millions were really at his son's disposal—then the Stock Exchange and its suddenly wobbly pillars had further reason to tremble.

The Exchange did show signs of nervousness, in that two days later it issued an elaborate justification of its conduct. In suspending dealings in Stutz, the Exchange explained, it had acted to protect the public from losses that might have resulted from the wild gyrations in the price brought about by the corner; "There is not a word of truth in the statement that the action . . . was dictated by a desire to benefit the short interests." As to Ryan's contracts for borrowed stock, the Exchange backed down from its previous position that they need not be honored, and took the new tack that it had nothing to do with the question; the settlement of the contracts was "entirely a matter for negotiation between the parties." The statement concluded on a note of warm self-congratulation: "The members of the Governing Committee of the Exchange are firmly convinced that in all actions taken in respect to Stutz Motor stock they have been guided solely by a sense of their duty to the best interests of the Exchange and of the public."

It remained for Ryan to spring the trap by calling in the stock he had loaned; should it not be forthcoming, as it obviously would not be, since it had long since been sold back to him, he would be entitled, under Exchange rules, to "buy it in"—that is, barring the unlikely event that there was still someone idiotic enough to sell it short, to buy it from himself on behalf of those who owed it to him, at whatever price he might care to set, and charge the cost to the unfortunate borrowers. Such, under the terms of the market game, are the consequences of selling short and getting cornered—unless, of course, the cornerer's contracts are invalid, and on this point the Protective Committee tacitly capitulated on April 20 by announcing that it was ready to accept impartial mediation on a negotiated-settlement price. (By this time the Protective Committee had admitted that it represented fifty-eight Stock Exchange firms that were caught short 5,500 shares of Stutz. The figure was euphemistically low, but the admission significant.) A mediation committee acceptable to both sides was formed, most of its members being understandably concerned representatives of the banks from which Ryan had borrowed millions of dollars to mount his operation, but it soon bogged down in resignations and pussyfooting occasioned by its desire to avoid publicity. Ryan postponed his "buying in" pending the outcome of the mediation efforts, but as the days dragged by without results he grew increasingly restive, and finally he announced his final deadline. He intended to buy in all the stock owed him on the morning of April 24, precisely at ten o'clock. "Patiently I have waited many days," he pointed out. In what market did he plan to make this interesting transaction with himself? Why, on the outdoor Curb Exchange, membership in which was accomplished merely by showing up on Broad Street, where trading went on in all weathers. And what would his price be? Ryan wasn't saying. On the twenty-third, frantic efforts were made by the Protective Committee to achieve a negotiated settlement, but in vain.

April 24 was a Saturday—still a half-working day in Wall Street then, as it was to continue to be until well after the end of the Second World War. On the fateful morning Broad Street was mobbed with brokers and finance fans waiting to see Ryan administer the *coup de grâce* to the shorts, whose close identification with the ruling clique of the Stock Exchange would make the carnage even more appetizing. The clerks who sat, as usual, in the office windows above the street, waiting to receive orders by hand signal from the brokers below, were all but falling from their perches in their excitement. Meanwhile, in the privacy of a law office nearby, the Protective Committee was at last considering capitulation. A broker named Colonel John W. Prentiss, who had assumed informal leadership of the group by virtue of his reasonableness, was urging the assembled short sellers that the time was long past for fulminations against Ryan, and that they had better come to terms with him in the few minutes remaining before ten o'clock if they valued their financial hides. After a few bad moments, his counsel prevailed. A motion was passed giving the committee full authority to act for all fifty-eight short sellers; then, at someone's apt suggestion, slips of paper were passed around on which each wrote the settlement offer he thought appropriate. The resulting figures were averaged, and Morse, the chairman, announced that the committee was now ready with its offer. A delegation then proceeded to the office of Allan A. Ryan & Company, at 111 Broadway, arriving there at nine-forty. "Do you want to see anyone?" Ryan's receptionist inquired innocently. The members of the delegation said yes, and on being ushered into Ryan's presence, stated that they, on behalf of all the shorts, offered $550 a share for all the shares due him. Ryan unhesitatingly accepted, and forthwith canceled his order to buy in the stock. At two minutes before ten, Colonel Prentiss stepped out of Ryan's office and said to reporters, "The Stutz matter is settled. The settlement price is $550 per share."

Everyone seemed to be happy except the fans on Broad Street, who had been deprived of their show. All agreed that Ryan had scored a great victory over both the short sellers and the Stock

Exchange, even though he had come down from his earlier prices of $750 and $1,000 per share; after all, his profit on the transaction was conservatively estimated at between a million and a million and a half dollars, and he was still virtual sole owner of Stutz. He said a few gracious words about Colonel Prentiss' "unremitting tact and judgment and consistent courtesy under trying circumstances," and then left for Hot Springs, Virginia. The short sellers, who among them had lost whatever sum Ryan had gained, nonetheless eschewed further recriminations; their representative, Morse, said simply, "The Stutz controversy is ended . . . we have concluded the matter."

IV

But everyone wasn't happy, and the controversy wasn't ended. Ryan's debts to banks, most of them due in the autumn or earlier, amounted to many times his profit on the corner; his obvious recourse was to raise the money now by selling off some of his Stutz stock, but that stock, without the Stock Exchange listing, was far from readily marketable, and if economic conditions should turn sour it might not be marketable at all. Soon after the settlement he exulted to his old mentor Schwab that on paper he was now worth $100 million—a fortune nothing less than comparable to his father's. Perhaps Ryan hoped that Schwab, like the taskmaster in the Parable of the Talents, would say, "Well done, thou good and faithful servant"; if so, he was disappointed, because Schwab skeptically replied that that might be true if Ryan valued Stutz at a thousand dollars a share, but exactly how was he going to realize that much, or anything like it? Ryan apparently had no ready answer.

And the Stock Exchange, far from being willing to suffer its humiliation in silence, was not through with him. All through May there were rumors that it was "investigating" him and his affairs, and on one occasion Ryan showed that his own rancor had not abated by saying to Clarence Barron that he would never resume his membership even if his intransigence cost him millions, and adding—heretically, but prophetically—that in his view the Exchange ought to be under the guardianship of Washington. For one thing, the Exchange was dragging its feet in the matter of selling his membership, which would bring him some $100,000. Then early in June the Exchange suddenly let it be known that Ryan's resignation back in April had not been accepted, after all. The reason for this belated revelation became clear a few days later when the Governing Committee adopted a resolution charging Ryan with being "guilty of conduct inconsistent with just and equitable principles of trade"; specifically, the committee said, he had created "an arbitrary and fictitious price" for Stutz and had then "exacted from the parties liable excessive and unreasonable amounts." The case was to be tried at a closed hearing at which Ryan was invited to appear to defend himself. The Exchange, it seemed, had declined Ryan's resignation so that it could throw him out.

In reacting to this development, Ryan disdained to point out the Exchange's about-face on the question of the settlement price, which earlier it had explicitly said to be none of its business, but which it now undertook to pronounce excessive and unreasonable. Instead, he merely characterized the charges as a whole as "ridiculous on the face," and concentrated his fire on the form of the planned trial and on the motives of those who were to judge him. "Your invitation to appear in a star chamber and join you in placing a laurel wreath upon the past and present conduct of your committees and to furnish myself as a sacrificial lamb is respectfully declined," he said. "The judgment of 'guilty' awaits only my appearance for formal signature and summary execution. . . . No man appreciates more than I that the Stock Exchange is the keystone of the commercial structure of the country. No man has greater respect for its ideals and traditions. . . . But no man deplores more than I that this great institution . . . should have so fallen that these powers are employed for private ends and personal vengeance. It is a sad spectacle indeed." The trial went off as scheduled, in the absence of the accused; after five hours of deliberation, the Governing Committee found Ryan guilty as charged and voted unanimously for his expulsion, and the next morning, after the Stock Exchange gallery had been cleared of visitors, the verdict was intoned from the podium. On the floor, it was received in silence. At his office Ryan said, "It is immaterial to me, and really I do not give a damn." Then he left, reportedly for the racetrack at Jamaica.

But there were other matters on which he could not afford to be indifferent. All summer the banks pressed him for the return of their loans, and meanwhile the stocks of the companies other than Stutz in which he had invested heavily—Stromberg Carburetor, Continental Candy, Chicago Pneumatic Tool, and Hayden Chemical—suffered such mysteriously precipitous losses as to suggest that his enemies, the bears, were clawing at him again. In one case, when one of his stocks suddenly collapsed on the very day when a new issue of it was being made, the claw marks were all but unmistakable. At the same time his troubles were compounded by a coincidental collapse of the national economy. Consumers suddenly went on strike against inflated prices, organizing "overall clubs" and "old clothes days"; money became so tight that some leading banks had trouble maintaining solvency; world trade all but returned to its wartime condition of standstill; and, most crucially for Ryan, stock prices in general began such a drop that by the end of the year one-third of the April value of all Stock Exchange issues would be wiped out. The gods of finance were intervening on the side of Ryan's enemies.

In August he brought a million-dollar defamation suit against the Stock Exchange's president and Governing Committee, naming again the Stutz short sellers who were members of that body. (The Exchange immediately replied that the accused members had not been present at the "trial"—thereby conceding implicitly, and perhaps inadvertently, that they *had* been personally interested in Stutz.) This was probably not so much an attempt to avenge his honor as a serious move to raise money. But far from being able to realize the million in damages quickly, Ryan found that he still couldn't collect even the relatively trifling sum due him for his Exchange seat; the Exchange had sold it in July for $98,000, and in November was still withholding the money from him on a technicality. Meanwhile, the bankers were closing in on him, and Wall Street gossip began to speak of his imminent bankruptcy. George J. Whelan, the cigar-store man, told Clarence Barron in November, "Allan Ryan is all cleaned out"; another Barron informant, a Boston broker, said positively that Ryan owed fourteen million that he couldn't pay, and added, "Ryan has known for thirty days that they had him. He is now eating out of their hands."

In such circumstances it was obvious that if Ryan would not turn to his father—and he wouldn't—his creditors would. Some time in November representatives of the banks to which Ryan owed money, including the Chase and the Guaranty Trust, made an indirect approach to the old man through his long-time friend and associate, Whelan. They received no encouragement. "You loaned Allan A. Ryan money without any regard to his father when you knew Allan was not on speaking terms with his father," Whelan pointed out to the bankers. "I don't see how you have any claim upon Thomas F. Ryan." The matter was complicated by the fact that the elder Ryan was the largest stockholder in the Guaranty Trust and, as Whelan put it, the bank's boss in a showdown. Therefore in a negative sense, by not opposing the Guaranty Trust's huge advances to his son early in the year, the elder Ryan had had a hand in them. Perhaps he thought that was enough. There is no evidence that he now showed the slightest disposition to commit his own funds to rescue his son, or that he had done so previously.

Allan Ryan's enemies at the Stock Exchange knew that they had him at last; they could sit back and leave it to the banks to be the executioners. Late in November the banks announced that they had formed a committee "to take charge of" Ryan's affairs; even though the bankers were careful to say that they believed he was still several million dollars in the black and that they confidently expected to get back all their money, this meant plainly enough that in fact they anticipated his failure. His credit ruined, a bankrupt in everything but name, Ryan for twenty months carried on a game, hopeless last stand. Only Schwab seemed to be still with him, putting in a good word for his protégé where he could. Ryan tried unsuccessfully to ally himself with John Shelton Williams, Controller of the Currency and a veteran critic of New York banks, particularly of their loan policies. (The banks expressed hurt surprise at this, protesting that they supposed Ryan *liked* them after all they had done for him. "I could never conceive that a man could be so mean," complained the president of the Chase, suggesting that that bank felt that its loan department was running a sort of social service, rather than a business, even in those days before it adopted its now-famous advertising slogan.) He got as his lawyer Samuel Untermyer, who as counsel to the Pujo Committee in 1912 had become the national symbol of opposition to the banks and their "money trusts." To win political friends, or to bolster confidence in his credit, or both, he somehow scraped together a forty-thousand-dollar contribution to the Democratic National Committee. But all in vain. On July 21, 1922, he filed a bankruptcy petition listing debts of $32,435,477 and available assets of only $643,533. For what satisfaction it might bring him, this made him one of the biggest bankrupts in the nation's history, even though later calculations showed his debts to be smaller.

Like a bombed-out house, a bankruptcy statement suddenly reveals, piteously and shockingly, to the indifferent or curious public gaze all the details of shattered private lives. Ryan's listed debts included $157.75 to Best & Company for children's clothing; $3,260.25 to Black, Starr & Frost for jewelry; $60.36 to Buckley School for tuition; $768.68 to Charles & Company for groceries; $134.08 to E. P. Dutton & Company for books and stationery; $13.75 to the Montauk Club of Brooklyn for dues; and $207.80 to the Plaza Hotel for theater tickets. They also included $66,000 due to T. Coleman du Pont, of the Delaware clan; some $300,000 to Schwab, the balance of the million from his mentor having apparently been paid off; slightly more than a million to Harry Payne Whitney, son of his father's old partner; about $3.5 million to the Chase National Bank; and $8.66 million to the Guaranty Trust Company. It was now plain enough what the banks had been concerned about.

Actually, Ryan's situation was somewhat less hopeless than the bankruptcy papers implied, in that they assigned no value to the vast quantities of Stutz stock—some 135,000 shares—owned by Ryan and pledged as collateral for his loans. These were to be sold at public auction, and Ryan's remaining hope of escaping bankruptcy was that they bring a good price. Allen Wardwell, lawyer for the Guaranty Trust, said a few days before the sale that the Stutz stock along with his other holdings would make Ryan solvent if the Stutz sold for $50 a share; he later revised the figure upward to above $60, but, in any case, there would be no question of Ryan's solvency if only the price were 100, which is about what it had been early in 1920, before the whole melee had begun. Unfortunately, though, this was all dreaming. During 1921 Stutz had sold on the Curb in the 50-to-100 range, but Ryan's bankruptcy and other reverses had knocked it galley-west, and in mid-July it stood at 5. Only an insane Croesus would bid 100 or 60 or 50 for 135,000 shares of it.

The auction took place on August 2, at the Exchange salesrooms on Vesey Street, and the Stutz stock was bought by a Guaranty Trust vice president for twenty dollars a share. Next day it was announced that the bidder had been acting for Schwab, who thereby became boss of Stutz. The banks thus recovered part of their loans, Ryan's bankruptcy was certified, the short sellers had their revenge, and the Stock Exchange ruled supreme. Its next equally determined challenger, a decade later, was to be not one man but the national government backed by an overwhelming majority of the people.

V

Schwab proved to be a less effective magnate in automobiles than in steel. Stutz cars went on breaking records in speed tests, but the firm's books showed deficits nearly every year. It did not share in the automobile industry's great boom during the twenties. (The open, bucket-seat Bearcat that became a talisman of the time was not a product of the time; it was a used car, the manufacture of which had been discontinued after 1920.) In 1932 the company was reduced to making grocery wagons. In 1938, a year before Schwab's death and two years before Ryan's, it quietly went broke.

At the time of the auction Schwab was asked whether Ryan would get back on his feet again, and he replied, "I hope he does—I think he will." In spite of several attempts, he never did. His hope, if he had one, for a new initial stake in the Wall Street game lay in his father, who, after all, besides being one of the last of the old financial freebooters, was also, to judge from his benefactions, one of the most generous-hearted. But his will, when it was read following his death in November, 1928, left his fortune to his other survivors, including Allan Ryan's sons, and mentioned Allan himself only twice. Once was to give him third option, after two other survivors, to buy any object in the testator's art collection. The other was to say, "I give and bequeath my white pearl shirt studs to my son Allan A. Ryan."

Chapter Three

The Almost Aristocracy

I

By way of scene-changing: In the fall of 1921 the national economic picture reversed itself in sixty days. The postwar depression
abruptly ended, and a new and more durable boom replaced it.
With one accord the familiar economic barometers all began to rise.
The recovery was officially smiled upon and encouraged by the
Federal Reserve System, which, beginning in 1921, progressively
reduced its discount rate from the postwar peak of 7 percent all the
way to 3 percent by 1924. The discount rate, through its influence
on the interest rates charged by banks and other private lenders,
tends to determine whether credit is hard or easy to get for everyone
from the giant corporation to the home-buyer in need of a mortgage,
and such a dramatic thaw in the money market promoted general
expansion, risk-taking, speculation, reckless spending—the flowers,
or maybe weeds, of free enterprise that had bloomed too soon in the
early postwar period and thus been blighted in the frosts of 1921,

and now were to grow over the rest of the decade to unmanageable, nightmarish size. Meanwhile the U.S. Treasury, under the leadership of an old friend of industry, Andrew Mellon, who had resigned directorships in no fewer than fifty-one corporations to assume the secretaryship in 1921, augmented the confidence and the profits of business by embarking on a vigorous and systematic program of reduction of corporate taxes.

Business was in charge of the country to an extent that it had not been since the post–Civil War era of railroad expansion; and its new leader was a newer kind of transportation, the automobile. Just between 1921 and 1923 the annual factory sales of passenger cars rose from under 1.5 million to over 3.6 million, and the total number of motor vehicles on the American roads from 10.5 to 15.1 million; by the end of the decade the latter figure would be almost 27 million, and the automobile industry would account for not quite one-tenth of all manufacturing wages and *more* than one-tenth of the value of all manufactured goods. Automobile stocks were to the stock market of the 1920s what electronics would be to that of the 1950s; by the time the really big market advances of the period were under way, General Motors, Fisher Body, Du Pont, and Yellow Cab were called the Four Horsemen of the boom, and it was a standard Wall Street joke to speak of the market collectively as "a product of General Motors."

(Of course, prosperity was not for everyone. The farmer, largely deprived of his huge wartime export trade, ill-equipped by temperament and technology to protect himself against suicide through overproductiveness, and virtually unassisted, in those days, by government, was in the direst of straits. The average price of all farm products was cut almost in half from 1920 to 1921, and was to regain only a fraction of the loss by 1927; per capita net income for persons on farms fell 62 percent between 1919 and 1921. These catastrophic declines, unprecedented in the country's agricultural history, meant defaulted mortgages and the failure of the rural banks that held them; in the great years of "prosperity" from 1923 to 1929, banks in the United States were failing steadily at a rate of nearly two per day. As for wage-earners, throughout the 1920s almost one-third of them took home less than $2,000 per year, a fifth of them less than $1,000. But poverty programs, and even federal farm-price-support programs, were not the order of the day.)

Thus well before the death of Harding on August 2, 1923, had brought Calvin Coolidge to the Presidency, what came to be called the Coolidge boom was already under way. And most of the other familiar totems of the decade were already established. Prohibition, in force since January, 1920, was already largely ineffective (the national death rate from alcoholism, at a record low in 1920, had crept back most of the way to its old normal level), and the speakeasy was a national institution. *Babbitt* had been published, and the book's hero's prototype was rampant in every Chamber of Commerce. New immigration laws had closed the Golden Door in response to a national wave of "nativism." As for Wall Street, in a country that had decided to be ruled by business enterprise it found itself a sort of rival to Washington. Its manners and morals, its important men, its social hierarchy took on in the public mind the sort of glamour more often associated with those of national capitals in times of high statesmanship.

II

J. P. Morgan the Younger—"Jack"—a kindly-eyed man with a white mustache and black eyebrows, with the tastes and bearing of an English gentleman, was the symbol and embodiment of Wall Street leadership, and his firm, in its bomb-pocked building at the Corner, was the leadership's citadel. True, the firm had lost some of its former temporal power in domestic affairs. The passage of the Federal Reserve Act in 1913, which coincidentally had been the year of the elder Pierpont Morgan's death, had marked the end of Morgan & Company's *de facto* status as the nation's central bank, and the rise of gigantic corporations with the capacity to finance their own growth out of retained earnings was beginning to deprive it of its purse-string power over corporate affairs. On the other hand, the war and its resulting devastation in Europe had left the firm far more important than ever before in international dealings, and, moreover, its 1920 acquisition of joint control with the du

Ponts of the hottest new industrial giant of them all, General Motors, showed that the old suzerain had not lost its vitality at home. But it was not only money power that Morgan & Company exercised over Wall Street in the 1920s. In addition, it was the style-setter, the court of last appeal, and to a certain extent the conscience of the place.

Its qualities were both established by and magnificently epitomized in Morgan the man and the partners he chose. A partner himself since less than three years after his graduation from Harvard in 1889, and the heir to many millions, as well as the management of the firm, on his father's death, he was born to the purple, and from the beginning had never shown any inclination to wear it without dignity and responsibility—according, at least, to his lights, which were worldly puritanism, class-consciousness, and solemn self-righteousness of late-nineteenth-century American Protestantism. Like his father, he permitted no divorces in his firm—not to partners, not to employees. The basis of commercial credit is not money or property but character, Pierpont Morgan the Elder had insisted, memorably joining his business philosophy to his religious one, before the Pujo Committee in 1912. He had explicitly placed character above brilliance as a business asset. His son Jack, in a favorite maxim, put the thought only a little differently: "Do your work; be honest; keep your word; help when you can; be fair." Like his father, he discountenanced the notion that he rendered separate accounts to Caesar and to God, and once he remarked sentimentally that he would rather lose money by trusting a man too much than gain it from trusting one too little. Yet his partner Thomas W. Lamont noted that the elder Morgan's "habit of swift, incisive thought" had been "amply inherited by his son, who joins to it, perhaps, a more sober judgment." Delicately bred and shy of publicity, Morgan the Younger was nevertheless courageous and physically strong, as he showed in 1915 when he overcame in hand-to-hand combat a would-be assassin who, armed with two loaded revolvers and a stick of dynamite, had invaded his mansion at Glen Cove. Very much a working professional rather than a rich dilettante, he yet maintained—or affected—a kind of elegant, aristocratic amateurism in his attitude toward banking. He and his partners never entered the Stock Exchange, preferring to delegate

44

their Exchange business to outside brokers. (A necessary institution, even a praiseworthy one, but not quite their sort.) His outward concern was always the style as much as the content of banking. When the counsel for a Senate committee once read back to him a crucial part of his testimony to it and asked him to make corrections if he liked, he replied only, "I should like it if the stuttering part were cut out of my answer. I am not used to this form of examination."

At times it almost seemed as if Morgan and his firm felt that they could afford a certain disdain for money and money affairs, per se. They conceived of themselves as statesmen of finance (which they were) rather than mere money-getters (though they were that, too). And yet the slightest hint that their statesmanship made them part of national government was in their view an unforgivable gaffe, because of their deep-seated Jeffersonian, Adam-Smithian prejudice against government and all its works. When Harold Nicolson wrote that at the outbreak of the First World War the Morgan firm "ceased to be a private firm and became almost a department of Government," Morgan wrote in longhand on the manuscript that had been submitted to him: "I have no right to ask you to alter this, but it will be interpreted as if we were reduced to the status of a department subordinate to the government." Nicolson, who tended to think of bankers as "rather low-class fellows," had supposed he was offering a high compliment; but he had reckoned without the lordliness of Morgan. One compliments the self-regarding mighty at one's peril. Morgan's partners pressed the matter harder than he, and the offending passage was changed.

These partners, whatever else they may have been, were the members of the most exclusive and influential club in the American financial world; the very furnishings of the private offices on the second floor at 23 Wall—wood-burning fireplaces, well-worn easy chairs and couches—created a clublike atmosphere of leisure and ease. If the gentlemanly tradition of Wall Street had been defeated at the time of the Civil War, as some historians argue, it was carrying on a strong holding action at the House of Morgan. The partners were extensions of and adornments to J. P. Morgan's personality. Like him, they tended to be Anglophile ("Our firm has never for one moment been neutral," Lamont said during the First

World War; "we don't know how to be!"), given to a certain unworldliness (real or affected), and Republican. All were Protestants of old American stock; they were the Old Yankee Trader gone high-brow, and as a matter of course welcomed among their number no one of other inheritance or faith. Their loyalty to their leader and their firm was so fierce as to be sometimes embarrassing in its mawkishness and even, to the irreverent, laughable in its parochialism. (Asked by the Pujo Committee in 1912 whether or not a certain action of the House of Morgan was defensible, a leading Morgan partner replied in passionate earnest, "I do not know why the House did it, but if the House did it, it was most defensible!" The line was to be publicly quoted, with entire approval, by another leading Morgan partner a generation later.) Up to shortly before the First World War, the ranks of partnership were not closed, to those otherwise qualified, by the lack of a college diploma; thus the American dream of the self-made man was honored. Indeed, although they were socially and ideologically fairly homogeneous, the partners were perhaps as much a physical as a social type, with a kinship more primitive than social background or like-mindedness. They were generally tall, slim, handsome, fair, with copious heads of hair that turned prematurely white; as early as the turn of the century it had been said in Wall Street, not quite wholly in irony, "When the angels of God took unto themselves wives among the daughters of men, the result was Morgan partners." Like a rare breed of dog or horse, they shared a certain aura, and the aura was necessary to the role they conceived for themselves. In a society whose leadership automatically goes to successful traders and their heirs and successors, they were pretending that they were not the heirs and successors of successful traders but rather men destined, somehow or other, to rule that society wisely. They were trying to invent an American aristocracy—themselves.

Henry P. Davison, son of a Pennsylvania plow salesman, no college man, last right-hand man of the elder Morgan, and active up to shortly before his death in 1922, epitomized the Morgan aura, and suggested the Morgan methods, in a wartime episode when he was chairman of the American Red Cross War Council. At a Detroit rally at which he was exhorting a crowd to contribute to the Red Cross fund drive, a rude and raucous voice suddenly called out, "We want to know what the Morgan firm is doing with all these hundreds of millions of dollars it collects for the Red Cross!" A hush fell, and Davison let it ripen for a few seconds. "Do you think that is an entirely fair question?" he asked finally. The interlocutor vigorously made it clear that he did. "Very well," said Davison, "I will tell you this: that the firm's entire connection with this fund consisted of a subscription from the partners of one million dollars, and a stipulation that not one penny be ever deposited with the firm." This information—previously withheld out of modesty, or shrewdly husbanded for just such a moment?—carried the day, and both applause and contributions were forthcoming. To combine success with righteousness—that was to be a Morgan partner, and if an element of what the churlish would call "taking advantage" seemed to creep in, that too could find roots in American Protestantism. It is entertaining, though perhaps a little startling, to note that Davison's partner Thomas W. Lamont later wrote that what struck him about the episode was that Davison had "made no attempt at platform guile."

Lamont was the quintessential Morgan partner of the 1920s, and after Davison's death the habitual spokesman for his senior. "Mr. Morgan speaks to Mr. Lamont and Mr. Lamont speaks to the people," it was said. Handsome and patrician as the best of them, Lamont was sometimes called "the soul of respectability." Like so many powerful Americans of his era, he had been raised in a parsonage, the son of a poor Methodist minister in Claverack, New York, brought up to believe that cards, dancing, and even sidewalk strolling on Sunday were sinful. After working his way through Harvard he went to New York to seek his fortune, and became a Morgan partner in 1911 at the age of forty. During the 1920s he was thought to be the "brains" of the firm, and besides being its spokesman he was its chief diplomatic emissary—to China, Japan, Mexico, and Egypt, for example—in transacting loans and giving financial advice; but it was not so much on the strength of his public work as on that of his immense private influence, his virtual open wire to the White House during the tenancy of Hoover, that Ferdinand Lundberg was to write that during the decade Lamont "exercised more power . . . has put into effect more final decisions from which there has been no appeal, than any other person." He became rich but not vulgarly so, and a leading benefactor of those respectable institutions, Harvard and Exeter. If there was a shadow of disappointment in the soul of respectability's professional life, it may have been a secret wish to have been a literary man; he began as a newspaper reporter, always had many literary friends, was angel to a literary journal, and for a short time had a fling at owning a New York newspaper, the *Evening Post*. If there was a weakness in his exemplary character, it must have been that most Morganian shortcoming, self-serving sentimentality. In his unrelievedly worshipful biography of his partner Davison, Lamont sharply criticized the authors who had dealt with the life of Morgan the Elder for writing without knowing their subject personally—and then he cheerfully went on to add that "Mr. Morgan never undertook to meet newspaper or periodical writers." Hardly the cool logic of a great banker. Toward setting the record straight as to Morgan's character, Lamont told of how on his own very first day as a partner of the firm, in 1911, he had heard the senior Morgan, informed that a New York bank with thirty thousand depositors of modest means was in danger of failing, immediately offer unconditionally to guarantee the deposits in full, with the comment, "Some way *must* be found to help these poor people." Lamont explained that he told the story only to "show the extraordinary impulse that always was in Mr. Morgan's mind, to try to help people out of difficulties, regardless of the cost to himself."

Well and good; the House of Morgan did guarantee the deposits, and ended up losing $200,000 as a result. But did Pierpont Morgan, that least sentimental and least egalitarian of men, really say, "Some way *must* be found to help these poor people"? The social historian Frederick Lewis Allen, a Pierpont Morgan enthusiast, couldn't believe he did, and other students of the subject consider the sentence about as likely to have come from the lips of Genghis Khan. "When that the poor have cried, Caesar hath wept," Shakespeare's Mark Antony said in his funeral tribute to *his* late senior partner, and the listeners were not expected to take the orator too literally.

A more inscrutable but not necessarily less characteristic member of the club in the 1920s was Dwight W. Morrow. His disdain for great wealth in his young adulthood went to an extreme even for a future Morgan partner; he used to have a nightmare, from which he would wake up screaming, that he had become rich. As a young lawyer, he told his wife that the mundane life of the New York bar was not for him, and that when he had made one hundred thousand dollars he intended to retire and teach history. Instead, in 1914, when he was not quite forty, he left the bar to accept a Morgan partnership and to become rich, and by 1925 the nightmare had apparently materialized, because he was desperate to escape Wall Street for some more elevating milieu. He eventually found it in government service, as Ambassador to Mexico, behind-the-scenes mentor to his college classmate Cal Coolidge, and United States Senator from New Jersey in the year before his death in 1931. But he scarcely found peace of mind.

The contrast between Harold Nicolson's biography of Morrow, a bland and syrupy paean to Morgan respectability and high-mindedness if there ever was one, and Nicolson's later-published diary notes, is startling and illuminating. "A Protean figure. There was about him a touch of madness . . . or something inhuman and abnormal. . . . He had the mind of a super-criminal and the character of a saint," Nicolson says of Morrow in the diary, written at the very time he was composing his innocuous book (of which he was later to speak contemptuously himself). Of some fatuous clubwomen in Pittsburgh who were oppressing Nicolson with clichés about the public, visible, respectable Morrow, Nicolson confided to his diary, "I longed to say, 'But this is all nonsense and you know it. Dwight Morrow was a shrewd and selfish little arriviste who drank himself to death.' "

That would have been at least as much of a lie as the pap Nicolson actually wrote. Still, it was what he longed to say to the ladies, and perhaps to put in his book; like the general public, and Wall Street in particular, Nicolson hankered to deflate the Morgan partners' eternal rectitude and catch them out as pious hypocrites. Morrow was a Protean figure indeed, and one suggesting a new dimension, unimagined tortured depths and contradictions, behind the elegant, gentlemanly façades of the aristocrats of 23 Wall. Were they the straightforward fellows they wanted to appear—or supreme stuffed shirts? Surely, like most of us, they were something of each. As naïveté can be the luxury of the well-placed, so false naïveté can be their weapon. Lamont, the product of the Claverack parsonage, surely *believed* twenty years later that he had heard Pierpont Morgan keening for the poor bank depositors; similarly, there is no reason to think Morrow doubted for a moment that he hated and despised wealth. It was part of the genius of the firm, perhaps the backbone of the moral grandeur that enthralled crass and skeptical Wall Street in spite of itself, that these questions could not be simply answered in the House of Morgan's heyday and still cannot be now.

III

Kuhn, Loeb & Company, just down the street physically but a good deal more distant socially, was the second most powerful firm in the Street. Four years older than J. P. Morgan & Company, it, along with its German-Jewish colleagues like J. & W. Seligman & Company, Lehman Brothers, and Goldman, Sachs, had been the first American investment bankers in the post–Civil War period, and when the upstart House of Morgan had so vigorously entered the lists, Kuhn, Loeb had met the challenge for dominance in a series of epic struggles that had culminated in a turn-of-the-century free-for-all for control of the Northern Pacific Railroad, with Morgan and James J. Hill arrayed on one side and Kuhn, Loeb and E. H. Harriman on the other. After that the two firms had entered into an armed truce that amounted at times to an alliance to repel new invaders. The territory gradually became broadly and tacitly divided between them: in a test of strength, industrial and utility financing to Morgan, railroads to Kuhn, Loeb. In the early 1920s Kuhn, Loeb had a total business as large as or larger than that of the House of Morgan, but had far less prestige and influence; in that regard it was not equipped to compete with the intangible but inescapable facts of nativism, Yankeeism, and Protestantism, which the men of 23 Wall embodied so fully and could trade on so adeptly.

But Kuhn, Loeb had its own well-cultivated air of breathtaking superiority. As Judge Harold Medina would say of the firm later, it had "a high-toned and exclusive character" stemming from the natures of the men, almost all of them related to each other by blood or marriage, who made it up, and from the singular way it chose to do business. The first Kuhn, Loeb partner not related in one way or another to one of the others had been accepted in 1911; in the early 1920s, vast as the organization was in regard to volume of business, it was still so much a family affair that there were only four partners. Its basic business ethic, called "our show-window policy" by the chief of those partners, Otto H. Kahn, was described by him with his characteristic elegance: "It is not we that go to the corporations and ask them to do business with us. We hope that we have established a reputation which is our show window, which attracts customers. We hope that it is our trade mark. . . . We do not go after them. That may be conceited, but we do not." Moreover, when corporations came hat in hand to Kuhn, Loeb, it was a point of honor that the firm never indulged in price competition, never accepted the applicants as new clients under conditions in which Kuhn, Loeb might be accused of having "stolen" them from another banking firm. Interestingly—and, in terms of social history, significantly—just this policy of which Kahn was so proud was finally to bring the firm afoul of the federal authorities, who insisted that the refusal to try to steal business from competitors was prima facie evidence of illegal conspiracy in restraint of trade. Thus gentlemanly values came into head-on collision with those of bureaucratic democracy.

Jacob Schiff, the financial genius who had brought Kuhn, Loeb to the fore and guided its destinies for almost half a century, had died in the fall of 1920, a few days after the Wall Street explosion (though not as a consequence of it). The new dominant figure, Otto H. Kahn, was an even more extraordinary man. He was far and away the greatest patron of the arts that the country had ever seen. "I must atone for my wealth," he said—rationalizing, reducing to an entry on a kind of moral balance sheet, the same guilt that gave Dwight Morrow nightmares. The Morgan Yankees did not seek to atone for their wealth, but rashly undertook a tougher metaphysical task—to justify it. Kahn's means of atonement was

51

equally characteristic. The Morgan Yankees might collect rare books and hobnob with literary folk; in Puritan tradition the printed word had been highly respected, but the theater had been considered wicked, and the performing arts were seldom for them. Kahn had grown up in a lush atmosphere of music-dominated European culture in Mannheim. Thomas Lamont might buy control of the *Evening Post* and finance the *Saturday Review of Literature*; Kahn bought control of the Metropolitan Opera Company, brought to it Toscanini and Gatti-Casazza and thereby ushered in its most glorious era, annually made up its deficit out of his own pocket, and at his death in 1931 was still its president and chief stockholder. He introduced to American audiences the Russian ballet and Paris Conservatoire Orchestra, gave paintings and cash to many museums, endowed many art schools, opera companies, and theatrical projects, and even put up money prizes for Negro artists. And, showing the vein of steel that made him so eminent as a banker, the same man could write admiringly of E. H. Harriman, whom even the gruff and unfastidious Pierpont Morgan loathed for his ruthlessness: "His was the genius of the conqueror, his dominion was based on rugged strength, iron will, irresistible determination, indomitable courage."

Kahn and the younger Morgan, both born in 1867 and in their prime in the 1920s, are a study in Wall Street comparison and contrast. Both attached great importance to personal deportment, liked to conceal their philanthropies, and were unashamedly Anglophile. But where Morgan's style of life ran to the vigorous, the outdoor, the heartily athletic, Kahn's emphasized the elegant frailty of a hothouse flower. Where Morgan radiated the faint anti-intellectualism of the country squire, Kahn was thoroughly intellectual and urban. Where Morgan's "English accent" was that of an American who had lived in England and went there often, Kahn was a *real* Englishman who through most of his life kept the British citizenship he had acquired as a young London banker. Where Morgan in his office was a monument of staid sobriety, Kahn, in his, liked to sing. Twin eminences in their time in their big-little world, they were allies and enemies—each regarding the other with a subtle mixture of respect and scorn.

IV

In financial life, where values tend to take the candid form of prices, issues that may be smothered or confused or euphemized in the rest of society sometimes stand out with crystal clarity. So it has been in Wall Street with the issue of the relations between American Christians and American Jews. From the earliest arrival of Jews in Wall Street in numbers, following the great mid-nineteenth-century migrations from Germany, there had been a degree of more or less overt anti-Semitism, especially noticeable in panics when scapegoats were wanted. Jay Gould, personally unappetizing and professionally a cheat of monstrous proportions, was often spoken of in the Street as a descendant of Shylock and was described even by Henry Adams as "the complex Jew"—although his ancestors had settled in Connecticut in 1646 and probably not one of them had been Jewish. Pierpont Morgan's hostility to Kuhn, Loeb in the years before the truce was a matter of professional rivalry more than of religious prejudice, but the latter question was by no means out of his mind. "Pierpont feels that he can do anything because he has always got the best of the Jews in Wall Street," Andrew Carnegie crowed after *he* had got the best of Morgan, or so he thought, in the deal that led to the formation of U.S. Steel. "It takes a Yankee to beat a Jew, and it takes a Scot to beat a Yankee!" Carnegie's and Morgan's cheerful assumption of the existence of "Jewish" ethnic traits, combined with the equally cheerful assumption of their own superiority, was of course wholly characteristic of American life at the time. Not so characteristic of it, though, was the respect Morgan felt for his Jewish rivals. They were competitors worthy of his mettle; after the Northern Pacific affair he would have been slower to think that he could "do anything." By accepting Jacob Schiff and his firm as an equal, Morgan, however grudgingly, admitted the Jews of Wall Street, or a few of them, into the American establishment. This happened at the outset of the twentieth century—considerably before the Jews of the rest of the United States were to achieve the same thing.

The old Morgan–Kuhn, Loeb armed truce was the very basis of Jew-gentile relations in Wall Street of the 1920s. Admission of Jews to the business establishment had been unaccompanied by their admission to the social one; in 1925 as in 1900, the clubs and drawing rooms of the Morgan Yankees and their like were generally closed as a matter of course to Jews, however cultivated and accomplished. (The chief exceptions were a few "Christianized" Jews with Anglo-Saxon names, who had been wholly accepted by the leading Protestants of the time.) You can do business with anyone, old Morgan had said with his genius for blunt prescience, but you can go yachting only with gentlemen. Perhaps, one may add, it all depended on one's definition of gentlemen; there is no evidence that the cultivated and accomplished Jews of Wall Street felt their lives to be blighted by these exclusions.

But there was a more serious aspect to the matter. Ironically, the very success of a few persons of Jewish background in winning their way early to the innermost and uppermost circles of Wall Street had had the effect, not of opening that way for others to follow, but rather of strengthening the will of the opposition to bar the path. Growing fear and resentment of adventurous and successful outsiders led to their exclusion where exclusion was possible. Thus in the 1920s, by which time the country's Jewish population had swelled to several times what it had been at the turn of the century, most of the Wall Street law firms hired no Jews at all, while some nine out of ten of the big banks followed the same policy (as, indeed, a few of them do today). In stock brokerage, according to one estimate, 60 percent of the firms adhered to rigidly anti-Semitic hiring policies, 15 percent gave preference to Jews because their customers were predominantly Jewish, and the remaining 25 percent were unprejudiced. The Stock Exchange was widely known to have an informal quota system designed to prevent Jews from gaining a foothold in its power structure. And there were office buildings on and around Wall Street that consistently refused to rent to Jews. While the connection of these conditions with the bitter old local business rivalries seems unmistakable, it ought to be added that they can surely be attributed in part to the national mood of the time—a time in which the blue-chip corporations went in for tokenism in the hiring and promotion of Jews, resort hotels openly advertised themselves as restricted to a gentile clientele, and some Jewish apartment-house owners in New York and elsewhere found it expedient to refuse Jews as tenants. American society seemed to find no anomaly in the fact that it had compelled such landlords to bar themselves from living under their own roofs.

Finally—to give life to statistics and to suggest the ambivalence of the Wall Street Jew-Christian relationship at its most elevated level—a true story. It is May 7, 1915, the morning of the sinking of the liner *Lusitania* by a German submarine off the Irish coast, with the loss of many American lives. Into the main room of J. P. Morgan & Company comes the white-bearded patriarch of Kuhn, Loeb, Jacob Schiff himself. There is a general stiffening of the partners in the room, J. P. Morgan among them; at the time, Kuhn, Loeb and Schiff are suspect of having German sympathies arising from ties of birth and long business associations, although in fact they, and Schiff in particular, are wholeheartedly for the Allied cause with the single reservation that they withhold their support from Czarist Russia, the land of pogroms. With a certain uncharacteristic timidity, Schiff approaches Morgan and murmurs regrets at "this most unfortunate outrage." Morgan makes a curt rejoinder and turns abruptly on his heel, leaving Schiff—the one banker of them all whom Morgan's mighty father had owned as an equal—to walk crestfallen out of the building alone.

After an awkward silence, Morgan says to his partners, "I suppose that I went a little far. I suppose I ought to apologize?" The silence grows longer and more painful, and then Dwight Morrow scribbles something on a writing pad and hands it to his senior partner. Morgan reads, " 'Not for thy sake, but for thy name's sake, O House of Israel!' " Morgan nods in agreement; then he gets his hat and sets out for Kuhn, Loeb & Company to apologize to Schiff.

The tentative approach, the brutal snub, the instant remorse, the Biblical quotation that almost unconsciously introduces a religious question where none had been, and finally the apology too late to do much good—it all encapsulates the emotional climate of the old rivalry that a past-haunted Wall Street carried out of the war into the 1920s.

V

Apart from those few ancient and unassailable German-Jewish investment banking firms, the Wall Street establishment in general was emphatically in the Morgan rather than the Kuhn, Loeb mold. Allen compiled a list of fifty of the most powerful Wall Streeters of the decade, and found them to be remarkably homogeneous. Although many had been born in the West or Midwest, their educational backgrounds were generally Eastern and traditional; eleven on the list had been to Harvard, four to Yale, three each to Cornell and Amherst, and so on. Far more than American business leaders outside of Wall Street in the time of Sinclair Lewis' *Babbitt* and H. L. Mencken's "booboisie," these New York financiers had the dress and demeanor of gentlemen; Wall Street, Allen pointed out, was a school of manners, and the place where the possession of manners or a good counterfeit of them had definite business value. About one in four of the fifty had been born into the financial ruling class, and those who had traveled furthest to achieve it tended to be not noisy and conspicuous mavericks, but the most sedulous apes of its characteristic style. Most of them lived on the Upper East Side of Manhattan (only four of the fifty commuted from the suburbs in winter), and had country houses in New Jersey or on the North Shore of Long Island, where they played golf, kept racing stables, and sailed (more than half of them owned yachts). They belonged, most often, to the Metropolitan Club in town and the Piping Rock Club in the country. Their extracurricular good works ran to trusteeships of universities and educational foundations, seldom to patronage of the arts or social-reform movements. Among the fifty, only about half were publicly identified with any religious denomination, and in the cases of many of those who were, the identification was clearly nominal or ceremonial. A sociologist, though, would have had no trouble classifying them as to religious standing: precisely, they were lapsed Protestants. Only seven on the list were of Jewish ancestry—all of these investment bankers except for the speculator Bernard M. Baruch—and apparently even fewer were Roman Catholics. Until the very end of the 1920s Catholics were excluded considerably more rigidly than Jews from the financial inner circle—although, as we shall see, they succeeded in drawing some inner circles of their own.

It was a time when Wall Street still claimed the chosen youth of the nation. The bright boys from the best colleges went there to be lawyers or bankers because that was the way one got rich and carved out a career—whether in law, finance, government service, or even politics. The dull boys from the same colleges, the well-born athletes and playboys, pleasant-mannered, socially at ease, intellectually incurious and indolent, drifted there because it was the natural thing to do and was also the easiest place for them to make a living. "I've always thought that there was very little wit wanted to make a fortune in the City," says one of Trollope's acerbic characters of the gilded Victorian youths who went from Oxford or Cambridge to London's financial district. So it was of the correct young men from Harvard, Yale, or Princeton who went to Wall Street in the 1920s to sell bonds. "Everybody I knew was in the bond business," says Nick Carraway, the young Yale graduate in the exemplary novel of the era, *The Great Gatsby*. "So I supposed it could support one more single man. All my aunts and uncles talked it over as if they were choosing a prep school for me, and finally said, 'Why—ye-es.' " Yes, indeed; the Nick Carraways found that in the bond business connections were an entirely adequate substitute for wit; all one needed was good customers, and for good customers there were always one's relatives and the well-heeled acquaintances one had made at school and college. Like Nick Carraway, one did not consider business hours the important part of one's life. It was in the evenings, at the long, long parties in New Jersey or on Long Island, that one really came to life, to stay up until three or four in the morning and then catch just enough sleep to make it possible to drowse through another day downtown. Like few Americans, privileged or not, before or since, these young Wall Streeters strongly oriented their lives to leisure rather than to work.

Even in the more rigorously competitive business of stock brokerage, where the ups and downs of the market presumably went their neutral way without regard for birth or breeding or schooling, those things could still be of advantage. The key to success in stock trading was exclusive information, and the distribution of such information was arranged, informally but nonetheless carefully, along social lines. There was Metropolitan Club information and Links Club information, there was even Harvard-Yale-Princeton information and Williams-Amherst information, and a possessor of any such information would no sooner give it to someone outside his own circle, or withhold it from someone inside, than a Mafia man would betray a colleague to the police.

A caste, then—and a rather pale, uninteresting one at that—engaged in perpetuating itself? To a certain extent, yes. ("They're a rotten crowd. You're worth the whole damn bunch put together," Carraway says finally to Jay Gatsby, the self-made man, and thus reaffirms the American gospel of social mobility.) But there was something else. Along with the indolent, charming snobs there were the almost-genuine aristocrats; the country's most brilliant and public-minded men were still more apt to be found in Wall Street than in Washington or the universities. To work in the small town south of Fulton Street in those years was to have the possibility of meeting, if not of becoming, the great of one's time or of a time soon to come; and if it seems strange that a nation's school for leaders should have been a place dedicated solely and simply to the practice of dealing in money, it must seem almost miraculous how little the quality of leadership shown by the school's graduates apparently suffered.

Recall, then, some of the men, actively working in the Wall Street area on financial matters in the middle 1920s, who were already celebrated in a wider world or were soon to become so.

Of the elder statesmen already full of years and honors, but with more years, honors, and their heaviest responsibilities ahead of them, there were Charles Evans Hughes and Henry Lewis Stimson. Both were lawyers back at their Wall Street desks between assignments in the wider world. Hughes, sixty-three years old in 1925, had come about as close to being elected President as is possible without actually *being* elected, and was by all odds, President Coolidge notwithstanding, the country's first citizen; a former Associate Justice of the Supreme Court, he was just back from a four-year term as Secretary of State, and five years later would leave Wall Street again to return to the bench and become the Court's Chief Justice.

Stimson, approaching sixty, had been Taft's Secretary of War in a bygone time, would be Hoover's Secretary of State in the near future, and at last, incredibly, would return to the War Department an aeon later in social time and be charged with primary responsibility for the decision to use or not to use the atomic bomb against the Japanese. In 1925, unmindful of this dreadful burden to fall upon him in his old age, he was briskly treading Wall Street thinking about mergers and estates and perhaps a divorce or two.

Among men in their fifties, we find, besides Lamont and Morrow, a third equally establishmentarian figure, the West Virginia–born corporation lawyer and conservative Democrat John W. Davis freshly returned from having lost the 1924 Presidential election to Coolidge. Still in their forties in 1925, and very much on the Wall Street scene, were the Morgan partner Russell W. Leffingwell, a former practicing lawyer who had been Assistant Secretary of the Treasury from 1917 to 1920, and Herbert Lehman, an active partner in his family's famous firm, Lehman Brothers, and before long to become Democratic Governor of New York State, and subsequently a Senator. Somewhat less prominent in the financial community just then was a lawyer in his forties, with offices at 52 Wall Street, who had done a stint as Assistant Secretary of the Navy, had run into a setback in the form of a spell of bad health that had left him crippled, but was nevertheless back on his feet and in a decade would become, among other things, Wall Street's bitterest enemy. Few readers need be told that his name was Franklin D. Roosevelt.

Wall Streeters in their thirties in 1925 included John Foster Dulles, then a rising but not especially heralded lawyer; Averell Harriman, like Lehman a partner in a family banking firm; James Forrestal and Ferdinand Eberstadt, rising young men at Dillon, Read & Company; Robert A. Lovett, at Brown Brothers; John McCloy and Thomas K. Finletter, recent recruits at the Cravath law firm; Sidney Weinberg, a Brooklynite who had started as an office boy at Goldman, Sachs & Company, now a new member of the Stock Exchange and eventually to become the chief adviser to the Ford family and a director of perhaps more blue-chip corporations than anyone else living; and Joseph P. Kennedy, an aggressive stock speculator who had left Boston the previous year to get into the thick of Wall Street, and would remain in the thick of American life one way and another for almost forty years to come.

Taken as a group, these men made up a galaxy the like of which Wall Street has not seen since. Yet among the youngest Wall Streeters of the time, the men born around the turn of the century and thus still fledgling financiers in 1925, we find hardly any who would later distinguish themselves in public service. It is not hard to deduce why. The financial careers of that generation were to suffer an early blight due to circumstances beyond their control, and immediately afterward the character of national government would change abruptly and perhaps permanently: whether Democratic or Republican, government after 1932 would take to recruiting talent for appointive posts from the universities and from business rather than from finance. Wall Street as the nursery of statesmen was already, without knowing it, in its last years.

But two young men, each to become a public figure in his way, cannot be overlooked.

James Paul Warburg, the witty, ebullient, and debonair son of a Wall Street giant—the Kuhn, Loeb partner Paul M. Warburg, often called the father of the Federal Reserve System—was one of the brightest and most interesting young bankers of the middle twenties. Born in 1896 in Germany, he had had a bilingual, two-continent childhood, made a brilliant record both academically and socially at Harvard, flown the precarious crates of the U.S. Navy in the war, and then rapidly attained to a key vice presidency of the International Acceptance Bank, a sort of commercial-banking off-shoot of Kuhn, Loeb. True enough, his father had founded the bank, but there was little question in the mind of anyone who knew him that Jimmy Warburg could have made his way without benefit of nepotism. At the age of twenty-five, for example, he had been offered the post of Assistant Secretary of Commerce by Herbert Hoover, and had turned it down on the ground that he considered himself too young. In addition, he was that rare bird, a serious professional banker whose interests and friendships in the worlds of the arts and entertainment were more than skin-deep. He was a Sunday painter of racy nudes, he sometimes played poker with the celebrated Algonquin group (with results that must have raised their regard for banking as an intellectual discipline), and his house on East Seventieth Street was a permanent salon frequented by the likes of George Gershwin and Sigmund Romberg. Indeed, he was actually a professional in both the arts and entertainment. Was he not a published poet—and not vanity-published, either? Was he not the lyricist of some quite successful popular songs? No one knew quite which way Jimmy Warburg was going, but there seemed little question that he was on his way—and he was.

Richard Whitney, older than Warburg—he was already in his middle thirties in 1925—was quite a different breed of cat, and was also further along the road to success. Indeed, he had emphatically arrived at it, and no wonder; he possessed impeccable connections, as good an education as the nation could offer, and the inborn ability to lead. Entirely unrelated to the New York Whitney clan stemming from the turn-of-the-century transit king and partner of Thomas Fortune Ryan, he was the scion of seventeenth-century Massachusetts settlers who had crossed on the *Arbella*, the ship that followed the *Mayflower*, the son of a Boston bank president, and the nephew of a former Morgan partner. At Groton School he had been captain of the baseball team, acting captain of the football team, manager of the school play, and that most awesome of schoolboy authorities, a prefect; decades later he was still a well-remembered favorite of his headmaster, the Reverend Endicott Peabody. At Harvard, while not distinguishing himself especially in academic work—he said later that intellectual pursuits had had no attraction for him, and that he had chiefly enjoyed "factual" subjects such as history—he had rowed on the varsity crew and been taken as a matter of course into the Porcellian Club, and so great was his enthusiasm for his entire Harvard class, not to mention the efficiency of his memory, that many years later he could entertain and astonish his friends by reciting the first, middle, and last names of every member of it. After Harvard he had spent a year with a Boston brokerage firm and then headed for Wall Street, where he had bought a Stock Exchange seat in 1912 and formed his own firm, Richard Whitney & Company, bond specialists, in 1916. Meanwhile, his elder brother George (also Groton and Harvard, also Porcellian) had married the daughter of a Morgan partner and by 1919 had become one of the most prominent junior Morgan partners himself. As for Richard, he had married the daughter of a former president of Wall Street's beloved Union League Club and onetime business associate of Pierpont Morgan. In all these circumstances, he had naturally become the "Morgan broker"; when Morgan partners had transactions to make on the Stock Exchange that they fastidiously declined to frequent in person, it was usually he who made them. When the gods of 23 Wall materialized on the earthly market across the street, the bodily form they took was that of Dick Whitney.

It was an impressive form. Obviously this position alone gave Whitney great influence and even power, but he had personal qualities that made people notice him, too. If this outline of his status makes him sound like a Nick Carraway some years later, his personality was actually more like that of another Fitzgerald character, the snobbish, arrogant athlete, Tom Buchanan. Tall and muscular, with athletic build only slightly run to fat, always impeccably groomed, and handsome in spite of heavy features, with a liking for wearing formal clothes to work, he cut an imposing figure in the Street. He had a toplofty way of being able to deal perfectly factually and equitably with people he considered his social inferiors—which meant most people—and at the same time leaving no doubt of just how he considered them; he was master of the bully's art of flattering people by seeming to treat them as his equals while at the same time reminding them they weren't. But despite his snobbishness, he had business friends of all sorts, and his office hiring practice, unlike that of so many other firms, was not anti-Semitic. He lived on a grand scale at his house in New York and on his five-hundred-acre estate near Far Hills, New Jersey, where he rode to hounds, raised champion Ayrshire cattle, and augmented a staff of household servants with a platoon of twelve "outside hands"—herdsmen, grooms, a jockey.

Such were the lives of two of Wall Street's comers—broadly speaking, one a Kuhn, Loeb man and the other a Morgan man.

VI

... And at the end of Wall, its single Gothic Revival spire rising like the hat of a worldly monk, its chancel extending a cliff overhanging Trinity Place, its green graveyard covering the bones of Hamilton, stood Wall Street's church, Trinity. As befitted the occupant of that position, it was Protestant (specifically, Episcopal) and rich (the balance sheet in the late twenties showed annual productive assets of the parish, mainly real estate, at $14 million, and annual net income from investments, after deducting all expenses and taxes, at over $700,000; meanwhile, the one-acre plot on which the church stood was appraised by the current real-estate market at roughly $40 million). "Trinity is entirely surrounded now by tall buildings constantly rising higher, some of them the highest in the world," wrote the Reverend Caleb R. Stetson, who had succeeded the future Bishop Manning as Trinity's rector in 1921, in the Parish Year Book and Registry at the end of the decade.

> One has the feeling that the forms of Mammon are like a circle of ravenous wolves waiting to pounce upon the only open space left in this section, the only witness to the things of the spirit in the midst of the great temples of materialism. But here the church has stood since long before the United States was born, since the time when Wall Street was really a wall built to protect the city from the attacks of Indians and wild beasts. . . .

He went on to say that the permanent population of the parish area, consisting chiefly of seamen originally from Middle Europe along with a smattering of Greeks, Armenians, and Syrians, was constantly growing smaller as new office buildings displaced old residential tenements, and that it had recently dropped below five thousand. The Sunday congregations, as always, came largely not from this tiny contiguous population (made up largely of Roman Catholics) but from uptown. The ground physically surrounding it was mission territory to Trinity—and as Stetson interpreted that mission, it was not just to the residents but to the immeasurably larger working population, the people who made Wall Street Wall Street, the hundreds of thousands who surged in each morning to occupy the temples of materialism and then surged out again at night. Every weekday at noon, Trinity held a half-hour service for downtown workers, at which the rector or one of his assistants exhorted those caught up in the excitement and absorption of money dealings to remember the things of the spirit; and, in addition, an actual Trinity missionary, the Reverend William Wilkinson, climbed a box in the open air on the Street each lunchtime to deliver a short sermon bringing the message directly to the heathen. The outdoor sermons generally were well, although perhaps not reverently, attended; the church services generally were not.

There was a reason: a Wall Street saying had it that a man seen entering Trinity was a man in trouble. Evidence of the urge to pray was a cause for tongue-clicking and a sign of impaired credit. "Poor Jones! There he goes into Trinity—he must be cleaned out." But Trinity would have its day yet.

Chapter Four

So Near the Apes

I

One spring day during the late 1920s, a small group of Americans, acting in a time-honored tradition, met secretly and hatched a plot to make themselves some quick money. The method they chose was manipulation of the price of the stock of Radio Corporation of America, then one of the hottest issues on the market. Under a formal partnership agreement, duly approved by their lawyers, they committed themselves to deal in one million shares—valued, at the current price, at ninety million dollars. They then enlisted, for a fat fee, the services of Michael J. Meehan, the Stock Exchange member best in a position to carry out the manipulation because he acted as the floor specialist for Radio stock. At the start of the operation the stock stood at 90. Using a series of carefully contrived feints and maneuvers shrewdly and deliberately calculated to deceive the investing public, Meehan in a few days brought in thousands of unsuspecting buyers from the general public, and thus drove the price up to 109. At this point the men in the small group sold out their stock, and the public buyers were left holding theirs while the price quickly settled back to 87. The whole thing took just over a week, during which Meehan, along with his associates in handling the operation, earned a "management fee" of $500,000. The men in the group, who had spent the week in their offices doing no more than approvingly watching the stock ticker record Meehan's virtuosity, divided a net profit of just under five million dollars.

This sort of thing, although legal at the time, was not very different in method or intention—only in the sums involved—from the confidence games that had flourished in the United States back at the turn of the century. It was, after all, another form of not-quite-outright larceny requiring high intelligence, great mental dexterity, and no violence. Yet the participants in the Radio operation were not criminal types of the sort of Yellow Kid Weil and the other celebrated con men. They were, on the contrary, rich and eminent Americans, national leaders whose names were known and honored everywhere. Among them, for example, were Walter P. Chrysler, founder and head of the Chrysler Corporation; Charles M. Schwab, the sainted steel man; Mrs. David Sarnoff, wife of the Radio Corporation's president; Percy A. Rockefeller, nephew of John D.; Herbert Bayard Swope, celebrated editor of the *World;* John J. Raskob, Democratic National Chairman; and Joseph Tumulty, former aide and confidant of President Woodrow Wilson.

II

Speculation, trading for the principal purpose of taking a chance on a gain at the risk of a loss, has gone on in stock exchanges since the day the first of them was organized in Amsterdam in 1602. This need shock no one; by its nature a stock exchange rivals a racetrack or a roulette table as a natural medium for taking money risks, and, furthermore, speculation in commercial goods, rather than in pieces of paper representing stores of goods or the hope of acquiring them, had gone on for centuries before 1602. Most people, if asked to account for the urge to speculate, would certainly reply that it is rooted in human venturesomeness, acquisitiveness, and love of risk for its own sake, but the British sociologist Elias Canetti has a rather more engaging and original explanation. "The essence of trading is the giving of one object in exchange for another," he writes.

The one hand tenaciously holds on to the object with which it seeks to tempt the stranger. The other hand is stretched out in demand towards the second object, which it seeks to have in exchange for its own. As soon as it touches this, the first hand lets go of the object; but not before, or it may lose both. . . . The trader remains on his guard during the whole transaction, and scrutinizes every movement of his opposite number. The profound and universal pleasure men take in trading is thus partly explained by the fact that trade is a translation into non-physical terms of one of the oldest movement patterns. In nothing else today is man so near the apes.

In Wall Street in the later 1920s, where speculation in stocks reached a degree of intensity and subtlety and an extent of public participation probably not matched anywhere before or since, it is doubtful that it occurred to any of the speculators that they were recapitulating the movement patterns of their subhuman ancestors swinging from tree to tree. Nor did this occur to the explainers and defenders of speculative activity. On the contrary, those explainers and defenders, led by the authorities of the New York Stock Exchange, emphasized as lyrically as their gifts would allow the creative, human, even almost superhuman accomplishments of speculation and speculators. "Of all the peoples of history the American people can least afford to condemn speculation in those broad sweeping strokes so beloved of the professional reformer," wrote the Exchange's official economist. "The discovery of America was made possible by a loan based on the collateral of Queen Isabella's crown jewels. . . . Financing an unknown foreigner in the hope of discovering a mythical Zipangu cannot by the wildest exercise of language be called a 'conservative investment.'" Such statements as that, which might have startled some of the speculators themselves with the grandeur imputed to their activities, evoked from the Princeton economist Joseph Stagg Lawrence the comment, "The Stock Exchange is the stage whereon is focused the world's most intelligent and best informed judgment of the values of the enterprises which serve men's needs. It is probable that upon this stage can be discovered the aristocracy of American intelligence."

The critics of unrestrained speculation, whose voices were relatively few and muted in the age when the business of America was business, questioned the argument's factual basis, insisting that actually stock speculation had played only a minor role in the growth of American enterprise. But they went further and questioned its morality. They maintained that, as practiced in their time, it was an outrage to the elementary sense of fair play. The earlier Wall Street battles, from Vanderbilt vs. Drew through Morgan vs. Harriman and on down to Allan Ryan vs. the Stock Exchange, had been waged among insiders armed with comparatively equal weapons. But now, for the first time anywhere, the public in large numbers was coming into the arena of speculation, and the question was whether its members, peering for portents at their financial pages and stock tickers in towns and villages around the country, were not hopelessly overmatched by the knowledgeable Wall Street professionals on the spot on the Exchange floor or handy to it in offices within a few blocks. As John T. Flynn was to put it a few years later, "The game of speculation is one played by some three or four thousand insiders and some half a million outsiders on terms of complete inequality." The outsiders, he said, "are permitted to see only a part of their own cards while their professional adversaries have access to the cards of all the players as well as their own."

The form the dispute was most apt to take was a semantic haggle about whether or not speculation was gambling. Emphatically not, said the Stock Exchange—and for good practical reason: quite apart from any moral obloquy attached to gambling, in New York State it was illegal and gambling debts unenforceable, and so if speculation had been judicially pronounced to be gambling, the Exchange would have instantly become incapable of functioning. In advancing its point, the Exchange's economist, who had an intense affection for professors who saw things Wall Street's way, was apt to dust off old Professor Henry C. Emery of Yale, who back in 1908 had drawn up a set of distinctions between speculation and gambling of positively medieval fineness. In their public statements, though, the Exchange leaders tended to deal with the problem through flat assertion rather than logical argument. Asked to make the distinction, the top Exchange spokesman once replied that speculation was "good," since it "has built this country," while gambling, on the other hand, was "bad." So there you were.

The chief instrumentality through which the Wall Street insiders, with Stock Exchange approval, sheared the gullible public lambs was the stock pool (of which the Radio operation was a classic example). The point of a pool manipulation was simplicity itself: it was a way of inducing the Stock Exchange ticker tape to tell a story that was essentially false, and thus to deceive the public. Then as now, the stock ticker tape (as distinguished from the Dow-Jones financial news tape, which does not concern us here) printed no news or comment—only the price and volume, along with the letters identifying the particular stock, of each transaction as it occurred. As such it was every speculator's prime source of information as to what was going on at any given moment; fortunes had been made by clever plungers using no other sources. It was also entirely neutral, giving exactly the same information to everyone, inside Wall Street or out. "The tape doesn't lie" was the sucker's folk wisdom; but, in fact, the tape could be made to lie. Even though it continued to record each transaction as faithfully and impartially as ever, the nature and sequence of those transactions themselves could be so arranged, by the people doing the transacting, as to make the watcher of the tape, in his innocence and greed, buy a gold brick.

The group of capitalists pooling their resources would first pick out a stock suitable to their purpose because it had glamour appeal to the public, and because there were comparatively few shares on the market, making for ease of manipulation. They would then accumulate a large block of those shares, through inconspicuous buying over a period of weeks or months, or, better yet, by getting the company's management, which was usually involved in the pool, to give them an option to buy a certain number of shares at the current price whenever they might choose within a stated period—say, three or six months. They would, if possible, make an ally if not an actual partner of the stock's specialist on the Exchange floor; normally he was involved as either broker or dealer in a large percentage of all transactions in it, and it was he who, holding in his hand the supposedly secret book listing all outstanding orders to buy or sell the stock, had access, in Flynn's metaphor, to the cards of all the players. Finally, they would hire their key man, an expert in manipulation called a pool manager (who, as in the Radio case, might be the specialist himself). Then they were ready to go.

On behalf of the pool, the pool manager, as broker, would begin buying and selling shares of the stock at frequent intervals, in no apparent pattern. Often he would buy and sell it back and forth between the members of the pool, or between them and their relatives, and these essentially spurious transactions, accomplished with the sympathetic help of the specialist, would be so weighted that the price of the stock would begin to rise slightly. In speculators' jargon it would be "active and higher"—a fact that would be advertised to tape-watchers by the constant appearance of the stock's symbol on the tape as each transaction was recorded. Thus the stock would be called to public attention, and the notion of making a quick profit in it planted in the public mind. The eager tape-watchers would gradually begin to buy—cautiously and tentatively at first, then, as the activity continued to increase and the price to rise, more and more boldly. Now the pool manager's operations would become more delicate. On some days he would abruptly switch to the selling side, simply to create confusion; then just when the public was about to decide that the picnic was over, he would come back in with a torrent of buying that would sweep all along with him. Finally, in a skillfully conducted manipulation, the thing would become self-sustaining; the public would in effect take the operation over, and in a frenzy of buying at higher and higher prices would push the stock on up and up with no help from the pool manager at all. That was the moment for the final phase of the maneuver, the pool's liquidation of its own stock, often spoken of indelicately as "pulling the plug." With a mousiness in sharp contrast to the elaborate fanfare with which he had begun his buying, the pool manager would begin feeding stock into the market. The price would respond by turning downward, gradually at first, then more rapidly as the pool manager's trickle of sales mounted to a flood; and before the public could collect its senses, the retreat would have become a rout, the pool would have unloaded its entire bundle profitably, and the public would be left holding the suddenly deflated stock. At the end of such a successful roller-coaster ride the price of the stock would be back at about where it had been at the beginning, and it remained only for the members to divvy up the spoils and go home.

Pool managers with some justification thought of themselves as artists. A few low-class ones, looked down upon by the masters of the fraternity, resorted to such expedients as arranging to have the stock they were manipulating plugged in brokerage-house market letters, or they deliberately circulated false rumors, or they bribed newspaper writers to write favorable stories. This was the equivalent of the use of violence in the con game. But just as the best con men disdained to use violence, so the best pool manipulators disdained these artistically inelegant practices. Their medium was the tape; they took pride in their skill to make it *and it alone* create precisely the effect upon the public that they wanted. If—as seems quite unlikely—any of these artists of the tape ever happened to read Professor Lawrence's paean to speculation, in which he had spoken of the aristocrats of American intelligence at the Stock Exchange, one feels that they would have been sure exactly whom he meant, and would have nodded their heads in approval. They would have been sure he meant them.

In practice: a pool conducted in the stock of Radio in March, 1928—not the one already described—raised the stock's price 61 points in four days. A minor pool in Hudson Motor Car Company later the same year brought a return of $105,467.29 (as stated in the letter of remittance from the pool's broker, which document came to light later) to just one of its participants, a dummy corporation behind which was concealed the president of the Chase National Bank. A pool in Anaconda Copper early in 1929 brought a big return to the president of another revered bank, the National City, who happened also to be the chief public sponsor of Anaconda stock at the time. And so on.

Does it all sound too easy and unsporting, the rich and politically powerful secretly mobilizing their vast resources of money and skill to flummox the struggling middle class and even the poor—those much-heralded bootblacks and newsboys who were being drawn into the market by the lure of easy money? Well, there *was* an element of risk; sometimes the suckers refused to play their assigned

71

role, some pools failed and lost money. And there was a sporting element of sorts, too. The con game was not the pool's only traditional antecedent. A great pool like the 1929 Radio one had some of the attractions of the hunt, of elegantly dressed socialites mounted on blooded horses joining forces with trained hounds to corner and slaughter an unsuspecting fox or rabbit. The kill was not the main point; what counted was the ceremony, the status that came with acceptance into the hunt; the businessmen in pools were the well-groomed riders, the socially inferior but technically proficient pool managers were their schooled hounds, and the public, of course, was the rabbit. One observer wrote that what brought businessmen into pools was "the lure of action, of quick profit, the thrill of battle, the call of the chase . . . the glamor of admission into a charmed circle, the attraction of a mysterious enterprise, and the social aura of association with the elect."

To repeat, there was for practical purposes nothing illegal about pools. The evils of stock manipulation were recognized in the common law in its ancient proscription of the offenses of "engrossing," "regrating," and "forestalling," but these charges had long fallen into disuse in American practice. The question of whether stock manipulation constituted common-law fraud was moot before 1930. Disapproval on the part of Wall Street's own authorities was nominal and easily allayed. "Wash sales"—transactions with oneself to create a false appearance of activity in a stock—were outlawed by both New York State and the constitution of the Stock Exchange; so one satisfied the rules and achieved the same aim by making the spurious trades with one's partners and associates. Specialists were forbidden by the Exchange to participate in pools—so they did it in their wives' names, without objection. Pools in themselves were not considered improper; the president of the Exchange reported later that his staff had investigated the 1928 Anaconda pool and the 1929 Radio pool and found nothing out of order. Asked what, if not manipulation, *had* accounted for the odd gyrations of Radio that March, he replied in a puzzled tone that Radio just seemed to be a "mystery stock."

Official frowns from Washington, then? Prior to 1928, none at all. President Coolidge and his fervently business-loving Secretary of the Treasury, Andrew Mellon, subscribed fully to the view that unrestrained stock speculation was a virtually unmixed blessing to the economy. At the smallest passing sign of an economic downturn, at the faintest hint of business pessimism in any important public figure, one or both of them would unfailingly come forward with optimistic pronouncements of their own, and the market would rebound in response. Only once, and then briefly, does the possibility seem to have occurred to Coolidge that a restraining hand might be beneficial. In 1927 Professor William Z. Ripley of Harvard brought out *Main Street and Wall Street*, in which, although he did not single out pools, he took up in detail a good many other devices being used by corporations to mislead their stockholders and by stock manipulators to mislead investors. "The first duty is to face the fact that there is something the matter," Ripley wrote. "I am conscious that things are not right. The house is not falling down— no fear of that! But there are queer little noises about, as of rats in the wall, or of borers in the timbers." Coolidge invited Ripley to the White House for a conference. He listened carefully to what the professor had to say, nodding now and again in apparent agreement that there was something the matter. When Ripley had finished, Coolidge took the cigar out of his mouth, leaned forward, and asked, "Is there anything we can do down here?" Under existing legislation, Ripley replied, the President was powerless; whereupon Coolidge leaned back and heaved a sigh of relief—one load off his mind.

Nor did the public object to pools, any more than it objects to roulette wheels with a double zero. It loved them because it thought it could turn them to personal advantage; someone else would be the sucker. Bona fide market letters, not under the control of pool managers, would confide to ordinary brokerage-house customers that the inside information was that General Motors or Radio was to be "taken in hand" at 2 P.M. The customers knew what that meant, and they would rush to climb aboard in hopes of taking a short ride to profit with the big money; and some of them were actually clever, coolheaded, and self-controlled enough to pull it off, getting out with a profit before the plug was pulled. So avid was the public for news of pool activities that pool operators, who in earlier times had as a matter of course maintained the strictest secrecy, eventually found that they could take advantage of the avidity.

They need merely drop the hint that a pool was in effect, and their work would be half done. At last the point was reached where pools were reported in the newspapers while they were in progress, almost as if they were sports events. The *Wall Street Journal*, without revealing its source, more or less reported the classic Radio pool day by day, commenting on each day's gyrations in the stock without using the word "pool," but in language of unmistakable purport to the cognoscenti. On March 21, the day after the operation's end, appeared the entirely candid and accurate note: "It is said that the one-million-share Radio pool has been terminated with a net profit of five points to the underwriters." The five points—or, to put it another way, five million dollars—had come out of the pockets of the public, which had now been trained to manipulate a stock, to its own ruin, almost by itself.

So with just about everyone—the fleecer, the fleeced, the public authorities—treating pools as if they were hardly less commendable than Fourth of July celebrations, it clearly would have required self-examination of almost superhuman rigor for their organizers, operators, and participants to have concluded that what they were doing was evil.

Still—a Chrysler, a Rockefeller, a Schwab, a Democratic National Chairman, New York's leading bank presidents, as spiritual cousins to Yellow Kid Weil? It speaks eloquently of the climate of 1928 and 1929.

III

Much has been written about what the master speculators and manipulators of the 1920s did to the investing public, to each other, and to the national economy, but since ours is a tale of men, with their times as background, we deal here chiefly with what they did to themselves.

Jesse Lauriston Livermore was the *éminence grise* among them, by 1920 already a historical figure as well as a leading actor in the stock-market drama, even though he was hardly into his forties at the time and would still, for years to come, retain the white-blond hair and smooth, ruddy complexion that made him look uncannily like a college boy. His talk, too, recalled a past time, peppered as it was with old-time rural slang expressions—"those birds," "well, sir," "sore as a pup." He was the quintessential turn-of-the-century American farm boy who had come to the city and found his knack and his passion in making money by trading. The American philosophers of the time of his birth (1877) had spoken of that pursuit as if it were a kind of religion, and Livermore had come close to making it one for himself. He left school and his father's Massachusetts farm in his early teens and went to Boston to try his hand in the bucket shops that flourished there and in other cities in the 1890s. Making book in stocks for hopeful tinhorn plungers, and juggling the book so that the plungers all but invariably lost, these institutions practiced in its most blatant form the small-time larceny that the country winked at in the name of free enterprise; and Livermore, a raw youth whose voice had hardly changed, almost immediately achieved the tinhorn's dream of turning the tables on them. So uncanny were his judgments of short-term stock movements that the bucket shops soon began refusing to pay his winnings or accept his accounts. At fifteen he was a certified "ringer," forced to resort to false names and disguises to get his bets accepted—but usually in vain. Thus frustrated by too much success, he moved on to the big league, Wall Street, just before the turn of the century. After some initial setbacks in the unfamiliar surroundings, he got his bearings and made his first big killing selling Union Pacific short on a hunch, just before the 1906 San Francisco earthquake; and in the money panic of 1907 his well-timed bear raiding was so massive and demoralizing to the whole market that the imperial Morgan took notice of him, an outland upstart of thirty, by sending emissaries to ask him to relent. The following year he lost a fortune trying to corner the cotton market, and then he went through a decade of spectacular ups and downs, culminating in a short-selling coup in the postwar depression that left him established, apparently permanently, as a man of great wealth. It was his third killing on a national disaster, and because it was well publicized as such he became the object of much public enmity, which left him unaffectedly bewildered. Wasn't selling as legitimate a market transaction as buying? If not, could markets exist? How, then, could an ethical question be involved? If you accepted the market system, as those who criticized him professed to do, he was right.

Livermore in the 1920s was an invisible genie of the market, feared, envied, his wires sometimes tapped, his name often invoked, his face seldom seen. When the market rose, the rumor would spread, and often be printed in the newspapers, that Livermore was buying, was on a bull raid; when it dropped, that he was up to his old bear tactics again. Sometimes the rumors were true and sometimes not; Livermore kept his own counsel. He operated in secrecy and usually as a loner. Although he managed a few pools for others early in the decade, he did not join them himself, preferring in his operations for his own account to take no accomplices. Late in the decade his base of operations was a secret suite of offices eighteen floors above Fifth Avenue, equipped like a large brokerage office with private telegraph wires, dozens of telephones, a standard quotation board kept up to the minute by young clerks, and a staff of trained statisticians to supply him instant information. Doormen and elevator operators answered inquiries by saying that there was no such office; the telephone company told those requesting his number that none in his name was listed. All this for no purpose but the conduct of his personal investments.

Thus a Livermore legend grew, but Livermore, fact-bound, money-obsessed, did not intentionally foster it; legends were not for him. In his occasional written or spoken comments, with candor rare in Wall Street he called the market a game and spoke of a profit not in the usual ringing clichés about free enterprise and individualism, but as "taking money out." He did not hesitate to refer to his "manipulation" of stocks, or the "advertising" he did by churning a stock to get it on the tape; manipulation, in his canon, was within the rules of the game unless it involved "deliberate misrepresentation," in which he was never known to indulge.

His leisure life did not escape his obsession. He had yachts, special cars, fancy estates in several countries, fancy women; but time and again at Palm Beach or Deauville or Cannes a hunch would overtake him and he would rush to the nearest telephone or brokerage office, and then cut short his vacation to hurry back to his only home, Wall Street. He never acquired urban social polish—or, apparently, tried to. Culture in any form was not his dish. He liked to tell a story of a stock trader who was asked, "What do you think of Balzac?" and replied, "I never trade in them Curb stocks"; the trader might have been himself. Formal religion did not interest him, but once, explaining one of his setbacks to a friend, he showed the residue of the New England Calvinist in him: "It might have been the plan of Providence to chasten me." Which meant by implication, of course, that when he won, that might have been Providence's plan, too.

Why is there something so depressing about this single-minded and simplehearted man? Perhaps because his obsession looms in retrospect as a crippling disability; perhaps because he is a kind of gigantic real-life close-up of the kind of American European intellectuals like to imagine, and indeed, because he came so uncomfortably close to being the embodiment of a prevalent American dream. And yet we pity him at our risk, because his ghost may rise up to call us what we cannot call him—a hypocrite.

Other prominent speculators came to Golconda from other physical and social backgrounds. There were the Westerners out of the automobile business or the Chicago grain pit: William C. ("Billy") Durant, grandson of the Civil War Governor of Michigan, founder of General Motors but long since displaced as its master, who by 1925 had won three stock-market fortunes and lost two, and whose vast bull pool with the multimillionaire Fisher Brothers ("Body by Fisher") and other Westerners was jocularly called "the prosperity boys"; and Arthur W. Cutten, whose precise, almost pedantic operations in the grain pit had put him among the dozen richest men in the country, and who in 1925, although he loathed New York with the relentless loathing of a loyal son of the Middle Border, moved on to Wall Street seeking new fields to conquer. But the most cohesive group of them, and the one most interesting as a social phenomenon, was made up of Irishmen from the slums of Eastern cities.

IV

These men came out of what the old Wall Street aristocrats, Protestant and Jewish alike, had long regarded as virtually a servant class. But it was, of course, no longer anything of the sort; identified with big-city politics, the Democratic Party, and active opposition to Prohibition, the Irish found their champion in Alfred E. Smith, and the virulence of the campaign along religious lines that defeated him for the Presidency in 1928 showed the force of Protestant America's ungracious reaction to that emergence. The Wall Street Irishmen, never dreaming of becoming Morgan or Kuhn, Loeb partners, glorying in their Irishness and Catholicism, turned those attributes to account by setting up their own command post where they rallied their forces and hurled defiance, often mixed with comic derision, at the older local settlers. The line of Wall Street endeavor most readily open to them was stock speculation, and that was the line they took.

They brought to it a zest, humor, and high-spiritedness all too lacking in the dour Livermore, in the grim Prohibition-boosting Durant, and in Cutten with his pince-nez and stiff collars and early bedtime. Perhaps inevitably, they usually "got their start" through the benign condescension of established men who found them worthy, or entertaining, or both. Mike Meehan, mastermind of the Radio pools, had started out in 1917 as a theater-ticket broker, scraping up aisle seats to Broadway hits for partners and executives of Morgan, Lehman, and Goldman, Sachs. The partners and executives rather liked the youngster, chubby and red-faced and high-pressure as he was, and some of them helped him set himself up as a Curb broker; he did so well that after a couple of years he moved on to the Stock Exchange. He was on his way then; a decade later he lived at the Sherry-Netherland, his firm owned eight Stock Exchange seats, he was a close friend of all the Democratic mighty starting with Al Smith and John Raskob, the walls of his inner office were lined with Shakespeare bound in calf, he was still as noisy and irreverent as ever, and the Morgans and Lehmans and Goldman, Sachs regarded him with fascinated horror. Meehan originated the idea of branch brokerage offices on ocean liners, and his firm maintained them on the *Bremen,* the *Berengaria,* and the *Leviathan.* Sometimes he and his associates, bent on some bull or bear caper attracting attention to which would not come amiss, would enter the Exchange in a phalanx—Mike Meehan, Esmonde O'Brian, Richard O'Brian, John Moyland, J. P. McKenna. In bulling his beloved Radio from a 1928 low of 85¼ to a 1929 high of 549, in the absence of any dividend payment by the company, he not only accomplished undoubtedly the most spectacular and probably the most disgraceful stock manipulation of the decade; he also, some observers feel, did more than any one man to make the public love the stock market and to plant the seeds of the "people's capitalism" of the era after the Second World War.

Bernard E. Smith, Ben to his friends, grew up around the turn of the century in the shabby Irish neighborhood in the far-West Fifties of New York, left school without graduating, sold newspapers and bummed around the country for a while, sold cars, got a job as a clerk in a brokerage office, and there befriended the firm's rich Protestant customers, who regarded him as "a diamond in the rough." He was rough, all right—an incessant practical joker and kidder, whose kidding, later in his life, was apt to have the harsh edge of a none-too-veiled assault on whatever his former patron regarded as good and sacrosanct. A smallish man with broad shoulders, blue eyes, and an open Celtic face, he returned to stock brokerage in the early postwar years as an office manager, and again found a use for his ability to entertain the quality, to make them like him because they were helping him. It was the very blue-blooded broker Stuyvesant Fish who sponsored him for membership in the Stock Exchange in 1926. Percy Rockefeller, whom he had met in earlier years when he had been an automobile salesman, was now his fast friend and fellow participant in pools. Smith took part in many of the biggest bull pools of 1928 and 1929, and actively managed some of them. Yet despite the fact that he profited handsomely from them, he was not at heart a bull. He had gone broke playing bull in a passing market setback in 1926, and well remembered the experience. With a certain coldness of eye, call it realism or cynicism, Ben Smith—a Puritan of his own kind, who never smoked or drank liquor, beer, wine, tea, or coffee—saw through the ballyhoo of the Coolidge boom to its underlying insubstantiality; he felt a certain contempt for the pieces of embossed paper he was getting rich dealing in, just as he felt a certain contempt for the grave, pious, statesmanlike stuffed shirts who stood behind the boom, and who had served as steppingstones on his way. He was still relatively little known, but his day in the sun was coming.

Joseph Patrick Kennedy of Boston, born the same year as Smith and in somewhat similar circumstances, made his name and his pile a little sooner. He was more ambitious, more Protean, probably more ruthless; moreover, unlike Smith, he had an establishmentarian inside him waiting to be let out. Having broken away from a comparatively humble job with Hayden, Stone & Company's Boston branch, in 1922 he set up his own office behind a door that grandly read "Joseph P. Kennedy, Banker." He quickly made a reputation as an aggressive stock manipulator, and in 1924 he got the assignment of defending Yellow Cab Company, John D. Hertz's Chicago-based taxicab operation, against a bear raid on its stock that seriously threatened the financial position of its owners. Hertz raised the money for a bull pool, and Kennedy, having taken a train from Boston and established himself with a ticker and a battery of telephones at the Waldorf-Astoria in New York, managed it brilliantly, routing the raiders, ending the decline in the stock, and doing it all so deftly that at the end of a month he was able to return the pool all of its money, besides earning himself a handsome commission. A few months later Yellow Cab stock dropped abruptly again, and Hertz, suspecting Kennedy himself of being the bear raider this time, threatened to punch him on the nose when they met next. The punch was never delivered; nor was the double-cross ever definitely pinned on Kennedy, but to his biographer Richard J. Whelan "it would not have been unthinkable." In 1926 Kennedy picked up his brood of infants and young children (among them John F., aged nine, and Robert F., less than one year) and moved with his wife to Riverdale, north of Manhattan, so that he could operate in Wall Street without long-distance commuting. For the rest of the decade he was one of its major operators, specializing in motion-picture stocks.

Smith wanted money as his equalizer with life; Kennedy took money for granted and set his sights on power. Apart from his skill and ruthlessness, his greatest asset was a rare social adaptability that, as Whelan says, permitted him to be equally at home with Meehan or Smith and with Wall Street patricians like Jeremiah Milbank and the loftiest of corporation executives like Owen D. Young of General Electric. Thus he had a dimension lacking in most of the hard-driving and quick-thinking Irish rowdies who carved out a place for themselves in a hostile Wall Street that would have much preferred to be able to go on thinking of them as cops, firemen, ward heelers, or bartenders. But even for Kennedy there were limits. By early 1929 he was rich, powerful, and well known in the

Street, and had even gained a certain reputation for wise conservatism by giving a wide berth to the wilder pool operations. Then one day he strolled into 23 Wall Street and casually asked to see J. P. Morgan. It was a move he must have been planning for some time; he was a calculating man who did not suffer slights gladly, and he must have believed that his influence had reached the point where Morgan would be curious to meet him, or, failing that, would judge that he could no longer afford to snub a man of such stature. For once he had miscalculated—Mr. Morgan, he was told shortly, was too busy to see him.

V

Meanwhile the mood of Wall Street's solid backbone—its Nick Carraways, the proper young men of good family and good education who had come to it as a matter of course, and in the normal course might expect to go on to become its and the nation's statesmen—was changing. It was not that these men were corrupted by the example of the well-publicized killings being made by plungers from the lower social orders; rather, they were changed by easy success, by business life's unexpected compliancy, by how easy they found it to do well at what they had thought was going to call on all their efforts.

Their manners changed. They had been brought up in the old national tradition, going back to the Founding Fathers, of the generalist and the amateur. One did not discuss business on social occasions; in particular, one did not discuss it with women. But now suddenly women themselves talked about business—or rather about the stock market—all the time. If sex had been their favorite subject earlier in the decade when changed national mores had made it newly available to them as conversational material, now sex banter had become a bore; another social change had abruptly opened up another new and perhaps equally fascinating topic. Stock-market talk was no longer considered unfeminine. Brokerage houses maintained separate board rooms where women speculators, whose numbers now ran into the hundreds of thousands, could watch the tape and discuss it without the distraction of male presence; if women are, as they have been accused of being, chronic and inveterate gamblers, their emancipation had at last proceeded to the point where they could indulge this passion openly, in deed and word. And the young Galahads of Wall Street who counseled them and accepted their bets—how could they bring the dinner-table conversation to some more traditionally genteel topic when all the ladies wanted to talk about was Radio and Steel and Anaconda? And in any event, why should they try? What the young brokers had always thought of guiltily as shop talk had suddenly become fashionable social conversation.

It was being done everywhere, in the low saloons as well as the high salons. A perceptive British correspondent newly arrived in New York wrote later: "You could talk about Prohibition, or Hemingway, or air conditioning, or music, or horses, but in the end you had to talk about the stock market, and that was when the conversation became serious." The tradition of the well-rounded amateur, in American social conversation, was temporarily dead.

Worse than his shop talk was the young Wall Streeter's mounting sense of infallibility. Let us glance at one such man—call him Leeds. The descendant of a line of New England clergymen, and a parsonage boy himself, he had come out of Harvard and gallant war duty in the Air Corps to become a broker. He was a modest, candid, and engaging fellow, and he was soon doing well. His aunts and Harvard friends entrusted their money to him, sparingly at first, then more liberally as the market went up and Leeds began to appear to them as a budding financial genius. As the decade wore on and the great boom developed, he made more and more money, even small paper fortunes—*always for his clients;* not that he was not accepting their commissions and thereby himself becoming well-to-do, but in his well-bred and scrupulous way he always gave the benefit of his most sober judgment to his clients first. There might be brokers who did otherwise (as, of course, there were) ; as for him, this was his code. He liked to explain it, with jocular self-depreca-tion, by saying that he had always preferred bartenders who didn't drink themselves. Thus his inherited conscience was not merely assuaged, it was vastly gratified; business gradually became for Leeds, in his own mind, almost a form of social service, of living by the Golden Rule. And as he made more and more money for others, so he came to believe more and more in the remarkableness of his own gifts, and to think of his benign dispensation of them in more and more grandiose terms.

No matter that most other brokers were making lots of money for their clients too, that there were long stretches when it would actually have been difficult for any broker *not* to do so; those who deal successfully in stocks, even the professionals, almost always persuade themselves that theirs is a more or less isolated experience brought about by their own unusual acumen. And now Leeds' friends and clients began to find his gentlemanliness yielding little by little to arrogance. They began to notice an edge of superiority in his manner with them, and sometimes after he had had a drink too many they had to admit to each other that he was getting to be something of a megalomaniac bore. In the time of a stock-market cult, he was coming to conceive of himself as a high priest. And then gradually the change spread through his whole character; there was a certain tendency to treat himself too leniently, a certain erosion of standards of behavior, a certain loss of self-control. Leeds was no longer the man he had been before, they had to admit. "Ill fares the land, to hastening ills a prey," they might have quoted, but didn't, "where wealth accumulates, and men decay."

But of course, wealth was not accumulating for all, even all involved in the market, and thereby hung the generally untold tale of the boom, the tale of the disappointment, regret, mean recriminations, and bitterness of those who saw others getting rich but did not get rich themselves. Unrestrained euphoria and bland overconfidence, we tend to forget, have their inescapable opposite side. For every buyer of stock there is a seller; for every purchase that leads to a profit there is a sale that leads to the loss of a profit that might have been. Many people watch the prices of stocks they have recently sold more closely than the prices of those they still own; thus they show themselves to be more involved in fantasy than in reality, more concerned with justifying past actions than in planning future ones. In short, to be human. Think of those who got out of the market, say, in 1926 or 1928, and then all through 1929 (or almost all) cursed themselves every time they scanned the financial pages for letting a fortune slip through their fingers as a result of their foolish prudence.

Nor can their tempers have been improved by the din in their ears from the Bruce Bartons and John J. Raskobs of the land, who were forever telling them on radio and in the popular magazines and books that in selling their stocks—"selling America short"— they had been not only foolish but also downright unpatriotic and perhaps unchristian as well. (Barton's *The Man Nobody Knows*, presenting Jesus as the "first businessman," whose parables were "the most powerful advertisements of all time," was a great best seller of the Coolidge era.) The sour, dog-in-the-manger mood of those who had lost their chance contributed as much to the American mood of the time as the bland fulminations of the boosters. Hear the wise Barnie Winkelman, a lawyer who handled estates and closings: "A few operators can play the game of finance unemotionally, accepting losses and profits quickly and urbanely. The average man is unfitted for such decisions. . . . Seas of regret and remorse wash the land of purchase and sale. Among considerable portions of the community the sale of securities or real estate at less than the highest attainable price is a major calamity to be regretted for the rest of one's life." There were many among the losers of the boom who, with nothing of their own at stake any longer, were hoping and waiting for a crash that would prove them to have been right and put an end to their envy of others. The mood of the time was two contrasting moods.

Summing up the America that he found on his arrival on these shores in 1929, Claud Cockburn denied that it reflected excessive materialism. He found something "tragic and even noble in this grotesque scene"—that "it was a brief enactment of what was essentially an old American dream. . . . If the attitude of Americans to the stock market boom proved anything, it proved that they believed in miracles . . . that if you try hard enough you can make wonderful things happen." But a few years earlier another brilliant Englishman, John Maynard Keynes, not speaking specifically of Americans, had written in more somber terms of what happens to respectable and responsible people in times of excessive speculation:

> Amidst the rapid fluctuations of his fortunes, [the businessman] loses his conservative instincts, and begins to think more of the large gains of the moment than of the lesser, but permanent, profits of normal business. The welfare of his enterprise in the relatively distant future weighs less with him than before, and thoughts are

excited of a quick fortune and clearing out. His excessive gains have come to him unsought and without fault or design on his part, but once acquired he does not lightly surrender them. . . . With such impulses so placed, the businessman is not free from a suppressed uneasiness. In his heart he loses his former self-confidence in his relation to society, in his utility and necessity in the economic scheme. . . . He of all men and classes most respectable, praiseworthy, and necessary . . . was now to become, and know himself half guilty, a profiteer.

In Wall Street in 1928 and 1929 the sense of half-guilt, and the cause for it, was seeping upward through the ranks of respectability to the very top.

Chapter Five

Things Fall Apart

I

The perfect public forum for the mighty of finance was the
transatlantic shipboard interview. In those times an annual summer
trip to Europe, combining business with pleasure, was considered
all but *de rigueur* in the upper reaches of Wall Street, and in the
absence of transatlantic air service an ocean liner was the way of
getting there. The appearance of a powerful man's name on a
passenger list was just about the only routine occasion for advance
public disclosure of his whereabouts, and probable ready avail-
ability to reporters, at any given time. Thus each June and July, as
the advance of summer gradually converted the city into a caldron
that would steam intermittently until Labor Day or after and the
North River piers came to echo with the farewell hoots of departing
leviathans, the newspaper reporters culled the lists for the names of
Morgan partners, Stock Exchange officials, or famous pool operators,
and, finding them, took pains to be on deck with pad and pencil
shortly before departure time.

As for the mighty men, they could refuse interviews or sequester
themselves in their staterooms if they so desired. But often they did

not so desire. On the contrary, they sometimes selected their departures and arrivals as the moments to make their public statements, invariably referred to in the press as "rare." The fact that their presence on the ship was public knowledge gave them the opportunity to present themselves as reluctant subjects, men trapped into interviews that they could not in democratic courtesy refuse; in fact, they often came on board with carefully prepared and memorized statements. The circumstances gave them a chance to say what they wished to say while, to outward appearances, maintaining the financial traditions of conservative reticence, unavailability, dignity, and mystery.

So every early summer and early fall, the papers would be full of these "rare" public statements from the "usually unavailable" nabobs, and sometimes the market would be rocked by the wash from the statements. The great liners came to be the royal processions of American finance. The mighty men left for Europe, and the market, reacting to their buoyant words, bellowed *"Bon voyage";* they landed at Southampton or Le Havre, and the market cried "Bravo"; their stately conveyances again approached New York, and, as Winkelman wrote, "great salvos of welcome arose from the floor of the Exchange."

Around midnight on Saturday, July 31, 1926, the Morgan partner Thomas Cochran, having boarded the liner *Olympic* shortly before so as to get a night's sleep before her early-morning departure, consented to an interview with a ship news reporter. The following Monday at just past noon, the Dow-Jones financial news ticker carried the result into banks and brokerage houses in Wall Street and around the nation. Among other things, Cochran was reported as having said, "General Motors running at its present rate is cheap at the price, and it should and will sell at least one hundred points higher."

Doubtless many of the Dow-Jones subscribers rubbed their eyes and looked at the broad tape again. The elder J. P. Morgan, once asked by a reporter what the market was going to do, had replied with magnificent evasiveness, "It will fluctuate." Evidently times had changed. Not only was a leading voice from the imperial Corner, 23 Wall Street itself, stooping to tout a specified stock with an explicit future-price prediction, in the terms usually associated with the more importunate sort of brokerage-house telephone sales-man. That in itself would have been enough to cause jaws to drop. In fact, as the *New York Times* said later, "there was no precedent on Wall Street for such an episode." But, in addition, Cochran was—and was publicly known to be—very much of a General Motors insider, in a quasi-fiduciary relationship to the company. J. P. Morgan & Company was General Motors' banker, the firm had huge holdings of the corporation's stock, and some of its partners were General Motors directors. Since the General Motors board had met recently and since it could be assumed that Morgan partners were in the habit of communicating with each other, there was reason to believe that Cochran knew what had taken place at the meeting, and his words appeared to be what was called—although not in Morgan circles—a feedbox tip.

Within minutes, more than half of all the brokers and traders on the Stock Exchange floor were clustered around the post where General Motors was traded. Before the day was over, more than a quarter-million shares of the stock had been traded and its price had risen from 189½ to 201. It was much the same the following day: other listed stocks, and the other trading posts on the floor, were virtually neglected in the frenzy to buy GM, which rose 12½ more points. On Wednesday Cochran, a thousand miles at sea but fully informed as to the brouhaha, sent a radiogram intended for publication in which he disclaimed the interview only partially. He had "authorized" no statement predicting the future price of the stock, he said; otherwise he stood by the interview. Wall Street had no trouble deducing what had happened—the shipboard reporter had violated the time-honored rule of Morgan partners, which they shared with kings and presidents, that they never be quoted directly except by specific permission. Cochran's message from mid-ocean had saved his face before his partners, but it had not really much mitigated the strangeness of his and his firm's action. Regardless of what he had authorized, the fact remained that he, apparently with his partners' approval, had blatantly plugged a stock in which they were interested.

Next day, as GM continued to soar, the *Wall Street Journal* praised Cochran for his frankness, expressing the view that it was a sign of public-spiritedness when corporate insiders shared their favorable inside information with the public rather than keeping it for their own use. But this was rank heresy; even assuming Cochran had disclosed any secrets, which he hadn't, the form of "disclosure" in which he had indulged was all too close to wanton and self-serving manipulation; surely the proper means of corporate disclosure of favorable news was a corporate statement, not an interview with one insider. That the tip was no bum steer became clear soon enough—on August 12, when General Motors announced a 50 percent stock dividend, worth $600 million to its stockholders, which soon sent the stock on up to new heights. So those who had acted on Cochran's words had made money, pots of it, that might otherwise have gone to insiders like himself, and to this extent he might indeed be said to have worked in the public interest. But something more important had happened. J. P. Morgan & Company had descended from its pedestal. Perhaps just once—perhaps in part, yet not wholly, through a reporter's ignorance or bad faith—it had lent itself to the spreading puffery and free-wheeling morality of the growing speculative boom.

> Things fall apart; the centre cannot hold;
> Mere anarchy is loosed upon the world.

II

Things didn't visibly fall apart in 1927; instead, it was the year the big boom got going in earnest. A year after Cochran's interview the Dow-Jones industrial average stood half again as high as at the time of it. Charles Lindbergh's flight to Paris that May had helped by attracting attention to aviation stocks, but much more than that, it had helped psychologically, by bolstering national confidence in the unlimited possibilities of life—particularly life in America. What if there had never been such a stock market before, in this or any country? There was going to be one now. Nor was the boom all hopes and fantasies; in spite of a mild recession toward the end of the year, business in almost all its aspects was good, giving the stock market a sound underpinning. Who better than President Coolidge, for whom the boom had already long since by common consent been named, to put the new spirit into words? On November 17, 1927, he said that America was "entering upon a new era of prosperity." So the New Era was born; the phrase meant permanent prosperity, an end to the old cycle of boom and bust, steady growth in the wealth and savings of the American people, continuously rising stock prices. . . .

There was only one recognized cause for concern. As more and more people sought to share in stock-market prosperity, more and more borrowed money in order to do so. They borrowed it from brokers, who permitted (or, rather, encouraged) them to buy stocks on a cash margin—sometimes a very thin margin, say 10 or 20 percent of the value of the stocks they bought, with the balance being borrowed; and the brokers in turn borrowed from banks, in what was called the call-money market. This had been standard practice for years, but now the total sum of banks' loans to brokers suddenly began to rise to alarming new heights, and the credit structure of Wall Street began to look top-heavy and insecure. Such a contingency, too, had long since been anticipated, and the machinery to control it existed. It was chiefly to permit the regulation of credit, through the establishment of a master interest rate on loans and the adjustment of bank reserves, that Congress in 1913 had established the nation's central bank, the Federal Reserve System, charged to act in the interest of monetary stability, and independent of political direction even from the President himself.

In 1927 the Fed, as regulator of the economy, might have been expected to restrain wildly proliferating stock-market credit by raising its master interest rate, the so-called discount rate, and reducing bank reserves. It did the opposite. At a famous—or infamous—meeting on July 27, its officers decided on a course of making money *easier* to borrow rather than harder. It was something like the police issuing guns to people on the streets in a time of threatened riot, and it was an action that has since been blamed for many unhappy events that followed. To explain it, we must know something of the extraordinary man who, as the Fed's dominant force, was the nearest thing Wall Street in the 1920s had to a philosopher-king.

His name was Benjamin Strong, he was governor of the Federal Reserve Bank of New York, and he was quite probably the most dedicated central banker the country has ever had. He was a tall, handsome man with a large nose and ruthless eyes—a Morgan-partner type—racked with secret sorrows and ill health, and relentlessly self-driven. Born in 1872 in a small up-Hudson town, he came from a long line of Yankee merchants and traders, but did not grow up wealthy; he wanted to go to Princeton but never got there, and started working in Wall Street at sixteen. In 1898, married and the father of four, he moved with his family to suburban Englewood, that era's dormitory of Morgan partners, and there met and became friends with the great ones—Henry Davison, Thomas Lamont, later Dwight Morrow. But for special circumstances he would surely in due course have become a Morgan partner himself. In 1900 he was appointed treasurer of the Englewood Hospital, of which Davison, five years his senior, was president. In 1904 Davison made him secretary, and in 1909 vice president, of the Bankers Trust Company; the man he succeeded in each post was Thomas Lamont. Obviously he was riding a trolley leading straight to a desk at the Corner. But then in 1913 the Federal Reserve System came into being (largely in belated reaction to the Panic of 1907), and the two leading bankers among its founders, Davison and Paul M. Warburg of Kuhn, Loeb, decided on Davison's protégé Strong as the man to head the System's New York bank. (Interesting, though hardly surprising, that when it was decided that the economy needed a degree of regulation, Morgan and Kuhn, Loeb should choose the man for the job.) Strong at first refused. He—along with Davison and Warburg—had opposed the structure for the System as approved by Congress, consisting of a network of regional banks directed by a board sitting in Washington; Strong like most Wall Streeters felt such an arrangement would inevitably make the System subject to political influence regardless of any disclaimers, and wanted a single central bank in New York, on the model of the Bank of England. But now, at the insistence of Davison and Warburg, he relented; in 1914 he assumed the governorship of the new Federal Reserve Bank of New York.

His life was unhappy and uncomfortable, and destined to become more so. In 1905 his first wife had killed herself (and Davison had taken the Strong children into his household). In 1916 his second wife left him. The same year he was stricken with tuberculosis, still, in the same era in which *The Magic Mountain* was written, known with dread as the White Plague; attacking first his lungs and later his larynx, the disease was tc keep him away from his desk more than a third of the time over the twelve years, the years of his greatness, that remained to him. But his thoughts were seldom away. Emotional and physical adversity goaded him to harder work, and even when in sanatoriums or on sunny vacations he restlessly bombarded his bank colleagues with memoranda that came to have the force of ukases. He lived for central banking because he had little else; and, in particular, the task to which he applied his iron will was that of making the Federal Reserve Bank of New York in practice what he thought it should be, and what Congress had refused to make it in theory—the ultimate and dominant force in the System.

To a great extent he succeeded, partly because of his bank's convenient physical presence in the country's money center (a taken-for-granted characteristic of all other leading central banks), partly by the force of his personality, partly because most of his Washington rivals, the early governors of the Federal Reserve Board, were undistinguished and unqualified political appointees; the incumbent governor in 1927, for example, was a former Marion, Ohio, crony of Warren G. Harding's with no banking background at all. Strong by that time was almost a figure of Greek or Shakespearean drama; so ill now that he could seldom be at his desk, but at the top of his powers as a banker and leader, he was from his sickbed the virtual tyrant of the Federal Reserve System. "The Fed" meant "Ben Strong"; it did nothing without him. His passion now was European recovery, the adaptation of United States monetary policy to that end, and perhaps behind that passion, more than anything else, was the deepest friendship of this lonely man's life—with Montagu Norman, governor of the Bank of England.

For whatever reasons, in the early postwar years Strong's fierce, restless attention turned more and more to international monetary cooperation—not the bureaucratic, official kind at which the League of Nations was making a few ineffectual stabs, but a more mysterious, secretive, highhanded sort achieved behind closed and guarded doors, over the best food and wine, among the esoteric little international band of central-bank governors. Anglophile by nature like the Morgan partners he so admired, Strong had a large, perhaps a decisive, part in the return of Britain to the gold standard in 1925 at the old $4.86 dollar parity—a gallant but blatant overvaluation reflecting not economic reality but nostalgia for Britain's glorious past; it could probably not have been accomplished without loans to Britain of $200 million from the Federal Reserve, arranged by Strong, and another $100 million from the House of Morgan, arranged with Strong's help. But in 1927 Strong found himself under pressure at home. A growing faction in Washington, privately championed by Secretary of Commerce Herbert Hoover, began urging a higher discount rate and a generally restrictive money policy designed to dampen stock speculation. Such a policy would be anathema to Strong's European central-bank friends—particularly Norman, who came to New York especially to plead for lower American interest rates to stop the continuing outflow of Europe's gold to the Golconda in the New World, and thus help defend the exposed position of the pound. Various other American officials, on one side of the question or the other, had other motives; indeed, the largely behind-the-scenes debate on the subject that raged through the summer of 1927 was a little classic of cross-purposes. Hoover, the careful engineer, counseled restraint; Coolidge, urged by Hoover to put pressure on the Fed, characteristically found a legal justification for taking no action at all, in the Fed's statutory independence of the Executive; Mellon, the business-loving boss of the Treasury, was all for continuing cheap money to finance continuing expansion; while Carter Glass and a handful of other Senators complained bitterly that Fed policies were channeling practically all available credit into Wall Street to the further detriment of the nation's struggling farmers.

Strong cared little for any of them. He was no New Era man, no rubber stamp for Coolidge or Mellon; rather, he nursed his own fixed idea—that America must have low interest rates that would stop the gold inflow from Europe—partly to eliminate its inflationary effect here, and partly to save Europe's own economy. And the latter idea seems to have begun to assume the proportions of an obsession in his mind. Like any central banker, Strong was an economic nationalist, committed to putting his own country first in a clash of interests. But in this time of confusion as to what America's interests *were*, his ties to England and Norman dominated his mind. Through the spring, while Strong was convalescent in North Carolina, the Fed's policy seemed to waver. In the summer he was better and back on the job, and the Fed acted. In August the discount rate suddenly went down from 4 to 3.5 percent at most of the Federal Reserve banks. The governor of the one in Kansas City, where solicitude for the woes of Europe was not ordinarily notable, was asked by an astonished questioner why he had done it. "I did it because Ben Strong wanted me to," he replied. One Reserve bank, that of Chicago, balked, exercising its prerogative to refuse to comply with the Board's wishes unless directly ordered to do so; early in September, at Strong's behest and in defiance of all precedent, the Board gave the order and Chicago was forced to submit. The cost of this victory for Strong was internal discord. The vote within the Board was only four to three, showing that his mastery was slipping away; but he was still master, and the deed was done.

The sequel is well known; the market went roaring upward and credit expanded faster than ever. Early in January of 1928 it was announced that over the course of 1927 brokers' loans to speculators had shot up from $3.29 billion to $4.43 billion. There had never before been anything like such a rise in a year, and when Coolidge commented that he did not consider the rise enough to cause unfavorable comment, even Wall Street was dumfounded. That March was the high-water mark of pool operations; it was also the month when Cadillac sales in New York City hit an all-time high. On the twenty-seventh, an avalanche of trading broke all previous Stock Exchange records. April and May were more of the same. In mid-May the daily volume of Exchange trading was so high that lights burned in the Wall Street office windows far into the mild spring evenings, and the St. George in Brooklyn Heights, the hotel nearest Wall Street, reported scores of unexpected late arrivals each night—financial-district workers who had been forced to stay too late to go home. The Exchange doctor reported that in spite of constant overwork no members had recently suffered nervous breakdowns. "They're all making money," he explained dryly.

As for Strong, he was in London now, sick again for what was to prove to be the last time, comforted by the company of his friend Norman, and his grip on the reins of the Fed was loosening at last.

He could take satisfaction in the fact that his policy of the previous year had achieved its purpose; the pound and Europe's economy looked stronger for the moment—but, he must have asked himself as he read the news from Wall Street, at what cost, and what more to come?

III

Wall Street's bull market collapsed [yesterday] with a detonation heard round the world. . . . Losses ranged from 23½ points in active Stock Exchange issues to as much as 150 in stocks dealt over the counter. . . . It was a day of tumultuous, excited market happenings, characterized by an evident effort on the part of the general public to get out of stocks at what they could get. Individual losses were staggering. Hundreds of small traders were wiped out. . . .

The sales were countrywide. They flowed into the Stock Exchange not alone from New York brokerage houses but from every nook and corner of the country. . . .

The newspaper was the sober *New York Times;* the date was June 13, 1928 (repeat: 1928). If the break was in reaction to any identifiable event, the event was the realization by the Republican National Convention that the boom's patron, Coolidge, meant what he said and could not be drafted for another term in the White House. But if it hadn't been that, it would probably have been something else; a moment had come when what the market needed to set off a collapse was not a reason but an excuse.

The collapse was short-lived; the detonation did not reverberate. In a matter of a few days the June 12 losses had been recovered, whereupon the market moved on into new higher ground at a brisker rate than ever. By August the Dow-Jones industrials were 20 percent above their June low; by November, 50 percent.

All that had happened was that the engine of the boom had coughed once, then resumed its former smooth purr. The question became, Had the cough meant anything? Could it be forgotten as some sort of chance occurrence of no significance, or was it time to stop and take the whole machine into the shop for a check-up? The country as a whole and Wall Street itself divided on the question, and now hindsight, with its graceless finger, points out to us which were the wise and prescient, or else lucky, men of the time on the one hand, and which the deluded—or unlucky—on the other.

Back at the beginning of 1928 a group of Senators raised a hue and cry against rising brokers' loans and stock speculation. Their argument was agrarian, Populist, and long familiar in American life—that the sharks of Wall Street were absorbing the money supply of the country and thus depriving the real producers, the farmers. Not surprisingly, the protesting Senators came mostly from the farm states of the old frontier and Middle Border—Borah from Idaho, Brookhart from Iowa, Capper from Kansas, La Follette from Wisconsin, Mayfield from Texas, Pine from Oklahoma—where the prevailing attitudes were so often those of an earlier America: states where for many the bounds of a day were sunrise and sunset, where Prohibition and the more dour forms of Protestantism reigned, where the Eastern seaboard, and especially New York City, was automatically suspect of lawless saloons and foreign ways and libertine gambling in stocks. The struggle, one commentator wrote, was "founded upon a clash of interests and a moral and intellectual antipathy between the wealthy, cultured, and conservative settlements on the seacoast and the poverty-stricken, illiterate, and radical pioneer communities of the interior"; the same writer went on to say that "the Puritan instincts of the [farm] community are scandalized by the spectacle of men and women 'doing nothing' and enjoying the fat of the land which honest folk can get only by the sweat of their brows." This was oversimplification to the point of cartooning; for one thing, the eminently Puritan farmers of New England in an earlier time had been inveterate gamblers and had helped finance their very War of Independence through lotteries, and for another, we have seen how many of the stock-market speculators of the 1920s were neither cultured and conservative nor products of the Eastern seaboard. Still, the Senate Banking and Currency Committee's hearings on brokers' loans in February and March of 1928, during which one witness after another denounced the plutocratic manipulators and the harm they did to men of the soil, served to polarize the issue in the public mind. From then on, the East was broadly thought to approve and promote the stock boom, the West to fear, suspect, and resent it. Coolidge, Mellon, and company notwithstanding, beginning in 1928 the country was far from unanimous on the market. The venom against it that was to break out a few years later did not come from nowhere.

Even the "wealthy, cultured, and conservative" East—Wall Street itself—came to be divided. Not at the Stock Exchange, to be sure; the authorities there spoke with one voice in defense of speculation, which, after all, was the Exchange's main activity and the source of its vast prosperity. But at the great investment-banking houses, even the mighty and monolithic Morgan and Kuhn, Loeb, there was a certain discreet choosing up of sides. At Morgan's, Thomas Lamont was a staunch New Era man, scoffing at the notion that the market was unsound, while Russell Leffingwell was openly skeptical. At Kuhn, Loeb, Otto Kahn was a hearty backer of the boom and a heavy investor in it himself, while his close associate Paul Warburg during 1928 and 1929 was gaining a reputation as a Cassandra by repeatedly predicting a collapse unless speculation were brought under control.

That the Federal Reserve Board was seriously divided within its own counsels was first shown in the close vote on the matter of cracking down on wayward Chicago. In 1928, under political pressure, and deprived of its indigenous driving force by the decline of Strong, it progressively reversed its easy-money policy. In three steps it raised the discount rate from 3.5 to 5 percent; at the same time bank reserves available for lending were reduced by Federal Reserve sales of government securities on an unprecedented scale. At the beginning of the year the Fed held $616 million in such securities, most of them bought under Strong's expansionary policy during 1927; a little more than a year later, in the early part of 1929, constant and vigorous selling had reduced the portfolio to below $150 million. Strong in London took no part in the decisions leading to this startling turnabout, but he apparently favored or at least condoned them; he is on record as having recommended a 5 percent discount rate in one of his famous communications, sent that May. Had he decided, then, that he had been wrong the previous year, and wished to make amends? Or that conditions had reversed themselves—that the pound and the franc and the mark were safe, and that at last the primary concern was stock speculation at home? Or was he too ill and tired now to keep up the fight? We do not know; he was not destined to explain.

The effects of the new Fed policy began to be felt in the second

97

half of 1928 and were to be felt in full force early in 1929. Nation-wide, interest rates rose and the classic concomitants of dear money followed: building construction fell off, the borrowings of state and local governments were postponed, small businesses starved for the want of new funds. And meanwhile stock speculation—the chief target of the policy—went its merry way as if harassed by nothing more than a persistent mosquito. We have seen how the market shot up during the second half of 1928; over the same period brokers' loans increased by another $1.5 billion, or more than they had increased during the whole of 1927—the year of Strong's easy money! In short, the new Fed policy was an instant and spectacular failure. Loans from his broker now cost the speculator 8 or 9 per-cent; early in 1929 they were to cost him 12 percent and more. But how could an interest rate of 8 or 12 percent a year deter a man, or woman, who fully expected to use the money to make a profit of 100 percent in a month or even a week? Traditional monetary restraints were useless because they had come too late. The speculative virus was past being checked by that medicine.

And the physician, the Federal Reserve, which might have ob-tained from Congress the power to use such drastic and untradi-tional remedies as arbitrarily setting minimum margin require-ments on stock purchases, was powerless because it was, relatively speaking, headless. Strong was dying. Back from Europe in August, he was informed by his doctors that he must give up all work at once. He offered his resignation to the Federal Reserve Board and to the New York bank; it was tabled. In September he wrote Montagu Norman of his situation, and got a moving reply: "Dear old friend, how hard and cruel life is. . . . But what a stage ours has been over these ten or twelve years! . . . Whatever is to happen to us—wherever you and I are to live—we cannot now separate or ignore these years. . . . God bless you and my love now and ever." After a last-hope operation, Strong died in New York in October.

God bless Ben Strong! In hindsight he was to be accused by Hoover of "crimes far worse than murder" and by most financial historians of being the single chief cause of the coming crash; but he was a better man than most of his detractors, and was cursed by fate as well as by his own tragic flaw; if he had been given another year of life, his full attention would surely have focused on the American situation and his firm hand might have done much to set things to rights in time. As it was, he left behind, as so many big men do, a power vacuum, a shattered institution, weak, divided, and lacking enterprising leadership. Things had indeed fallen apart when disintegration could least be afforded.

IV

What did a New York banker have to do to make money in early 1929? Lend it in the call-money market at 10 or 12 percent, at a time when he could, if he chose, borrow it from the Federal Reserve at 5 percent. As simple as that; both transactions were cut and dried, requiring no business initiative and involving practically no risk, and although starting in early February the Federal Reserve Board officially disapproved of the practice, it continued to be done. Bankers, like royalty in a constitutional monarchy, were in the position of being handsomely paid simply for existing. A plum tree had been grown, tended, and brought to fruit just for their shaking. No doubt the situation had come about through inadvertence, rather than as a result of any conscious conviction of the American people or their government that bankers deserved the rights of royalty; but it does not seem too much to suggest that a prevailing national attitude not very different from this had been a contributing factor.

Specifically, the situation had come about as follows. Despite the Fed's restrictive efforts, speculation not only continued but actually accelerated during January, 1929, a month during which the stock indexes rose another 20 or 30 points and brokers' loans another $260 million. On February 2 the Fed, having failed so signally to produce results with higher interest rates and sales of government securities, resorted to what is called "direct action" and others called "moral suasion"; it announced publicly its belief that "the Federal Reserve Act does not . . . contemplate the use of the resources of the Federal Reserve System for the creation or extension of speculative credit." In other words, please don't shake the plum tree any more for a while. That such a sudden prohibition of what had long been standard practice was virtually unenforceable seemed clear; the Fed was appealing to the better natures of the nation's bankers. Or—weak and vacillating as it was at the time—it was merely trying to save its face and its conscience, to wash its hands like Pilate. Certainly it seemed to back away from any vigorous prosecution of its wishes when, three days later, it issued a statement that it had "no disposition to assume authority to interfere with the loan practices of member banks so long as they do not involve the Federal Reserve banks," and a week or so after *that* it seemed to be almost pleading rather than commanding when it wrote to the various member banks reminding them that it was now their duty to prevent the use of their funds for speculation *"as far as possible."*

At all events, speculation went on—and Federal Reserve funds, hugely augmented now by money from American corporations and even from Oriental potentates lured into the New York money market by the soaring interest rates, continued to be used to some extent to finance it. The chief effects of the Fed's efforts were another sharp stock slump, amounting this time to a genuine baby crash, during March, and finally, on the twenty-sixth, a wild climax in the clamor for more call money that sent the rate rocketing up from 12 to 20 percent. Whereupon a leading banker—President Charles E. Mitchell of the mammoth National City—took matters into his own hands by coolly and brazenly defying the Fed's warning; he simply announced that his institution had on hand twenty million dollars, borrowed from the New York Federal Reserve Bank, that it would be happy to lend for speculative purposes at once. The mutiny prospered. The squeeze was instantly ended, panic was averted, the call-money rate settled back to a mere 15 percent, and the stock market resumed its upward course. Overnight the mutineer Mitchell became a national hero, replacing Coolidge as the great patron of the boom. As for the injured and insulted Fed, it dared attempt no action against Mitchell, maintaining a sullen silence. It was beaten again.

So bankers were free to resume shaking the plum tree without even feeling guilty about it. Government "interference" was humiliated and discredited; now anything went. In such circumstances one might have expected bankers, at least the most important, prestige-laden, and supposedly conservative among them, to lie low, to accept quietly the profits that flowed to them so effortlessly, to take the occasion of the happy market (a God-given market, one of them seriously called it later) to pursue sporting, cultural, or scholarly interests. But most of them were hard-driving, self-made men, ill-equipped by background or temperament to leisure activities. They were the sort of restless, competent, limited men that the system and the spirit of their times brought to the top of their profession everywhere except in the few tradition-bound firms like Morgan and Kuhn, Loeb. They had to have something to do, and they found things.

V

The same Charles E. Mitchell who so successfully bested the Fed was also the man who during the boom did most to destroy the old American image of the banker as a cautious guardian of traditional values along with other people's money. A big, heavy-set, broad-shouldered, good-natured man with a bold jaw and features that expressed power rather than sensibility, he was a born supersalesman. As he saw it, the principal business of his bank—and it was the biggest commercial bank in the country—was not lending or conserving money but peddling securities, common stocks included. This in itself was untraditional enough—bankers were supposed to swear by bonds, and to look upon all but the most deep-dyed of blue-chip stocks with suspicion—but Mitchell went much, much further in his iconoclasm. Not content to wait with customary bankerly discretion for customers to come in and ask for securities advice, he believed in hawking his product, going out into the towns and villages to find customers and, if necessary, cram the product down their throats. True enough, banks were restricted by law in their freedom to trade in securities; but Mitchell's bank (like others in his time) circumvented the restrictions with insolent ease through the use of a flimsy dodge called a "security affiliate"—a separate, paper company wholly owned by the bank and sometimes even sharing, down to the last man, the bank's officers and directors, yet free to plunge in the market at will because of its nominal status as a nonbank. F. L. Allen was not alone in finding the institution of the security affiliate "a masterpiece of legal humor."

The methods of Mitchell and the National City Company, the

National City Bank's affiliate, were without precedent. He simply thought of securities as merchandise like any other, and handled them accordingly. Maintaining a staff of hundreds of salesmen with offices in dozens of cities around the country, he pressed his men to move the merchandise as relentlessly as if it were shoes or hair oil. There were contests, prize money awarded to salesmen according to elaborate point systems—one point per share of General Mills common disposed of, four points for Missouri-Kansas-Texas preferred, and so on. Mitchell was nothing if not candid about his view of his business; he habitually spoke of the securities trade as a form of "manufacturing," to be conducted like any other form. Once he explained, "We have a certain portion of our organization—and it amounts to a large force—devoting itself to the manufacture of long-term credits suitable for public distribution, and for the analysis of the production of other manufacturers." The manufactured goods were, of course, pieces of paper priced at hundreds or thousands of dollars each, and representing promises that were by no means always kept. Many of the products of Mitchell's manufactory were bonds of foreign countries with notoriously shaky treasuries, and in 1927 Thomas Lamont felt impelled to speak pointedly, with unmistakable intent, of "American banks and firms competing on an almost violent scale" to sell foreign bonds.

But a rebuke from the House of Morgan did not deter Mitchell; soon after that his National City Company successfully sold the two ill-fated issues of the Republic of Peru that were to make the term "Peruvian bond" for years a rueful metaphor for nearly worthless securities. About this time Mitchell switched his major effort to common stocks; in 1929 his affiliate pushed out more than a million shares of highly speculative Anaconda Copper, and more than a million of those of his own bank, the National City. By then Mitchell's affiliate was blithely participating in Stock Exchange pools; it was taking wild speculative flyers with what, after all, was basically the bank depositors' money; it was actively soliciting the holders of National City bank balances to get their money out of cash and into the stocks it was sponsoring; and Mitchell himself, taking a modest basic salary of $25,000, had pressured his bank's board of directors into voting him such a lavish incentive bonus that for the first half of 1929 his personal compensation amounted to just over one million dollars. Every traditional banking inhibition was flouted, all the bars were down, and the man who had lowered them, far from being subject to censure now, was reaping general approbation along with money. Imagine an old-style American banker in a Midwest farm town—one who eschewed stock speculation on principle as his father and grandfather had always done, who lent cautiously in local mortgages, who never solicited business because he believed that salesmanship was alien to the fiduciary aspect of his profession, and who scrupulously absented himself from the board room when his own remuneration was under discussion—considering the doings of Charles E. Mitchell. He might have found himself confused. He might have had a sense of the world gone mad and of himself as a caricature of a fuddy-duddy, goody-goody old fool.

Albert H. Wiggin, boss of the nation's *second* biggest commercial bank, the Chase National, is a study in comparison and contrast to Mitchell. Nine years the elder of the two, he, like Mitchell, had sprung from modest surroundings in the Boston area. Each in his way had the standard environmental impedimenta of successful American financiers—Wiggin was a clergyman's son, Mitchell had worked his way through college; each began his business career in the humblest of positions; each reached the presidency of his mighty bank at an early age, Wiggin at forty-three and Mitchell at forty-four; each was shrewd, aggressive, and single-minded, little distracted by outside interests, cultural or otherwise. But in temperament the two were opposites. Where Mitchell had the glib tongue and brusque good humor of a high-class carnival barker, Wiggin was reserved, almost scholarly in demeanor. In the public conduct of the Chase's affairs Wiggin was relatively traditional, even though his bank, too, appreciated and availed itself of the legal humor of a security affiliate. But in his private dealings for his personal account, he was considerably more daring than Mitchell. The latter could usually show that his garish actions were in the interest of his bank's stockholders, and thus could lay claim to the honored virtue of corporate loyalty. Not so Wiggin; the bank might pay him $275,000 a year for guiding its destiny, but when he saw a chance to profit at its expense, he did not feel bound to deny himself.

In 1928 a national bank examiner reported that Wiggin "dictates

103

the policies of the bank" and was "the most popular banker in Wall Street"; the previous year the popular dictator, without informing the bank examiner or virtually anyone else. but without breaking the law either, had formed several "personal holding companies" to enable him to speculate in stocks while concealing his identity and minimizing his taxes. By this means he played the market with notable success and participated in pools in various stocks; but his favorite vehicle for speculation was the shares of the company he knew best, the Chase National Bank. The president of any corporation is, of course, the nominal employee of its stockholders; therefore, stripped to essentials, Wiggin's speculative operations in Chase stock consisted of trying to make money at the expense of his nominal employers, and between 1927 and 1929 he succeeded to the extent of several million dollars, doing it so discreetly and deftly as not to so much as cause them even a ripple of annoyance.

Then he went a step further. Beginning in July, 1929, Wiggin— as astute as ever—began to see the prospects for the stock market in general and Chase stock in particular as dim. Accordingly, through one of his personal companies he sold over 42,000 shares of Chase stock short. He was then in the curious position of having a vested interest, and a huge one, in the deterioration of the institution he headed. Just as corporate officers are usually encouraged to own stock so that they will have added incentive to put out their best efforts, so Wiggin, with his short position in Chase stock, had provided himself with incentive to produce his worst efforts. This was legal; the audacity of his action was such that the question of forfending it by law had apparently never come up. Moreover, it was perfectly timed. When the account was closed that November, the whole market had collapsed as Wiggin had foreseen, and the profit to his personal company came to just over four million dollars. And no one—for several years—was the wiser; when Wiggin retired in 1932, the Chase's executive committee thanked him fulsomely for his uncounted services to the bank and unanimously voted him a life pension of $100,000 per year.

Enough; here and elsewhere, Mitchell and Wiggin have been overpilloried. Undoubtedly Mitchell wasn't the most overaggressive among the bankers of his time, nor Wiggin the most perfidious; they were only the most prominent offenders. Even Wiggin seems to have acted acceptably by his own curious lights. He had a faculty for convenient, sentimental self-deception; it was he who later spoke feelingly of the 1929 market as a gift from God, and he maintained to his death, with evident sincerity, that his Chase short sales had been entirely proper. Victims of a *Zeitgeist* if ever men were, these two were reflectors as well as creators of the collapse of old values, the falling-apart of things, in the sphere of commercial banking.

VI

All this and more came out later. In the summer of 1929 the surface of Wall Street was a mixture of placidity and mania—stock averages at record highs and still headed upward, the dissenters momentarily routed, the dubious pastimes of some of the most trusted leaders hidden from public view. Even with all that we know now, it remains hard to see that summer whole. The present generations, and perhaps those to come too, are doomed by the technical imperfections of old films and phonograph records to see the life of the 1920s, its nuances of mood, in distorted perspective. Of earlier times we have virtually no aural or moving visual record; of later times we have technically perfect ones. The twenties are the limbo between, and if (as Richard Avedon has said) there is something in the way a woman moves that speaks with unique eloquence of the time in which she lives, there is a gap in our knowledge; only with an intellectual effort can we avoid thinking of 1929 as a time when people walked like jerky puppets and talked in tinny voices. But let us try, as best we can, to look at Wall Street as it was in August, 1929, to catch its essentials in a frieze:

It is the month of Wall Street's traditional vacation, when even the most dedicated and the most obsessed drift off to mountains or seashore to wait, restlessly, for Labor Day and rebirth. But this year they have not drifted away. Stock Exchange volume for the month is a record for August and not far from a record for any month of the year. Coast to coast, more than half a million are playing the market on margin and perhaps as many more with cash. The days, for the most part, are unexpectedly and blessedly cool and dry; Golconda's climate lacks the usual seasonal sniff of Hell. Not only

105

do the regulars stay in town; newcomers have arrived in great numbers. They are men and women who are sacrificing their own vacations, or else have simply chucked their jobs, to spend their days sitting, or more likely standing, in the brokerage customers' rooms watching the quotation board report the glorious news, and to share in the benefits. They arrive early to read the brokerage houses' "morning letters" informing them confidently which stocks will rise how much that particular day, which will be "taken in hand" by a pool at what hour, which companies have favorable news to come out shortly. By Stock Exchange opening time, all along Wall and Nassau, Broad and Broadway and Pine, the customers' rooms are jammed—there is standing room only and perhaps not even that, there is a premium on positions from which the quote board can be seen. Still, they all are sure it is worthwhile being there, right on the scene; they feel themselves to be part of something tremendous, and perhaps, too, they feel their physical presence in Wall Street makes them insiders, gives them some slight advantage over those who are maintaining the same vigil elsewhere—the barber or chauffeur or cab driver whose ear is cocked for a tip his important client may let fall, even the important man himself who has given up his vacation not in substance but only in spirit, and, sacrificing a seat in the sun, is glued all day to one in an office in Bar Harbor or Newport or Southampton or in a Catskill Mountain hotel. Brokerage house branches have suddenly made their appearance at every important resort, and the wires between them and their home offices hum all summer long.

Many of those now crowding Wall Street have burned their bridges. They have thrown over their jobs on reaching some predetermined goal, a paper net worth of $50,000 or $100,000 or $200,000; they have bought expensive houses and mink coats for themselves or their wives, and look forward to lives of leisure and affluence spent at this easy and entertaining game. Moreover, in their short time on Wall Street they have come to feel a sense of belonging there; the scars on Morgan's are *their* scars and the grave of Hamilton in Trinity Churchyard is *theirs*. They have a new life and, if they wish, they can even partake of the very symbol of belonging. The most change-resistant of institutions, the urban club, has gone democratic on Wall Street; luncheon clubs, most of them no more than six months old, are everywhere, ranging from fancy cafés to one-arm counters in bare rooms, and membership is just a matter of knowing somebody—anybody—and paying a fee.

At lunch hour the streets of the district are jammed from building line to building line. Even at the height of the morning and afternoon business hours the streets are full of pedestrians, talking, gossiping, shouting to make themselves heard over the din of the new office-building construction going on everywhere. But at noon the crowds on the streets grow so thick that no car can pass, and the construction sounds are stilled for the workmen's lunch break. A visitor from England, charmed by the silence broken only by talk and footfalls, is reminded of Venice. He finds the atmosphere "savagely exciting," and, as an outsider watching the performance of a rite he does not understand, he feels loneliness and a certain alarm. He is not reassured when his American friend and guide breaks into a cool explanation of Wall Street and the American business system to say, abruptly and cryptically, "All the same, I don't really believe it."

All through the days, and long into the evenings, the talk, talk, talk goes on. There are tales of fortunes just made and of fortunes about to be made—above all, talk of fortunes. There is no talk of panic; the spring crisis is in the past now, brokers' loans are soaring faster than ever but that is considered healthy now, there is no money squeeze and call money has settled back to a reasonable 6 or 7 percent. The market averages stand 34 percent above the March low and 76 percent above early 1928. When, on the ninth of the month, the New York Federal Reserve Bank raises its rate to 6 percent, nobody pays much attention; the Fed is a figure of fun now. There is constant talk about the new investment trusts, Blue Ridge and Alleghany, Shenandoah and United Corporation and hundreds more, that are the latest thing in stocks, a billion and a half dollars' worth of new ones put on the market since January; paper companies with staffs of only half a dozen people, existing merely to hold and trade in the stocks of other companies, most of them elaborately designed to "move fast" by the application of "leverage" in their structure, they are considered flimsy and over-speculative by some, but why should they be? Weren't Alleghany and United sponsored by that pillar of conservatism, J. P. Morgan

& Company, and hasn't Alleghany gone up from its February offering price of 20 to 56, United from its January offering price of 25 to 73? There is talk about John J. Raskob's article in that month's *Ladies' Home Journal* entitled "Everybody Ought to Be Rich," in which he explains how savings of $15 a month wisely invested in stocks will do the trick in twenty years, and talk about how the Stock Exchange, emulating so many of the companies whose shares it lists, has just declared a "stock dividend" to its members—one-fourth of a seat to each holder of one. There are jokes about well-fed, broad-beamed Exchange members *needing* a seat and a quarter each, these days.

Money is king—but there is something else. It is a high, wild time, a time of riotous spirits and belief in magic rather than cold calculation, a time of Dionysius rather than Apollo. People speak of "luck" and "the breaks" more than of earnings and dividends. They have given up their month at the lakes and beaches not in the puritanical spirit of "business first" or "come, labor on," but in the hedonistic spirit of living more fully and not missing life's chances. It is almost as if they believed the market existed for taking chances not on money but on happiness.

On the seventeenth the *Île de France* and the *Berengaria* depart on transatlantic trips, the former eastward and the latter westward, each fully equipped for speculation with floating brokerage offices; when the *Berengaria* arrives in New York six days later, passengers tell of how every day the office on the promenade deck has been so mobbed that quotations had to be passed by word of mouth to passengers who couldn't get near enough. The same week, there is much favorable comment on a new book, *Wall Street and Washington,* by that renowned Princeton economic authority Joseph S. Lawrence, in which he scores off the Federal Reserve for its insolent meddling with Wall Street ("an innocent community" mercilessly persecuted by "flannel-throated fanatics" in Congress) and suggests that anyone who favors stronger regulation of the stock market is undoubtedly an all-round bluenose and probably an advocate of Prohibition to boot. This is the kind of talk the tape-watchers dote on, and when it comes from a cloistered professor, so much the better. As the month draws to a close and the Stock Exchange decides to forgo its usual Saturday session and declare a full three-day holiday over the Labor Day weekend, there is further cause for jubilation. There are rumors, cited even in the *Times,* of many large pools being formed to buoy the market during the autumn, and it is said that a single brokerage firm has received invitations to join no fewer than five of them; meanwhile four important railroad stocks, Santa Fe, Union Pacific, Chesapeake & Ohio, and Norfolk & Western, are all nearing the magic price of 300 in what appears to be a race. Nobody doubts that they will all reach it; the only question is which will reach it first.

So, assuming one can get hold of a reservation—the railroads and the Trimotor airliner to Boston are all overbooked—one can take that three-day weekend with no fears for the future. And yet—can one really believe it?

VII

When the crash finally came, it came with a kind of surrealistic slowness—so gradually that, on the one hand, it was possible to live through a good part of it without realizing that it was happening, and, on the other hand, it was possible to believe that one had experienced and survived it when in fact it had no more than just begun.

The market did not all crash at once. Large segments of it had been depressed for a year or more. The 1929 boom was, in fact, quite a narrow and selective one. It was a boom of the handful of stocks that figured in the daily calculation of the Dow-Jones and *New York Times* indexes, and that was why those well-publicized indexes were at record highs. It was also a boom of the most actively traded stocks bearing the names of the most celebrated companies, the stocks mentioned daily by the newspapers and millions of times daily by the board-room habitués—and that was why it was constantly talked about. But it was emphatically not a boom of dozens of secondary stocks in which perhaps as many investors were interested.

As a matter of fact, a good part of the stock market had been more or less depressed all through 1929.

The soaring of the averages made a rousing spectacle. Yet the highest September, 1929, price of Celanese was 66; its high in 1927 had been 118. The September high of Cluett, Peabody was 46; its high in 1928 had been 110. The September high of Consolidated Cigar was 62; its high in 1928 had been 100. The September high of Freeport Sulphur was 43; its 1928 high, 105. The September high of New York Shipbuilding was 27; its 1925 high, 88. The September high of Pepsi-Cola was 10; its 1928 high, 19. The September high of Philip Morris was 12; its 1927 high, 41. The list, even if confined to well-known stocks, could be extended to astonishing length. The motor stocks, in particular, were in a virtual industry-wide depression. Studebaker, Hudson, Hupp, and Graham-Paige, at that peak of the most celebrated stock boom in history, were down from their previous highs by 22, 25, 43, and 55 percent, respectively. And even General Motors, the very bellwether of the boom all through the decade, was down over 10 percent. The persistence of the idea that all stocks were going through the roof in the autumn of 1929 is a monument to the power of popular myth.

But if a sort of slow, partial crash, invisible except to its victims, had been occurring over a period of at least three years, Tuesday, September 3, 1929—the day the market averages reached the all-time highs that were to endure for a quarter of a century—was not a day when the public at large gave its attention to such a matter. It was the first day after the Labor Day recess, and thus by traditional stock-market reckoning the start of the active season, almost the start of a new year. The fact that it was a record-setting scorcher in New York, with a maximum temperature of ninety-four degrees and brutal humidity, did not deter the mobs from thronging back to the downtown customers' rooms and trading in such volume as to set a September record. Thus unaware of its achievement, in the atmosphere of a steam bath, the market of the twenties achieved its Everest. Next day there was a general, if unsensational, decline. The daily column of market comment in the *Times*—unsigned, but presided over and often written in those days by the paper's justly celebrated financial editor, the learned Alexander Dana Noyes—contained the sober remark, "The pace of advancing prices during the past week has been so rapid, and so regardless of the money-market position, as to inspire a growing sense of caution even among convinced speculators for the rise." The following day,

September 5, there occurred the curious phenomenon ever afterward called the Babson Break. A not especially well-known, and hitherto even less influential, financial adviser operating far from Wall Street—a frail, goateed, pixyish-looking man in Wellesley, Massachusetts, named Roger Babson—said to an audience at a routine New England financial luncheon, "I repeat what I said at this time last year and the year before, that sooner or later a crash is coming." As Babson implied, his earlier warnings had been roundly ignored. He was, in fact, widely thought of as something of a nut. Evidently it was a slow day for financial news, because at 2 P.M. Babson's words were quoted on the Dow-Jones financial news ticker and thus read in brokerage houses across the country. Without the slightest hesitation the market went into a nosedive that carried Steel down 9 points, Westinghouse down 7, and Telephone down 6 in a frantic last hour of trading during which two million shares were traded. The tiny cause and the huge effect, by any logical standard, were simply far out of proportion.

It was a prophetic episode—and so recognized at once. After the Babson Break the word "crash," entirely taboo a month earlier, suddenly became common currency in Wall Street. In its more conservative circles, the notion of an impending crash came within days to be fully as much the received wisdom as the contrary notion of an endlessly continuing boom. Babson was, of course, promptly and violently refuted by such New Era champions as Professor Irving Fisher of Yale; but five days later the Noyes column in the *Times* was still brooding on "the idea of an utterly disastrous and paralyzing crash" in a most disconcerting way. The *Times* found certain parallels between the current situation and that of 1907, when unbridled panic had come totally unexpectedly. The best reassurance the paper could offer was that now there were the new forces of the Federal Reserve and the investment trusts, which would presumably serve to help stabilize the market if necessary. Meanwhile, the market crept erratically downward until September 24, when there was another big break, this one unassignable to any cause at all and therefore dismissed as a "mystery decline."

October in Wall Street began in a mood of pessimism but calm. Rather spookily, brokers' loans kept increasing, suggesting that more and more people were still coming into the market. Why weren't their purchases raising prices? Or were they perhaps coming in on the short side? There began to be scary rumors of the formation of giant bear pools; Jesse Livermore was accused, and immediately denied it. Then there was a recovery, and everyone breathed easier. By the tenth the averages were back to about where they had been in mid-September. On the fifteenth the voice of the bull prophet Charles Mitchell was heard from the appropriate pedestal, a deck chair on an ocean liner; embarking for New York from Germany, he said, "The markets generally are now in a healthy condition." Irving Fisher chimed in with his soon-to-be-immortal opinion that stocks had reached "what looks like a permanent high plateau." It is not to be supposed that these statements were universally accepted; Mitchell and Fisher by this time had come to be monotonously predictable, and their views were ceasing to gain emphasis from repetition. Still, the market held steady for a week. Then on the nineteenth it sank again, in a huge two-hour break in the course of the second biggest Saturday-morning session ever.

By Monday the twenty-first it was clear that there existed the makings of the classic stock-market chain reaction downward: the decline in stock prices leading to calls for more collateral from margin customers; the inability or unwillingness of the customers to meet the calls, leading to the forced sales of their holdings; these sales leading to a further decline; and the further decline leading to more margin calls. There began to be hopeful talk of "organized support," the kind of massive pooling of resources in support of the market by the most powerful bankers that had saved the situation in 1907. "For the time, at any rate, all Wall Street seems to see the reality of things, and to discard the catchwords and newly-invented maxims of an imaginary political economy," said the Noyes column. The meaning was clear: sanity had returned, the New Era had become a thing of the past. The board rooms were less crowded now; the thousands of tyros who had jammed them in August were mostly discouraged if not wiped out, and had returned to their jobs and their old lives. The trumpets of the New Era still sounded, but they had a muted, valedictory sound now; Fisher dismissed the decline as a "shaking out of the lunatic fringe that attempts to speculate on margin," and Mitchell, on his ship's arrival at New York, could only say that the decline had gone too far. It went further that very day, with prices closing drastically lower in wildly confused trading that left the ticker an hour and forty-one minutes late; but the next day, Tuesday the twenty-second, there was a strong recovery.

So we come to Wednesday the twenty-third, a mild, clear fall day in New York, but a miserable one in the Midwest, which was swept by an early-season visitation of snow and sleet. This meteorological mischance, like the dazzling sun at the Battle of Hastings, has its niche in history. A market decline began early in New York; then the storm brought down many telephone and telegraph wires, and for the rest of the day a good part of the country was dependent on guesses and rumors as to exactly what was happening. Signs of panic appeared, and quickly fed on themselves. The day's trading of 6,374,960 shares was the second greatest in history; among the losses were 96 points for Adams Express, 70 for Commercial Solvents, 20 for General Electric, 43 for Otis Elevator, and 35 for Westinghouse. There was no piece of bearish news to account for it, but no one spoke of a mystery decline now.

By another mischance of retrospective interest, the vice president of the Stock Exchange was absent from the floor that day. He was the elegant Richard Whitney, now forty-one, the coming man at the Exchange. Not only was he its acting president in the absence on vacation of its president, E. H. H. ("Harry") Simmons, who was in Hawaii on a honeymoon, but so well known was his name and so great his reputation as a man of influence and leadership that the previous March, when President Hoover had wanted to confer with a Stock Exchange representative on the dangers of speculation, it was Whitney rather than Simmons whom he had summoned to the White House. On Wednesday the twenty-third of October, Whitney was away from Wall Street serving as one of the two stewards presiding over the climax day of the hunt's racing program of the Essex Fox Hounds, at Far Hills, New Jersey, where a crowd of some two thousand was on hand to rub shoulders with the figures of the society pages and watch perhaps the most fashionable of American turf events. Two horses, Speckled Beauty and Proposal, finished too close for the judges to decide between them, and according to protocol the stewards were appealed to. Whitney and his counterpart declared a dead heat. Two other horses had slipped on the damp turf and collided, sending their riders flying; there ensued an acrid argument between the two owners as to which jockey had been at fault, with the stewards again called upon to adjudicate. It was, then, a busy day for Whitney, though less busy than the day ahead would be.

That night an avalanche of margin calls went out, and a settled gloom hung over Wall Street. It thought it had had its crash, and was mustering its spunk to go forward. It little suspected that soon the thousands wiped out would become tens of thousands; or that the next day, when trading volume would be not six million shares but nearly thirteen million, would go down in memory as Black Thursday.

Chapter Six

Enter
the White Knight

I

From the Rector's report, Trinity Church Parish Year Book and Registry, covering the year 1930:

> The past year has presented many difficulties. . . . The problem of what we, as a church, could do to give comfort and help to the many who were in serious difficulties because of unemployment was a problem of the first importance. . . .
>
> I decided, after consulting with several experts in charitable and social service work, that the Church could best serve the community by taking care of her own people. The Vestry contributed a considerable sum of money. . . . I then appealed for voluntary contributions toward a fund to care for the poor of the parish. It is not possible or proper to speak publicly of the particular cases of dire need that were relieved, or of the many persons who were tided over periods of acute distress. . . . Times of adversity bring out the best and the worst sides of human nature. I am glad to find this year that people are turning to the Church for comfort and courage. . . .

The regular Sunday services, the Rector went on, had had a revival of good attendance; so, notably, had the weekday noon services. And, in addition, Trinity had found it appropriate to inaugurate a new program intended specifically to give comfort and courage to people of the financial community. Each weekday from eleven-thirty until one-thirty, a member of the clergy was stationed at a desk just inside the entrance to the church, to be available for consultation. The Rector wrote:

> If we could tell you of the various troubles and problems which are brought to us there, you would realize the great value of the ministry; but it is, naturally, impossible to speak of the matters which are brought to us. People unknown to us and to whom we are unknown are happy to be able to bring their troubles, which would in many cases be impossible to discuss with their own clergy, to a stranger whose business it is to assist if possible—frequently, and indeed usually, behind the screen of anonymity.

This new ministry was so popular during 1930 that at lunch hour there was often a small queue at the entrance to Trinity, waiting in turn for consultation and consolation—a bread line of the spirit.

As the congregation so often sang in "Lead, Kindly Light":

> I loved the garish day, and, spite of fears,
> Pride ruled my will: remember not past years.

The garish day was over, and the pride that had kept Wall Streeters out of Trinity Church was broken.

II

On the first great day of the crash—October 24, or Black Thursday—Claud Cockburn, the visiting British journalist, who was staying at the old Lafayette Hotel in Greenwich Village, had noticed a startling phenomenon as he was having breakfast with an American companion at a marble-topped table in the hotel's café. His companion kept distractedly jumping up and looking at the ticker machine at one end of the room—even though it was well before Stock Exchange opening time and therefore there could not possibly be anything on the ticker. With the percipience born of a foreigner's detachment, Cockburn saw (he would write many years later) that it was no ordinary day but one long to be remembered; it takes nothing less than a major air raid to change the social atmosphere of London, he would write, but New York—New York lives more externally. Walking toward Wall Street later that morning, after the tickers had already begun to beat out their sad and shocking story, Cockburn found himself part of a sort of silent army streaming in the same direction. In the Street itself, he found an enormous crowd; its sound was subdued, a kind of murmur, hardly more than a whisper, broken occasionally by the distinct, surrealistic cackle of an isolated hysterical laugh. (Photographs taken around noon that day of the front of the Sub-Treasury, across the corner of Broad and Wall from the Stock Exchange, show people standing on all its steps, lined up and looking blandly straight ahead as if posed to record the membership of some sort of organization. Their faces show no excitement or hysteria or chagrin. They stare in the way a caught fish stares as it lies on the beach or in the creel.)

Cockburn had a lunch date at the home of an important Wall Streeter. He was Edgar Speyer, former Edwardian English nobleman—he had been Sir Edgar and a Privy Councilor—and now, as an American, a millionaire partner in one of the oldest and most aristocratic German-Jewish banking houses. He and his wife lived in one of those lovely rose-brick Greek Revival houses on the north side of Washington Square, in an exquisitely ordered household with an atmosphere of culture and elegant calm, amid a gorgeous collection of Chinese paintings and porcelain. Luncheon, Cockburn found, was served by a young English footman under the supervision of a middle-aged English butler; and the meal was proceeding gracefully, with talk not of the stock market but of recently published poets—Mrs. Speyer was one—when everything suddenly went inexplicably and shockingly wrong. There was a disturbance, a sound of thumping and voices, behind the closed door to the corridor leading to the kitchen. The handle of the door turned slowly, and then the door moved open a few inches. Clearly, some sort of bizarre struggle was going on behind it. A moment later, when the butler and footman entered with a saddle of lamb, Cockburn caught a glimpse down the corridor of four or five maidservants of various ages standing behind the door in an excited and angry group. Having served the lamb, the butler and footman withdrew to the kitchen; there was more scuffling, after which a woman's voice was heard to shout the threat, "Go on, or else,"

> and then the door burst open and the butler, very red in the face, nearly bounced into the room as though he had been pushed violently from behind. . . . He closed the door and as collectedly as possible marched across the room to Speyer and in low apologetic tones begged him to come outside for a moment. Listening with an air of astonishment, Speyer, after a few seconds' amazed hesitation, left the room with him. Almost immediately Speyer came back again looking a little dismayed. He begged us to excuse him. The staff, he explained, had of course their own ticker-tape in the kitchen premises and they were all heavily engaged on the stock market. . . .

Speyer abandoned his guests for good then, leaving his lunch uneaten; his wife and guests finished the meal "under conditions of confusion and makeshift." The party was a disaster, a social enormity, a violation—perhaps the only one in his lifetime—of Speyer's most cherished principles of taste and decorum and hospitality, and Cockburn, shocked as one can be only by watching a man's being collapse before one's eyes, began to understand something of what the crash meant. Lives were crashing along with paper fortunes.

But Black Thursday was only the overture. The ticker, unable to keep up with the rapidity of transactions, ran until after seven o'clock that evening before completing the recording of trades that had stopped at three. A bankers' syndicate was formed to support the market, and the next day President Hoover said, "The fundamental business of the country . . . is on a sound and prosperous basis"; there was a two-day rally on Friday and Saturday, but on Monday the decline resumed, and on Tuesday the twenty-ninth, the worst day in the history of the Stock Exchange, the holocaust went far beyond the possibility of control and the national depression was on. The next day, John D. Rockefeller, Sr. came forward with *his* famous try at restoring confidence ("My son and I have for some days been purchasing sound common stocks") ; after another brief rally the decline was resumed again and went on day after day with such intensity that the machinery of Wall Street was all but paralyzed. By November 13, when bottom for the year was reached at last, of the eighty billion dollars that stocks listed on the Exchange had been worth in September, thirty billion was gone. Jesse Livermore said, "To my mind this situation should go no further." He was right, as far as 1929 was concerned. But 1929 was only the first act of the tragedy.

By December a mood of permanent crisis and settled gloom had descended on the Street. Workers there who opened their office windows on mild days heard a steady, low murmur coming from the crowd that gathered daily outside the Stock Exchange. One of those workers would recall a generation later, "The sound went on all through trading hours, and reached its peak around noon. It wasn't an angry or hysterical sound. That was the most ominous thing about it. It was a kind of hopeless drone, a Greek dirge kind of thing. It was damned distracting, I must say." The search for scapegoats had begun in earnest; new charges and indictments of stock swindles during the past summer and fall cropped up almost every day, and one Wall Street element after another—bucket shops, bear raiders, pool operations, put-and-call brokers, even the slowness of the Exchange ticker—was pointed to in turn as the cause of the crash. Meanwhile, the first tidal waves from the earthquake were already spreading across the city, the nation, and the world. The Russians were crowing that the crash proved their point—capitalism was decadent and doomed. Subway cars plunged under the New York sidewalks carrying carfuls of weirdly keening women. Coast to coast, there were no bread lines yet, but lifelong businesses and long-held insurance policies that had been pledged against loans to buy stock were being lost. College plans for young people were being canceled. Life styles were being changed—some thought for the better; Edwin Lefèvre quoted an intelligent traveling salesman as saying, "I firmly believe that there isn't a town of ten thousand inhabitants or over in the United States that hasn't at least one night club. In the past year and a half I have been in a hundred or more of them, and I'll swear that nine-tenths of the people I saw were having the time of their lives spending their uncashed stock-market profits. It struck me that these people had acquired the worst habits of the idle rich, without the riches."

Yet the real rich, especially the conservative rich, were the least hurt of anyone involved in the stock market—so far. Among the leaders of Wall Street there was much inconvenience but little catastrophe. J. P. Morgan, Thomas Lamont, and their partners could scarcely complain; their firm's profits earlier in the year so far overbalanced their losses in the crash that for the whole year 1929 J. P. Morgan & Company and its affiliate Drexel & Company increased their net worth by $27 million. The ancient George F. Baker told the *New York Times* that he had lost nearly $15 million, but on the other hand, a Wall Street rumor had him getting up from a sickbed at the height of the carnage and tottering to Wall Street over the protests of his doctor with the explanation, "I have made money in every panic in the last sixty years, and I do not intend to miss this one." Otto Kahn was reputed to have lost heavily and no doubt had—but not heavily enough to cause the slightest visible change in his exquisite way of life, his benefactions to the arts, or his showplace estate at Cold Spring Harbor.

The out-and-out speculators, whether or not they occupied seats of respectability, had fared according to their luck or their predilections. The bulls, naturally, were hurt worst. Billy Durant of the Midwestern "prosperity boys" pool would shortly be reduced to suing a broker for giving him a false tip that had cost him, or so he alleged, $75,000—a gambler squabbling with a tout. Arthur Cutten, the clean-living pool participant, found it expedient to reveal that he personally had been a heavy loser after it became known that people in his home town of twenty thousand had lost an aggregate of three million dollars on his tips. Mitchell of the National City, the "manufacturer," had during the awful week of October 28 borrowed twelve million dollars to support the stock of his bank, failed in the attempt, and then resorted in his desperation to a maneuver that would subsequently lead to his indictment for tax evasion.

On the other side, Wiggin of the Chase, the short seller of his own bank's stock, had, as we have seen, cleared more than four million dollars through his curious operations, during the worst period of the crash—and, in fact, as a result of it. Jesse Livermore, temporarily bullish at the start of the crash, had read the signs with his famous prescience, switched sides of the market in time, and come out still comfortably a millionaire. Mike Meehan, of the Radio pools and the shipboard brokerage offices, was all right, too.

III

Four other Wall Street figures and their fates merit our particular attention.

Ben Smith had become a national figure—a figure of villainy. The boisterous, bantering Irishman from the West Fifties was a big shot now: soon he would have a country house with a swimming pool in Bedford Village, be the American broker for Lord Rothermere, and become so inaccessible that reporters seeking an interview might wait a week or more before being called back, not by Smith or his secretary but by his public-relations representative. But Smith's new fame came not from his wealth but rather from the manner in which it was said, and conspicuously without his denial, that he had acquired it.

Caught in the mood of the moment, he had been on the bull side of the market in the summer of 1929 and had been badly hurt in the first wave of the crash. Then he saw the light. The whole boom, it was revealed to him, had been a huge sham and now the country was returning to reality. Smith's marked freedom from emotional ties with the Wall Street or national establishment now became a trading advantage. No loyalty to old school or class or even country blinded him to the truth; as Matthew Josephson said, he was a free soul. True enough, he had been swept along for a time by the mythos of the "New Era economics," and this pious sentimentality had cost him dearly. But now he was free of it; to him the New Era was a rejected religion—an alien one that, in weakness, he had embraced briefly and tentatively, under pressure of mass psychology, against his better judgment and deepest convictions. For Smith's true attitude toward the Morgans and Kuhn, Loebs and Mellons and Hoovers had always been "To hell with them" or something stronger than that, and now he was being proved right. Indeed, what was America itself to him? His life in it had been no bed of roses. "I was right in the first place and all along!" he exclaimed at the time of the crash. Before the first wave was over he had reversed himself and become one of the most lusty and vengeful of bears, lending the weight of his enormous short sales to the plunge of prices and profiting richly as the facts of financial life came at last into congruence with his caustic convictions.

"Never before has American business been as firmly entrenched for prosperity as it is today. . . . Stocks may go up and stocks may go down, but the nation will prosper." Thus the elder business statesman Charles Schwab, on December 10, 1929. He was enunciating the received view of the time, the view held by all those whose emotional commitment to the nation and its business, not to mention their own investments, was such that they were quite unable to countenance the notion of general national economic collapse—in short, to credit what was happening before their eyes. Smith, the free soul, could countenance and could see, and his response was not to make formal statements (he never made any of those) but to sell and sell and sell. And the response of the American public to Smith and his selling was characteristic of the time. When the newspapers made a legend of him, used his name to symbolize the dastardly and unpatriotic bears whose short sales were forcing the market down and down in a time when business was "perfectly sound," he began to be harried like a marmot. Day after day he received threatening phone calls and letters; his two daughters eventually had to have bodyguards. Smith was not intimidated. His enemies, he felt, were getting what they deserved, and so was he.

Inadvertently, Smith fed the legend himself by giving it a slogan and himself a nickname. At some point—at the height of the November 29 panic in one version, several months later in another—he rushed into the crowded board room of the brokerage house where he had an office and shouted over the noise, "Sell 'em all! They're not worth anything!" For the rest of his life he would be "Sell 'em Ben" Smith.

Joseph P. Kennedy, not so "free" as Smith because more ambitious for power (and certainly more committed to the national economic system) , apparently had made no millions selling short in the crash, but he had not lost any through buying or holding, either. Feeling that "only a fool holds out for top dollar," he had quietly taken his profits earlier in the year, and his biographer says that September found him "standing at a safe distance." Later he would write of the period, "In those days I felt and said I would be willing to part with half of what I had if I could be sure of keeping, under law and order, the other half"—but there is no evidence that in fact he had to part with half of what he had or anything like that much. That winter he could afford, financially and emotionally, to turn his back on Wall Street and go to Palm Beach, and the high-level negotiations and operations he carried on from that pleasant base were aimed not so much at making or keeping money as at forming new alliances that might be of use in the future. Kennedy did not need to be concerned about money now; his pile was safe, and his thoughts were turning to the conversion of money into power—the power that goes with being a king-maker, or, more particularly, a President-maker. A few months later, through the good offices of Henry Morgenthau, Jr., he would go to lunch at the Governor's Mansion at Albany to renew an old but slight, indeed rather hostile, acquaintance, dating back to the First World War, with Franklin D. Roosevelt. He would come away from this meeting convinced that he had found the man he wanted to be the next President. Thus his new career was launched.

James Paul Warburg, too, was among those who had survived the crash in a financial condition that permitted him to put his attention on matters higher and broader than personal survival. In the early aftermath he found himself working long hours to save not himself but his firm's clients, and, as a high official of an international bank, not grubbing over a two-point drop in Steel or Radio but worrying about such cosmic repercussions of the crash as the new drain of gold from the United States and the drying up of the American capital market. In 1930 he would spend much of the year abroad, looking out for his bank's European clients, and on his return would tell Wiggin of the Chase, over lunch, that he expected the upstart Adolf Hitler to come to power in Germany and subsequently to launch a new world war. Then Wiggin would call up the venerable Paul Warburg to say, "Your son is crazy. You ought to have him locked up."

So Kennedy and Warburg, two of the survivors, were turning their thoughts from money-making to statecraft; for half a century Wall Street had been the cradle of statesmen, but before long these two would be almost alone among Wall Streeters in having a hand in the national government.

IV

Richard Whitney was nationally famous—not infamous like Ben Smith, but famous as a hero.

It happened quite literally overnight: over the night of October 24–25. At a few minutes after noon on Black Thursday, when the panic was at its height, the stunned crowd in the Street saw a little group of well-known bankers trooping into Morgan's. Their names, which immediately passed in murmurs through the crowd, make a kind of Homeric catalogue of the banking chieftains of the time: Mitchell of the National City, Wiggin of the Chase, Prosser of the Bankers Trust, Potter of the Guaranty Trust, Baker of the First National; and inside the building to greet them as host was Thomas W. Lamont. The crowd, suddenly hopeful, guessed at once what it meant. The long-awaited "organized support" for the market had arrived; the bankers were meeting to commit millions of dollars to the defense of prices, to form a Morgan-centered consortium that, like the one in 1907, would stop the panic and save the country.

Nor was confirmation long in coming. Only a few minutes after they had entered 23 Wall, the chieftains departed, and Lamont held court for the press in his office, as was his custom. Silver-haired, looking cooler and more aristocratic than ever, gesturing idly with his pince-nez as he spoke, Lamont uttered the laughably and magnificently demulcent sentence, "There has been a little distress selling on the Stock Exchange, and we have held a meeting of the heads of several financial institutions to discuss the situation." It had been caused, he went on, not by any basic disorder in the national economy but by "a technical condition of the market." (Thus the new establishment line was promulgated at the very moment a new line became necessary.) Lamont did not say flatly that a support consortium had been formed, presumably because he knew that the existence of one was shortly to be demonstrated almost apocalyptically in action. At about one-thirty—by which time a rally of stock prices had already begun on the strength of word of the bankers' meeting and the Lamont interview—Richard Whitney appeared on the Exchange floor. Broad-shouldered, bull-necked, his face flushed from the previous day's outing at the race meeting, the gold Porcellian pig displayed on his watch chain, the Morgan broker strode to the post where U.S. Steel was traded and placed the most celebrated single order in Stock Exchange history—a bid for 10,000 shares at 205, the price of the last previous sale, although the stock was actually being offered at that moment at well below 200 and therefore Whitney was offering to pay several dollars per share more than he needed to. He then matched this grandly uneconomic gesture by proceeding to various other posts on the floor and placing similar orders for other blue-chip stocks—each in huge quantity, each at the price of the last previous sale. Within a few minutes his orders aggregated more than twenty million dollars, and everyone knew that the bankers' consortium was in action and that Richard Whitney was its floor man. The rally in all stocks sharpened and extended, and Black Thursday ended a good deal less black than it might have.

"Richard Whitney Halts Stock Panic," the headlines trumpeted next day. On that Thursday Whitney had been only an actor, and a good one, cast in the role of hero; his grandiose gestures had been consciously contrived for maximum effect. But in the days following, as acting president of the Exchange and field general in the bankers' battle for an orderly market, he fulfilled a function as genuine as Canute's against the sea. And somewhat more effective. Using his natural talent for leadership (or bullying, as some chose to call it) to maximum advantage, Whitney proceeded firmly, conscientiously, and imaginatively. On October 29, the day things got so far out of hand that whole basketfuls of orders to sell stock were simply forgotten in the confusion and stood unexecuted on the trading floor, in his capacity as acting president he called a noon meeting of the Exchange's Governing Committee to discuss the situation. Maximum secrecy about the very existence of the meeting was ordered, and successfully maintained, to prevent feeding the panic with new fuel; to this end it was held not in the stately Governors' Room as usual but rather in the office of the president of the Stock Clearing Corporation, a room tucked away in the Stock Exchange basement directly under the trading floor. Invited to the meeting, in addition to the governors, were two Morgan partners and some other representatives of the bankers' consortium; the

Morgan partners—just who they were remains uncertain even now, but surely one was Lamont and probably the other was Richard Whitney's brother George—were actually refused admittance for a moment by an incompletely briefed guard. The partners' efforts to slip into the Exchange building unnoticed had aroused the guard's suspicion.

Many of the men meeting to allay panic were near panic themselves. The consortium, as a matter of fact, was already in a state of collapse; its resources ($240 million, according to later reports, although some say less) were vanishing into the maw so fast, and so ineffectually, that the effort at supporting the market would clearly be a failure unless more funds were supplied, which they weren't: that day Lamont actually had to deny that the consortium had turned its coat and begun *selling* stocks. Whitney said later of the meeting, "The feeling of those present was revealed by their habit of continually lighting cigarettes, taking a puff or two, putting them out and lighting new ones."

The chief question before the group was whether or not to close the Exchange out of hand, perhaps for an indefinite period—something that in all the Exchange's history had been done only twice, in the dreadful Panic of 1873 and at the beginning of the First World War. Some maintained that in the present situation there was no alternative to such action; others, Whitney in their forefront, argued that it was "unthinkable." An indefinite closing, the opponents argued, would freeze bank loans on security collateral, render security holdings illiquid, and still further inflame the public imagination; bootleg markets like those of 1914 would develop in the streets, the national banking system and the economy would be all but paralyzed. Courage and fortitude were needed; the show must go on. The noes won. The Exchange stayed open until its normal closing hour that day. But the next day, the thirtieth, Whitney and his colleagues came up with a compromise. It was beginning to be obvious that the physical stamina of the Exchange employees, who for almost a week had been working practically around the clock in a losing effort to keep abreast of the paperwork, was being taxed beyond endurance. The Governing Committee decided on a plan of "special holidays" and shortened trading sessions. On Thursday the thirty-first the Exchange would open at noon instead of ten o'clock as usual; Friday and Saturday would be "special holidays" devoted to paperwork, and regular hours would be resumed the following Monday. Whitney, announcing the plan from the Exchange rostrum on Wednesday afternoon, resorted to one more of the dramatic anti-panic devices for which he was showing such a flair. Ordinarily, the tickers were stopped while the president of the Exchange made a public announcement to the floor; but on this occasion, to prevent the impression from being abroad that the Exchange might close down even for a matter of seconds, he saw to it that the tickers went right on chattering while he spoke.

The plan essentially worked. Needed time and relative calm were gained, and the notion of attributing the partial closing to practical and humanitarian motives rather than to panic proved to have been a brilliant stroke. It worked so well that the partial closing was extended; trading was shortened most days throughout November and was suspended entirely on several more "special holidays" without noticeably increasing public alarm. Still, the sickening decline of stock prices went on until mid-November, when, on its climactic day, the volume of trades went uncounted because the Exchange authorities simply stopped counting them. All through the weeks of crisis Whitney was masterly. Everywhere he went, on the street, at his clubs, at public functions, he found himself confronted with the same anxious queries, the same pleading, trusting faces; lives were disintegrating, and he was the man who could hold them together if anyone could. He said later that through the crisis he and his fellow authorities lived "the life of hunted things." But one may believe that part of him loved it; to command, to be thus relied on, to have the moral authority of a Groton prefect combined with the naked power of a potential temporal messiah is heady stuff, and Whitney had so superbly the patrician bearing, the aloof air, the broad shoulders, the steady gaze, the ready smile to carry off the role. The "cellar meetings" in the room under the Exchange floor went on; Wall Street finally got wind of them, and immediately concocted the quite unfounded rumor that Whitney and Lamont, using a periscope, were watching the activities above through a hole in the floor. As he and his fellow authorities left each meeting, Whitney would exhort them to keep up a bold front, regardless of their private feelings. In what, most ironically, can be considered a preview of a favorite tactic of Franklin D. Roosevelt in other dark days, he would say, "Now get your smiles on, boys!"

The boys went on smiling; and, at last, the market stopped dropping. Impressed by the rumors of bear raids, Whitney in November ordered a spot quiz of all Exchange members on their short positions in stocks; the results satisfied him that bear raiding was "so small as to be almost inconsequential," and the announcement of the results of the quiz was credited with helping stabilize the market. On November 30 the Exchange's Governing Committee passed a resolution of appreciation of Whitney's work in the crisis. "Great emergencies," said the resolution, "produce the men who are competent to deal with them."

Whitney himself spread the credit more generally, and generously, commenting that the events of the autumn had "increased our faith in this marvelous country of ours." Certainly they had increased the country's faith in him. Nor did the country know under what personal difficulties he had accomplished what he had. He said years later that he had lost two million dollars of his own in the crash—by which he certainly meant only paper losses on securities he held at the time; but that was bad enough, and the fact that he had financial worries that autumn will become abundantly clear in the course of this narrative. Yet over the critical weeks he seems never to have let such worries distract him for a moment from his responsibilities as the Stock Exchange's acting president, a job for which he was paid nothing. In truth, he had been magnificent: a born leader in his finest hour.

V

On the last afternoon of the year and the decade, wild bells of a sort rang out from the Stock Exchange floor; the annual New Year's Eve party, bigger and louder than ever, began an hour and a half before the close of trading with the installation of the 369th Infantry Band on a stand erected right in the middle of the floor. Noisemakers had been supplied to everyone, members and clerks alike; speakeasies had clearly been well patronized at lunchtime; when the final gong sounded at three, the pandemonium could be heard as far away as Broadway. And there was reason for celebration; not only was "it" thought to be over, but the fantastic trading volume that had gone with the crash had meant thousands of new clerical jobs and millions of dollars in commissions. Over the period since September, which had seen unemployment nationally rise from less than three-quarters of a million to more than three million, Wall Street, for those whose money was not in stocks, had become an island of temporary prosperity. This was none of Wall Street's calculated doing but an accident, a perfect irony; still, the contrast was not lost on the public. The first mutterings of generalized, unconsidered public hostility to Wall Street and all its works were being heard, and they would rise.

Whitney was Wall Street's symbol, so famous now that his moves and his quips were reported in the press like those of a movie idol. When in January he gave his barber a free trip to Florida as a whimsical reward for remaining silent while shaving him, the *Times* duly carried the story. Later that year Stock Exchange Post No. 2, the one where his famous "205 for Steel" bid had been made, was ceremoniously retired from the floor and presented to Whitney in tribute; he had it put on display in his office lobby. Simmons, the absentee Exchange president of 1929, had finally returned from his wedding trip in December, but he had long since decided to retire from the job at the end of his term, and when the new Exchange elections came around in April, 1930, it was a foregone conclusion that Whitney would be formally elected to the post he had actually been filling for a year.

It was a spring of great recovery and greater optimism. In April the Dow-Jones industrials touched a point 50 percent above their November low; no one could know that it was a point they would not touch again until 1954. In May the Secretary of Commerce said that "normal business conditions should be restored in two or three months"; the following month the Secretary of Labor chimed in, "The worst is over without a doubt." Also in June, President Hoover himself greeted a delegation of clergymen who had come to ask for a public works program with the cheery reply, "You have come sixty days too late. The depression is over." (Hoover never

129

said that prosperity was just around the corner; the now-indelible legend that he did may have arisen from the published indirect quotation of what he had said at a press conference in January—that he saw "definite signs that business and industry have turned the corner from the temporary period of emergency.")

But as recovery waned during the summer and fall and the public hostility to the Stock Exchange began waxing, Whitney took to the lecture circuit in its defense. By now he was accepted, in New York, in Washington, and coast to coast, as *the* voice of Wall Street. That a dandiacal snob with no common touch, and little interest in common people as individuals, should have been a master advocate before the public seems paradoxical, but Whitney, again like Roosevelt, had a gift of leadership that transcended class barriers or even personal inclinations. He had a positive taste for, and ability at, communicating with the public; indeed, he was a far better communicator than financier. Moreover, he flourished in a time when many Americans still actually preferred to be influenced and led by those they felt to be socially above them. His very aloofness and unwillingness to stoop to or compromise with public taste served to impress the public; it might not love him—few did—but it listened to him and believed him.

In September, 1930, he was lecturing the Merchants Association of New York on how the "business slump" was due to overproduction and artificially stimulated high prices. "To attribute business depressions to stock-market panics is to place the cart before the horse," he argued; in reality, stock prices were a "barometer" of business conditions, an effect rather than a cause of depressions; the current business depression could be traced back to May, 1929, rather than to September or October when the market had broken. The *Times*, in an editorial comment, found "much to support this interesting diagnosis," but added, prophetically, that Whitney's views tended to be "inexorable." October, 1930, the month applesellers first became prevalent on American street corners, found him making mild, self-serving remarks about the Stock Exchange to the well-bred and presumably sympathetic ladies of the Junior League: "We endeavor to have righteous men as our members and to have their business done in a straightforward way." The same month, on his initiative, he and his vice president Allen Lindley had dinner with Hoover at the White House. No statement came out of that occasion, although its occurrence was widely noted and interpreted as indicating warm relations between Wall Street and Pennsylvania Avenue; Lindley told the press afterward that the dinner had been "personal," and added, "It was a delightful evening. We spoke about everything."

During 1931—as stocks went on sliding and sliding until the averages stood at lower than half of their 1929 low, and as unemployment, which had soared from three to seven million during 1930, continued rapidly toward the ten-million mark—Whitney more and more went beyond the role of Wall Street advocate to assume the mantle of Wall Street statesman. In January he told the Boston Chamber of Commerce of his anxiety to dispel the idea that the Stock Exchange was "a machine which operates in arbitrary and unaccountable ways," and, using analogies dear to his sporting heart, drawn from baseball and football, he went on to try to do so. In April, the month he was renominated unopposed for his second term as Exchange president, he addressed the Philadelphia Chamber of Commerce on "Business Honesty." The notion that security frauds belonged to the past was, he warned, "absolutely false"; on the contrary, they were as rampant at that moment as at any time in the past, and were resulting in annual losses to investors running into hundreds of millions of dollars, much of it bilked from the poor or near-poor. Bucket shops, misleading company reports, over-speculative investment trusts were some of the leading agents of this deception, he said. Members of the Stock Exchange itself were not to be considered above suspicion. "The fraudulent security criminal is a coward," Whitney declared, and went on to assure his listeners that the Exchange officials, cooperating with civil authorities, were doing everything in their power to ferret out such criminals in their midst. It was a rip-roaring reformist speech, and a notably candid one coming from the man charged with protecting Wall Street's image, although it was later to come back and haunt him in quite a different context. In September he was sharply criticizing those who still refused to face the fact of depression: "There have been . . . too many empty platitudes, too great a lack of frankness and

131

realism, too much of an attitude of trying to whistle in the grave-yard at midnight. . . ."

The prefect was affirming that the school was in a mess, and taking his manly share of the responsibility. Well might he make the admission; the national economic picture was going from bad to worse. Over the summer of 1931 a series of banking panics and failures swept Europe; Hoover's one-year moratorium on inter-governmental payments, proposed in June and adopted in July, eased the situation only temporarily, and in September the once-imperial British pound, kingpin of world currencies for a century, was forced off the gold standard, adding new force to the hurricane winds of the economic storm over here. As the United States continued to cling precariously to the gold standard—that is, to sell gold in exchange for dollars to all comers on demand—a drain from its Treasury to foreign countries and to its own citizens began that within six months would cut the nation's gold reserve almost in half. Just in the five months between April and September, 1931, U.S. industrial production fell 18 percent, factory payrolls 20 percent, construction contracts 30 percent, and common stocks 40 percent.

And Whitney still dramatically rode the hurricane winds. On the morning after the British departure from gold—Monday, September 21, one more awful and thrilling day in Wall Street—he called the Governing Committee into session at nine-fifteen, three-quarters of an hour before opening time. Not a major stock exchange in the world was open except the Paris Bourse, and the question of closing this one was again on the table. Again the idea was rejected: both for practical reasons and as a matter of sacred principle, the market must continue to operate. This time Whitney did agree to a temporary departure from laissez-faire in the form of an emergency ban on short selling, to prevent deliberate exploitation of an already demoralized market, and announced the restriction from the rostrum just before the opening. Stocks dropped violently that day as expected, but over the next two days they rallied strongly, and on Wednesday morning Whitney announced that things were back to normal and short selling was again permitted. Another crisis bravely weathered: Whitney's public career finished out 1931 still at zenith.

VI

But all the time Whitney was playing this grand role he was in deep personal financial trouble.

It dated back to long before the crash, and its sources were by no means to be found in the crash. Out of personal inclination, and to maintain his and his family's pre-eminent social position, Whitney was a man who lived expensively; what with the Ayrshire herd and the horses and the debutante parties, later he would say that even at the depth of the depression his bills had run to over five thousand dollars a month, and that was probably a considerable understatement. And he had no personal fortune to support such a style of life. His original Stock Exchange seat had been bought with money borrowed from his family. The Morgan brokerage business brought him far more prestige than cash; specifically, it grossed something like sixty thousand dollars a year, but the firm's overhead was high and its other brokerage business not really extensive, since Whitney found it congenial to do his business chiefly with a few wealthy friends and relatives rather than with the public. At almost all times throughout his career the Morgan broker and now Stock Exchange president had needed money, and he had sometimes needed it rather desperately. Moreover, there can be little doubt that he needed it psychologically as well as practically. Big, strong in body and will, well-born, capable (and, for what it may mean, left-handed), he nevertheless had his demons. Always across his path there fell the shadow of his brother George, the Morgan partner, and much more than "ordinary" Morgan partner since by 1930 George had been chosen as the destined successor to Lamont as right-hand man to Morgan himself: his brother George, then, a little older, a little more handsome, a little more personable, considerably more sober-seeming, infinitely more astute in finance, considerably more successful by the ineluctable Wall Street yardstick of personal financial worth. The brothers frequented somewhat different social circles—Richard was much the more sporting of the two, George the more serious-minded and intellectual—but they shared membership in various urban clubs (the Knickerbocker, the Links), where George was inclined to be the Whitney who was taken more seriously, while Dick was often treated as a kind of amusing bad boy. Only in the personal fame that came out of his new role could Dick outshine his paragon of a big brother.

As early as 1921 Richard Whitney began getting through periods of temporary embarrassment by borrowing sums of money from George. At first, he always duly made repayment. Thus in 1926 he borrowed $100,000—not such a staggering sum between these bravos—to finance the purchase of a town house; George seems to have got it back on the appointed date. Meanwhile, like less prominent men desperate for money, he was beginning to plunge in speculative stocks. In 1923 he first became interested in the Florida Humus Company, a marginal venture devoted to experimenting with the exploitation of peat humus as a commercial fertilizer. Not long after that, he found himself attracted to another obscure Florida concern, Colloidal Products Corporation of America. These were wild-blue-yonder stocks from which most prudent brokers even in those manic years would have shrunk away in horror; but the broker who would soon be the most famous in Wall Street had an unshakable conviction of the rightness of his opinions, and the further sad and astounding fact is that he was a classic stock-market sucker. When his first investments in the Florida ventures did not prosper, Whitney's enthusiasm for them seemed to wax in inverse proportion to their success; he made the classic sucker's error of compounding his losses rather than cutting them. By the later years of the decade, when a general Florida economic collapse had reduced the stocks to what he considered to be bargain-basement prices, he was throwing huge additional sums into them in hopes of making a killing on a recovery. These huge sums consisted of loans obtained from his brother and one of his broker friends. During 1928 George Whitney loaned his brother, all told, $340,000, and a certain E. B. Schley came through with another $250,000—all unsecured, and all to help Dick Whitney gamble on finally joining the permanent rich through peat humus and mineral colloids.

In 1929 he was still at it. That February he wanted $175,000 more from his brother for the Florida investments. In March he wanted (and this time even he must have hesitated before making the request) half a million dollars more, this time to finance the purchase of an additional Stock Exchange seat that he felt he needed for the expansion of Richard Whitney & Company. Even though the 1928 loans remained outstanding, George Whitney provided these new sums—trustingly and fraternally, but also from a more practical motive. The Morgan partner had, to put it mildly, no faith in his brother's Florida ventures, and by now he had come to feel that Dick's most valuable asset, the credit of Richard Whitney & Company, was in jeopardy as a result of them unless the firm had additional and firmer assets to call upon. Then came the crash, and Dick's sudden rise to fame. But not to riches. In October, J. P. Morgan & Company advanced him $100,000 to help him handle the enormous daily clearings involved in the operation of the ill-fated bankers' consortium. This sum was returned on the last day of December, but his other unsecured loans were not. Quite apart from huge sums that he owed to commercial banks that were holding his securities as collateral, Richard Whitney finished out the decade owing his friend Schley a quarter of a million dollars and his brother George slightly over a million.

And so, impaled on stocks that he would not have dreamed of considering as suitable for listing on the Stock Exchange he headed, shielded from the consequences of his bad judgment by the seemingly bottomless generosity of his brother, the feared and worshiped voice of Wall Street in 1930 and 1931 was teetering on the edge of financial collapse. Calculations made much later with the benefit of hindsight established that as of June 30, 1931, the firm of Richard Whitney & Company, which dealt regularly in sums in the millions, had an actual net worth of about $36,000—and that figure did not even reflect its proprietor's unsecured personal loans! No one in Wall Street dreamed of such a precarious state of affairs—or almost no one. There was, it is true, a mounting sense of concern about Dick Whitney's affairs in the offices of J. P. Morgan & Company, where, as a broker for the firm and the brother of a partner, he was generally well known (although only slightly known to J. P. Morgan himself) and generally liked as an amusing and effective emissary from the raffish world of the Stock Exchange across the street. George Whitney did not tell even his partners the staggering extent of his personal advances to his scapegrace brother, but he did put the word around the office that he had less than complete confidence in Dick's business judgment. Accordingly, some time in 1930 or 1931 the Morgan partner Thomas Cochran made a discreet approach to Herbert G. Wellington, a prominent broker who was a great friend of Richard Whitney's. The trouble with Dick, Cochran said, is that he has bad investment judgment. "We all love Dick around here," the Morgan partner went on, in the breezy and unbusinesslike cadences that Morgan partners were famous for, "and we would like to help him reorganize his firm. He needs partners who aren't office boys." Then to the nub of the matter: would Wellington consider merging his prosperous firm, Wellington & Company, with Richard Whitney & Company?

Wellington, who was devoted to Whitney but no fool, said no. Then, having failed to help out Whitney through persuasion, the Morgan firm turned to direct action. The immediate problem was a $500,000 loan to Whitney from the Corn Exchange Bank that had recently come due but remained unpaid. To judge from later accounts, there was a good deal of stirring around in the Morgan offices about the matter—vague efforts to determine the actual worth of Whitney's Florida investments, shock at the results of these efforts, and, at last, much talk about doing the right thing and helping out a good fellow in a jam. The upshot was that on June 29, 1931, J. P. Morgan & Company loaned Richard Whitney $500,000 for ninety days, unsecured, at an annual interest rate of 5 percent—a stiff rate for 1931, by the way.

So the immediate crisis passed; the Corn Exchange was paid off with the Morgan money, and Whitney's debt transferred to a less importunate creditor. (The Corn Exchange could not have been too importunate, at that; Whitney had been a director of it at the time he had borrowed from it, another detail that had made the Morgan partners uneasy.) But Whitney remained locked in the disastrous Florida ventures, into which he had by now sunk a million and a half dollars, and when the ninety days were up and his loan to Morgan's came due, he could not pay it. It was amiably renewed and then, after another ninety days, renewed again. Happily for Whitney, they all still loved him at the Corner—though not, apparently, all so much as his brother George, who in September put up his own securities as collateral for his brother's loan, thereby taking over the risk. And Dick, still spending over five thousand dollars a month on family living expenses, still generally thought of as among the soundest men in Wall Street, and now, as the whole country knew, spending his days masterfully tiding the Stock Exchange over the crisis of a world depression, wound up 1931 owing almost two million dollars that he could not possibly pay. Now or ever, nothing but the perpetually continued indulgence of his creditors, or a business miracle in Florida, could save him from bankruptcy.

VII

Early 1932: unemployment above ten million and heading for twelve million, or not quite a quarter of the civilian labor force; industrial production nationally down to half its 1929 rate; industrial stocks listed on the Stock Exchange worth about one-fifth of their value at their 1929 peak; foreign withdrawals of United States gold running at a rate of $100 million a week, and more than a billion dollars' worth of currency and coin, much of it gold, being hoarded by terrified Americans—in sum, a nation in the throes of economic disaster. The heart of the Hoover Administration's effort to meet the crisis was the Reconstruction Finance Corporation, set up to pump federal funds into banks and businesses and, by saving them from failure, to enable them to provide jobs and thus cause the benefits to "percolate down" to the poor and the newly poor. In the absence of a penny of direct federal relief to the unemployed, and in a time of the virtual bankruptcy of private philanthropy, this was called, with a good deal of justice, a bread line for big business. With a Presidential election coming up in November, Hoover and the Republicans badly needed a scapegoat to blame for the general disaster. The one they found most readily at hand was Wall Street, and the particular aspect of Wall Street that they chose was that old bugaboo, short selling on the Stock Exchange.

The arguments against and for short selling on stock exchanges were—and are—complex but subject to being summarized briefly. The attack on it centers obviously on the capacity of organized bear raids artificially to depress the stock market and thus unnecessarily damage companies and their stockholders, as the bear raiders had ruined Stutz and Allan Ryan. Moreover, the very root purpose of making a short sale—to profit by the misfortunes of others—tends to make the practice, as the wise and thoughtful Otto H. Kahn once said, "inherently repellent to a right-thinking man." A prime political target, then; and the more so because the defense of short selling, to the eternal frustration of its defenders, has to be based on more sophisticated and therefore less readily grasped concepts. In the first place, a short sale can be looked upon as nothing more than a sale for future delivery—such a transaction as is commonplace and universally accepted in almost all forms of commerce, and the interdiction of which, in most forms, would be universally regarded as intolerable tampering with the free market. And there are other points to be made. For example, every short sale necessarily implies a later purchase by the short seller; thus short selling can be looked upon as creating a reservoir of potential buying power that will ultimately work not to depress the market but to buoy it. Again, in the absence of short selling, which is widely practiced by the floor specialists and traders who give the market much of its liquidity, stocks would tend to gyrate all the more wildly, increasing the risk to the unwary investor. And these theoretical arguments, which were all advanced by defenders of short selling in 1930 and 1931, seemed to be backed by practical experience; all recorded efforts to forbid or severely restrict short selling on stock exchanges over extended periods—in Holland in the seventeenth century, in France in the eighteenth, in England in the nineteenth, in Germany at the opening of the twentieth—had ended in failure. The short sale like the earthworm is an unprepossessing object that plays a useful role.

But these arguments did little to deter a President and a party politically *in extremis,* and it was one of the many ironies of the time that their archvillain in their search for the sinister Wall Street forces that they charged with thus bringing the country to its knees for private gain was the arch-Republican Richard Whitney.

As we've seen, Whitney had already been called upon to investigate bear raids (and by implication to defend short selling) once before, immediately after the 1929 crash. The outcry against the practice had faded out abruptly during early 1930 when the market had been rising. (Criticism of market techniques always mysteriously vanishes during rising markets.) But it began to be heard again early in 1931, and this time it carried a new note of urgency. That May the Stock Exchange, at Whitney's order, reacted by instituting a rule compelling every member firm to furnish every business day a record of the shares held short by the firm or its clients. This was a strong measure to keep tabs on just who was selling short, and how much, but it in no way actually restricted short selling, and it did not satisfy the critics. In October, the month after the sterling crisis had forced the emergency two-day ban against any and all short selling, Whitney and the Exchange went a step further, adopting a rule permanently forbidding short sales in stocks that were already on the way down.

Since the basic principle of a bear raid is to further depress a stock that is already on the way down, this was a formidable and long-overdue barrier to bear raiding—and one, incidentally, that still remains in force on the Stock Exchange today. However, the resourcefulness of market manipulators being what it was, it was not an entirely impassible barrier. With the election getting closer every day and the market still dropping dreadfully, the outcry went on. Indeed, it rose to a crescendo. In December the Senate passed a resolution calling for a major investigation of all the securities markets, with emphasis on the New York Stock Exchange and short selling; the impetus behind this move came from a Republican Senator from Connecticut who had heard a rumor that a group of Wall Street Democrats was deviously planning a series of mighty bear raids to coincide with the 1932 Presidential campaign, and thereby embarrass Hoover. How little the Senator understood Wall Street is suggested by his willingness to believe that a market manipulator, Republican or Democrat, would put large sums out at risk for a mere political motive. But that Senator and others were desperate enough to believe anything. Écrasez l'infame! In January, 1932, Whitney and some of his aides went to the White House again. This time he went at Hoover's summons, and the meeting does not seem to have been as amiable as the one fifteen months earlier; Whitney gave no public account of it, while Hoover reported, in his memoirs years later, that he had "warned Richard Whitney . . . that unless they took measures to clean their own house I would ask Congress to investigate the Stock Exchange with a view to Federal control legislation." Hardly another "delightful occasion," then; rather, the Presidential threat of federal control, already Wall Street's nightmare for a decade, probably marked the moment when the spirit of cooperation between Wall Street and Washington ended, and a long era of bitter, splenetic, and occasionally comical hostility between them began.

Early in March the Senate formally authorized its Banking and Currency Committee, under the chairmanship of Senator Peter Norbeck of South Dakota, to go ahead with an investigation of Wall Street and bear raids. Instantly Wall Street's back shot up. At the beginning of April, with the hearings scheduled to begin in hardly more than a week, a group of top-drawer Wall Street bankers headed by Thomas Lamont himself sent an injured memorandum of protest to Hoover, which he rejected in a self-righteous reply. And the very day after he sent this reply, Hoover learned that Wall Street was resorting to a less straightforward method of persuasion. A committee of powerful New York bankers, Republicans all, and actually brought together through the good offices of Secretary of the Treasury Mills, had been organizing a pool to support the badly demoralized bond market and thus help out the Administration in its extremity. Now the committee sent word to Hoover that various "important financial houses" were refusing to join the pool—unless the Senate investigation were called off.

Thus Wall Street in its turn stooped to threats, and in the same act left the implication that it had things to hide. This was a shattered Wall Street, defensive and desperate, very different from the one where Lamont had debonairly waved his pince-nez at reporters on Black Thursday, or the gallant and embattled one that Whitney had so vividly depicted to the country in the early aftermath of the crash. With Lamont reduced to pleading to be spared exposure, with Whitney standing to be scolded before Hoover like a schoolboy by his headmaster, with leading bankers trying their hand at blackmail, the Wall Street of spring 1932 had lost both its exuberance and its sense of responsibility. Walter Gutman has compared the Street at the height of the depression to a Cape Cod beach resort in November—its inhabitants mostly fled, its landscape racked by hurricanes. With business near a standstill between days of panic, with unemployed apple-sellers standing at the very

Corner, with responsible jobs in brokerage houses paying as little as ten dollars a week, with the cream of the nation's youth now avoiding the place like the plague, Wall Street was like a trapped animal: what remained of its spirit was contained in a sullen, dangerous self-protectiveness. Whether Hoover or the Senate ever seriously considered calling off the hearings is not recorded; in any case, a series of dramatic events on April 8, 1932, put cancellation or even postponement out of the question.

That day—a Friday—rumors arrived from Europe of a concerted attack by French speculators on the dollar, allegedly designed to force the United States to follow Britain off the gold standard. Whether as a result of such an attack or merely as a result of the rumor of one, the dollar dropped sharply against other currencies on the international exchanges and the already disastrous drain of gold from the United States accelerated. If the story of the rumor and its effects has a familiar ring in our own time, it only goes to show that some things endure in international money affairs; but in the case of April, 1932, there were further presentiments of skulduggery to add spice. Also on Friday the eighth, the French police suddenly seized all copies of *Forces*, a scurrilous weekly financial journal published by one Marthe Hanau, a sort of financial Mata Hari who had been imprisoned in 1928 after her banking and brokerage business had been exposed as a bucket-shop operation on a huge scale, and who now, having served her term, was engaged in harassing the dollar by disseminating fiendishly plausible lies. Meanwhile, at home, a rumor of unknown origin spread to the effect that a million-dollar bear raid on the New York Stock Exchange—this one commercially rather than politically motivated —was scheduled for the following morning, Saturday the ninth. In reaction to all this, the stock market, which had already been through a two-week sinking spell as drastic as any during the whole depression period, crashed sickeningly; and in this atmosphere of general crisis and hysteria the Senate Banking and Currency Committee acted. Hearings were precipitately scheduled to begin the following Monday morning, April 11, and Whitney, melodramatically subpoenaed at his home in New York late on Friday, was ordered to appear as the first witness.

On Monday morning he appeared. The haste with which the

hearings had been scheduled made for a great deal of confusion; the hearing room was jammed with spectators, some of them sitting on filing boxes, others for whom there were no seats of any kind leaning on the back of the witness chair where Whitney sat. Nationwide, public interest was intense—and, to the annoyance of the Senators and presumably of Hoover too, considerable public sentiment appeared to favor Whitney. He was still, in the public's view, the gallant Wall Street knight *sans peur et sans reproche*—an aristocrat worlds apart from the cynical moneygrubbers and manipulators who were the real villains of the crash, and at the same time a strong field marshal who might still be the man to lead the country and its faltering multitudes out of the valley of the shadow. On the printed page his name and his picture were everywhere. A fortnight earlier the artist-reporter S. J. Woolf had depicted him in *World's Work* as very calm and masterly, and had commented, "Richard Whitney belongs to [Wall Street's] seething hubbub, yet strangely is not a part of it." That week in *Collier's*, John T. Flynn wrote of him with grudging respect, "Whitney represents the highest type of Wall Street broker"—the same John T. Flynn who was already known as a radical critic of Wall Street, and who a year later would become an energetic staff member of the very Senate committee conducting the investigation.

By way of further aid to Whitney's and Wall Street's cause, the Senators were ill-prepared. Only two of them, James Couzens and Carter Glass, were versed in finance; one of them, who apparently had Richard Whitney mixed up with his brother, thought the witness was a Morgan partner. Their ignorance gave Whitney just the edge he needed, enabling him to turn what was supposed to be an inquisition into an economics lesson. Elegant in bearing, precise in diction, meticulous of grammar and Groton of accent, Whitney lectured them and corrected their errors with weary patrician tolerance. The burden of his position was that there was no need for an investigation, since the Stock Exchange could and did adequately police itself. Although it had no specific rule forbidding bear raids as such, it forbade and punished any action intended to "demoralize the market"—and since that was the precise intention of a bear raid, therefore a bear raid was effectively forbidden. It followed logically, Whitney pointed out dryly, that the supposed raid of the previous Saturday had been nonexistent. "A bear raid," said Whitney in his most pedagogical tone, "is a violation of the rules of the New York Stock Exchange. And it does not take place." Whether he meant that it was mythological like the unicorn or extinct like the dodo, he didn't say. He scoffed at the stories of Wall Street plots to embarrass the Administration. Once, spreading himself in the course of his patient explication, he depicted himself as a practical farmer, and used an illustrative analogy involving his prize cows in New Jersey. As for short selling, he put forward the standard arguments in its defense, and summed them up by comparing a market without it to a man with one leg. He explained the Exchange's system of keeping tabs on short sellers, and agreed to submit a list of the names of the current biggest ones. People who disagreed with him on the social and economic merits of short selling might be intelligent, he generously allowed—"but they are wrong."

So it went at first. But as day followed day with Whitney still on the stand, and still conceding not even the smallest point, tempers began to wear thin. The tribunes of the people, and the people themselves, began to catch the whiff of tyranny. Once, when Senator Couzens suggested that a broker may use his customers' stock to depress the market, the witness' smooth brow clouded and he snapped, "I deny that!"—whereupon he immediately recovered himself, smiled, and added, "No broker may do that." "You brought this country to the greatest panic in history," asserted Senator Brookhart of agrarian Iowa. "We have brought this country, sir, to its standing in the world through speculation," Whitney replied icily. On April 21, Whitney's ninth day in the witness chair, the committee disclosed the names of the 350 biggest short sellers, as contained on the list he had submitted. The names were one more disappointment for the committee since—apart from the redoubtable Sell 'em Ben Smith, who was short 13,500 shares of General Motors, 15,000 of General Electric, 5,000 of Anaconda, and so on—hardly a single one on the list had ever been heard of. "These obviously are dummy names in many cases," one chagrined committee member commented. That afternoon Chairman Norbeck, his patience exhausted by a typically unproductive exchange, suddenly stormed at Whitney, "You don't grant that anything in the market is illegal. You don't grant anything. You're hopeless." Whitney beamed benignly. A few moments later Norbeck abruptly dismissed him, subject to recall under his subpoena. Whitney and his counsel, Roland Redmond, were taken aback; they had, they protested, things they wanted to put in the record. "Oh, you will be back," Norbeck replied—a promise and a threat.

So Whitney and the Exchange came out unscathed. Clearly, he had won, but it was a Pyrrhic victory. One committee member was to comment later that Whitney had been the most arrogant and uncooperative witness he had ever encountered. The monolithic quality of Whitney's assumption of rectitude, his scarcely concealed sense of superiority to the Senators, the very fact that they had failed to extract even small admissions from him and had been made to look foolish along the way, all fed their frustration, anger, and desire for revenge.

With Whitney back in Wall Street and other witnesses in the chair, the hearings became more productive. Through May and June they went on, and after a six-month hiatus for the political campaign and election they were resumed the following January, to continue almost to the eve of Roosevelt's inauguration. It was in the course of them that much of what we know about the underside of American finance in the 1920s first came to light. Ben Smith and a fellow speculator, Thomas E. Bragg, explained with a certain defiant glee the ins and outs of the Radio and Anaconda pools of 1928 and 1929; the rise and fall of the Kreuger match empire and the Insull utilities empire, with enormous public losses, were detailed. And, little noticed in the record, there was the recital of a curious, premonitory small episode that threw a fleeting shaft of light onto the relations between Richard Whitney and the firm of J. P. Morgan & Company. A lady named Grace Van Bram Roberts, of Highland, New York, had in 1928 written to the Stock Exchange pointing out that the brokerage firm of Hayden, Stone & Company, adjudged guilty of fraud by the New York Supreme Court in 1920, had never in any way been censured by the Exchange. On behalf of the Exchange, Whitney had replied that he happened to disagree with the Supreme Court's decision, and therefore intended no censure action against Hayden, Stone then or ever. Now, in November and December, 1932, Miss Roberts addressed her complaint personally to J. P. Morgan the man, as Wall Street's last court of moral appeal:

> Your great house cannot be afraid of Mr. Richard Whitney or of Mr. Charles Hayden; and if you refrain from censure of their acts, you will be understood to approve them. Hayden was adjudged a cheat, and you did not appeal. Whitney is his defender. . . . For the financial district to defend these cheats is to invite a sweeping condemnation. If the members of this firm had cheated at cards or in a yacht race, they would have been expelled from their clubs. Will Mr. Whitney's false statements tend to establish public confidence at a time when the stock exchange needs confidence?

More than a month went by, and then Miss Roberts got the following reply:

> DEAR MADAM:
> Mr. Morgan directs me to acknowledge receipt of your letters of November 16th and December 12th and to say that he has the highest regard for both gentlemen you mention and feels sure that you are misinformed.
>
> Yours very truly,
> V. AXTEN, *Secretary*

So much, then, for Miss Roberts' complaint and the New York Supreme Court. But how curious, in the light of later events, that she had spoken of a yacht race!

VIII

That winter the doomed Hoover Administration moved swiftly toward its *Götterdämmerung*. After his election defeat Hoover repeatedly appealed to the President-elect for cooperation in the national interest in time of crisis, but Roosevelt rebuffed these overtures on the ground that what Hoover was asking for was abandonment of most of the New Deal's planned programs. While the political leaders squabbled, the economy tottered. A conviction that Roosevelt would devalue the dollar led currency speculators and firms with international interests to exchange United States currency in huge quantities for gold and foreign money, causing the

Treasury to lose gold at a frightful rate. Meanwhile, ordinary citizens came to fear, with good reason, for the safety of their bank deposits. By the hundreds of thousands, they lined up at the cashiers' windows to make withdrawals; some of the weaker banks could not meet the concerted demand and had to close; the closings led to more withdrawals from the surviving banks, forcing *them* to close, and so the panic fed on itself. As early as October, 1932, the Governor of Nevada had to proclaim a bank holiday, and an epidemic of failures in the Western states quickly followed. Early in February came the closing of a group of large Detroit banks that were unnecessarily vulnerable because of the precarious holding-company structure of their ownership. Then things went out of control. On February 14 the Governor of Michigan declared an eight-day bank holiday that prevented access of almost a million persons to a billion and a half dollars of their money. Further bank holidays followed in Indiana on the twenty-third, Maryland on the twenty-fifth, Arkansas on the twenty-seventh, and Ohio on the twenty-eighth. During February those lucky enough to get to their banks in time withdrew in all $900 million, or not quite one-sixth of the amount of currency in circulation at the start of the month. Gold coins, in their last days on the American scene, vanished into private hoarding virtually down to the last five-dollar gold piece.

In sum, the whole complex of coin and currency, of credit and trust, was paralyzed because the trust was gone, and as a result the country was ripe for chaos, revolution, and tyranny. By March 3, the day before the inauguration of the new President, banks remained open in only ten states, and what with insufficient gold left in the coffers to back the currency and insufficient cash left in the Treasury to meet the government payroll, the United States was technically bankrupt.

In the midst of this holocaust Richard Whitney was called back for a reprise before the Senate committee. It was a subtly different Whitney now. Crisis and criticism had changed him; his maddeningly unshakable rectitude had shaded into sourness. On the conduct of the Stock Exchange he was as inexorable as before, but now he felt free to expound his social and moral attitudes, and took every opportunity to do so. What he expounded was not attractive. To restore confidence, he insisted, the national budget must first be balanced; as a start toward that goal, federal spending should be reduced by cutting government salaries and eliminating pension payments to service veterans with disabilities that were not battle-connected.

Looking back on Whitney at this period, we must remember and consider his secret troubles. How vividly aware he must have been of himself as a shell—a public leader of men of substance, a private near-deadbeat! Such realization cannot be comforting to one cast in the role of crisis leader. But as human understanding is imperfect, so is the human capacity for forgiveness. The Senators and the country could not know in February, 1933, that the man advocating a balanced national budget had a spectacularly and shamefully unbalanced personal one. But they could know that a man who spoke as an aristocrat and lived as a millionaire was calling for sacrifices not from his own kind but from those he would have been the first to describe as far below him. By any standard, this was not the gallant knight; this was not *noblesse oblige*. Wall Street's long effort to invent an aristocracy seemed to have failed.

Chapter Seven

Gold Standard

on the Booze

On the eve of the inauguration of the new President, Thomas Lamont (Harvard '92) telephoned his old friend Franklin D. Roosevelt (Harvard '04) to suggest that he take no precipitate action on the banking crisis, critical as it might be. It was Friday night, and Lamont believed that the leading banks that still remained open, meaning chiefly the key ones in New York City, could pull through the half business day on Saturday; then perhaps a sweeping change in national psychology might take place over the subsequent day and a half, by opening time on Monday morning a measure of confidence would have returned, and the crisis would be over.

Roosevelt, of course, did not follow this advice. His first act in office was to declare a four-day bank "holiday" (which actually turned out to be eight days long, and for many banks much longer than that). What Lamont had been counting on to restore confidence was, of course, the national impact of the accession to power of Roosevelt and the New Deal. Rather oddly, in the light of later events, Wall Street at that desperate moment clearly had more faith in the restorative powers of the New Deal than the New Deal had in them itself.

Wall Street wanted to be led out of the wilderness, and was in no mood to be particular about the character of its savior. This trusting attitude persisted, even flourished, all through the new Administration's celebrated first hundred days, when, in a thrilling and unprecedented rush of action, it sent hurtling through Congress the National Industrial Recovery Act, the Agricultural Adjustment Act, the Tennessee Valley Authority, the Federal Home Owners Act, and the Farm Credit Act, along with—measures certainly not likely to evoke wild enthusiasm in Wall Street in normal times—the Banking Act, designed to break up long-established concentrations of money power (including the sacrosanct House of Morgan itself) by requiring the separation of investment banks from commercial banks, and the Securities Act, compelling the issuers of new securities to give the public a detailed account of the risks involved in buying them. After staying closed through eight business days while the worst of the bank crisis passed, the Stock Exchange was back in business on the morning of March 15. When Richard Whitney made the reopening announcement from his presidential rostrum, there was a whoop from the holiday-surfeited brokers on the floor, and in the course of that day's trading stock values increased by some 15 percent—a larger advance than had ever occurred in any single day during the entire boom of the 1920s. Brokers instantly began talking about the "Roosevelt market," even though the designation had certain macabre connotations of the "Coolidge market" of a few years back. As the weeks went on, the parallels to the earlier period increased. On April 20, the Exchange's biggest trading day in three years, the ticker fell far behind in its recording of completed transactions—as it had done so often in 1929. By the end of April thousands of brokerage-office employees—secretaries, clerks, messengers, and the like—who had been laid off and unemployed for the past one, two, or three years, were being recalled to their old jobs. Wall Street was a boom town again, in large part because of the infectious enthusiasm and optimism of the man (not yet That

149

Man) in the White House, who, as one of his associates put it, was "like the fairy-story prince who didn't know how to shudder." By mid-July industrial stock averages stood at more than double their Inauguration Day levels, and the four-month rise had been the steepest in Stock Exchange history.

II

Yet during this euphoric period a strange thing, almost unnoticed at first and then progressively more disconcerting and ultimately nightmarish, was happening to Wall Street. Its fixed star—money—had left its regular place in the heavens and begun to wander and dance and lurch. For generations the dollar had been held firmly fixed by a force that was accepted in banking circles as being equivalent to a natural law of astronomy, the gold standard—specifically, by the Treasury's pledge to redeem dollars with gold in any quantity for all comers at $20.67 per fine ounce. Now, with that pledge temporarily abrogated in the emergency, the dollar was free to fluctuate in the world markets at the whim of speculators, just like some humbler currency, or, indeed, like some untrustworthy common stock. The hundred days marked the beginning of a unique, and for many people hair-raising, period of almost a year during which the most secure wealth for Americans consisted not of gold, which they were now forbidden to possess except for industrial use or in the form of jewelry, and not in money, every possessor of which found himself involved intentionally or not in a game of chance, but in land or goods. Wall Street's sky had fallen.

It began to fall with a deceptive lack of clatter on Roosevelt's second day in office when by proclamation he decreed a temporary end to the export or hoarding of gold. This was a technical departure from the gold standard, but the emphasis was on the word "temporary," and in a time when the panic was causing gold to leave the Treasury for foreign shores or domestic hoarders' mattresses at a fearful rate, few even among the flintiest of bankers questioned the expediency of the move. With the very banks closed, the gold embargo seemed a comparatively minor matter; naturally, it would end when the banks reopened, or shortly thereafter. "It is ridiculous and misleading to say that we have gone off the gold standard," Secretary of the Treasury William Woodin reassured the nation shortly after the President's proclamation. The *Times* of London, whose nation had been off gold for a year and a half, pronounced that the prospect of the United States' taking a similar course now was "so unlikely that it may almost be left out of account."

What was misjudged by everyone in Wall Street, and for that matter by almost everyone in the New Deal up to and including Roosevelt's closest monetary advisers, was the stubbornly fixed purpose behind his temperamental attitude toward money matters. In the Presidential campaign the previous year he had vied with Hoover in proclaiming his devotion to "sound money," which presumably meant the gold standard; on the other hand, in January, two months after his election, he had said to a journalist that if the depression continued "we may be forced to an inflation of our currency," which sounded like just the opposite. His intimates were all but unanimous in their agreement that he combined virtual illiteracy in monetary affairs with unshakable confidence in the superiority of his own offhand notions about it to the accepted wisdom of the experts; that he treated the subject of money as a casual, rather amusing game that alternately bored and fascinated him; and that the game tended to bring out his strain of sophomoric humor. As one of the advisers, an accepted-wisdom man, put it, "You were up against a compulsive drive to do something in this area without ever being able to pin the man down so that he would really think about it."

The advisers themselves were a mixed lot. There was Secretary Woodin, a shrewd, folksy former industrialist from Pennsylvania, certainly not known for unorthodox economic ideas. There was Lewis Douglas, Director of the Budget, a hard-shelled sound-money man if there ever was one. There was Assistant Secretary of State Raymond Moley, former professor of public law at Columbia, and chief of the famous pre-election "brains trust," an ambitious, egotistical activist with a slightly sardonic gleam in his eye, who was supposed to outrank all others in access to the President's ear. ("Moley, Moley, Moley, Lord God Almighty!" sang the Washington wits who knew the Hymnal.) There was Herbert Feis, astute

151

and orthodox, economic adviser to the State Department since 1931 and the New Deal's only important holdover from the Hoover Administration. Serving without portfolio until later in the year, there was Henry Morgenthau, Jr., Roosevelt's old upstate New York neighbor and friend, the product of a family distinguished in diplomacy but as much of an innocent in monetary affairs as the President himself. And then there was the shadowy, publicity-shy figure of George Frederick Warren, professor of agricultural economics and farm management at Cornell; he had some odd and highly original ideas about government management of the relationship between commodity prices and the gold value of the dollar. These he was able to press upon Roosevelt and Morgenthau as a result of relationships that had begun, in Morgenthau's case, when the latter had been a student at Cornell; and in Roosevelt's case, it was said by Mrs. Morgenthau, when Morgenthau had brought Warren and one of his Cornell colleagues to Hyde Park to give expert advice on how to plant trees. "How different life would have been had Franklin and Henry not met those arboreal experts!" Mrs. Morgenthau remarked years later.

Finally, there were two men of Wall Street, one of them serving Roosevelt by choice and the other as a result of circumstance.

Jimmy Warburg, the spirited, song-writing young Lochinvar of Wall Street in the twenties, now at thirty-six the president of the International Acceptance Bank, had met Moley through Roosevelt's son James, whom he had known for some years. In February, 1933, Moley brought Warburg along with other potential aides to the President-elect's house in New York City. "Which of you gentlemen is Ikes?" Warburg recalled later that Roosevelt had asked at that meeting, whereupon the future Secretary of the Interior had stepped forward like a private at roll call to identify himself and diffidently correct the pronunciation of his name. Later, Roosevelt said to Warburg, "Ray Moley tells me that you are the white sheep of Wall Street." Warburg replied modestly, and with characteristic quick wit, that the distinction belonged more properly to his father, and that, so far as he knew, a white sheep did not necessarily beget white lambs. Roosevelt was delighted with this response, and shortly thereafter offered Warburg the job of Under Secretary of the Treasury. Warburg turned it down for personal reasons; nevertheless, although he knew he risked ostracism in the street of black sheep where he had his career, he took leave of his bank, moved into the New Deal's pet Carlton Hotel in Washington as an unofficial, unsalaried White House monetary adviser, and thereby became virtually the sole surviving strand of the old tradition of Wall Streeters high-mindedly in the nation's service.

The other Wall Streeter—George Leslie Harrison, Benjamin Strong's successor as governor of the Federal Reserve Bank of New York—cannot be counted as a preserver of that tradition because he made no choice to join the New Deal, nor was he chosen; his job itself, ostensibly outside politics and not subject to political appointment or dismissal, was the only permanent one directly linking the center of finance to the center of government. His office was in the heart of the Wall Street area—in that area's most imposing structure, the New York Fed's Florentine *palazzo* on Liberty Street —and his duties included serving as the government's banker in all foreign dealings, so he and the new President were stuck with each other whether they liked it or not. A Yale and Harvard Law School graduate, a former legal secretary to the legendary Justice Holmes, a careful bureaucrat and a tactful diplomat, Harrison was a handsome, heavy-set, pipe-smoking, crinkly-eyed, confidence-inspiring sort of man—the more confidence-inspiring, perhaps, because he walked with a limp as a result of a childhood accident. He was destined over the months ahead to have his talent for diplomacy put to the comically excruciating test of adjudicating among Roosevelt and his wilder-eyed henchmen, the irascible commercial bankers of Wall Street, and the lordly central bankers of Europe.

III

In April there were rumblings from the West, and resounding echoes of them in Washington. The nation's farmers were in a state approaching open revolt. Prices paid for their output had fallen piteously low—the index of wholesale farm commodities stood at about 40 percent of its 1926 level—and as a result, they were caught in a seemingly hopeless bind. Even though they sold every crop they grew, the prices were insufficient to meet their mortgage payments, and they were being dispossessed by the tens of thousands. There began to be incidents of violence; one day late that month, in Le Mars, Iowa, a mob of masked farmers dragged a judge from his bench to a crossroads and nearly lynched him in an effort to force him to promise to stop signing mortgage foreclosures. But criminal assaults on legal authority could serve no purpose; what the farmers chiefly needed was the classic remedial measure for debtors in hard times—a deliberate governmental inflation of the currency such as Bryan had preached so long and so eloquently, that would raise prices and enable the farmers to pay off in cheap money the debts they had contracted in dear money. Inflation talk raged in Congress, and came to a climax in an amendment to the Agricultural Adjustment Act offered by Senator Elmer Thomas of Oklahoma, authorizing the President at his discretion to issue greenbacks or resort to practically any other known inflationary measure.

To hard-money men in and out of Wall Street the Thomas Amendment meant financial anarchy. Its adoption would mean that the country had definitively abandoned its monetary religion since 1879, the gold standard. But there seemed to be no indication that Roosevelt wanted the Thomas Amendment or that any similarly drastic move was in the wind; on the contrary, during the first half of April government licenses to ship gold abroad in spite of the embargo were issued to several banks, apparently indicating a gradual return to the old gold standard. Then on the evening of the eighteenth, Roosevelt held a White House meeting ostensibly to discuss the forthcoming International Monetary and Economic Conference, plans for which had been inherited from the Hoover Administration, inviting to the meeting, among others, Secretary of State Cordell Hull, Secretary of the Treasury Woodin, Moley the Almighty, and the monetary men Douglas, Warburg, and Feis. It developed that the President had other things than the conference on his mind when he unexpectedly instructed Moley to prepare the Thomas Amendment for Congressional passage and his signature. Then, turning to the rest of the group, Roosevelt blithely informed them that the country had just "gone off gold" and asked them to congratulate him.

They didn't; instead, according to Moley, "hell broke loose," with the trio of monetary experts, in despair at the casualness with

154

which the momentous step seemed to have been taken, frantically lecturing Roosevelt on the pitfalls and horrors of inflation for two solid hours, and even finally invoking the ghastly example of Germany in 1923, when the worst inflation in history had caused a state of chaos in which skilled workers had gone on strike for the equivalent of eight cents an hour and the going price for a luncheon chop, on one occasion, had risen from 600,000 marks one day to 1,500,000 the next. But Roosevelt, seemingly rather entertained by the storm he had provoked, remained coolly adamant. Later, after walking the streets with Warburg most of the night, Douglas exclaimed sepulchrally, "This is the end of Western civilization."

Next day came the public announcement that the country was off the gold standard, and, from Wall Street, some astonishing reactions. The stock market leaped ahead in wild trading. That was logical enough; if the dollar was going to be cheaper—and leaving the gold standard could mean nothing else—then it made sense to transfer one's assets out of dollars into stocks, and quickly. What was more astonishing was the total absence of anguished or angry protest from Wall Street on ideological grounds. The big bankers, the Wiggins and Mitchells, who only a few years earlier would surely have been howling for the President's impeachment, had apparently been so reduced in self-assurance by the depression and its panics that they were humbly silent while their world toppled under this casual push from the White House. What was "the end of Western civilization" to a leading government bureaucrat was a matter for no comment by those whose stake in the thing meant by "Western civilization" was greatest. George Harrison, starting his career as the man in the middle, gingerly explained to the Federal Reserve officials that Roosevelt had acted because "something had to be done to prevent Congressional excesses," and the officials meekly accepted the explanation. What was most astonishing of all, though, was the swift and decisive approval of Roosevelt's move by the greatest banker of them all. From 23 Wall came a public message signed by J. P. Morgan—apparently the only formal statement of his career, apart from one that had followed British devaluation in 1931: "I welcome the reported action of the President. . . . It seems to me clear that the way out of the depression is to combat and overcome the deflationary forces."

"Number 23" had spoken; heresy was enshrined, and, as a result, Wall Street remained calm. Whatever else it was, the Morgan statement represented a master stroke of government-business cooperation. But how in the world had it come about? Had the champion of hard money, the very prince of creditors, undergone some kind of conversion and become overnight a sort of Wall Street Bryan—an inflationist champion of the downtrodden debtor class? It was sheerly impossible. Was the House of Morgan, then, engaging in secret conniving and deal-making with the White House, as it had allegedly done so often during the Coolidge and Hoover Administrations? Interestingly, a newspaper column by the prodigiously influential Walter Lippmann, expressing the view that maintenance of the gold standard would only worsen the depression, had appeared on the very morning of the day of the fateful White House meeting—and Lippmann was known to have close ties with the House of Morgan. Such a hypothesis is intriguing but not convincing. After all, Roosevelt in his campaign had caustically criticized the ties between Hoover and Morgan's, and (it came out much later) had even rejected his friend, the Morgan partner Russell Leffingwell, as a possible Assistant Secretary of the Treasury on the ground that "We simply can't tie up with '23.' " More likely, the explanation for this most enigmatic action of Morgan's life, and perhaps the most enigmatic in the House of Morgan's long history, lies in a private letter Leffingwell wrote Roosevelt a few days later in which he said, "Your action in going off gold saved the country from complete collapse." It would seem, then, that the feeling at "23" was that a time had come when only heresy could save the temple itself from falling along with everything else. If so, the Morgan statement was a statesmanlike act, the climax—and perhaps the end—of the best old Wall Street tradition.

Now the dollar was a speculative security; anyone who owned it was playing a volatile market. It could no longer be exchanged for gold, but, in the foreign-exchange markets in the European capitals, it was still exchanged freely and regularly for French francs, which were still firmly tied to gold. From the relationship of the current, fluctuating dollar-franc rate to the old fixed rate when the dollar, too, had been on gold, it was possible to calculate each day just how much the dollar was now worth in terms of gold. Immediately after

Roosevelt's announcement the dollar dropped to 88½ cents; it steadied for a while, then fell further during May when the Thomas Amendment was signed, making inflation formally the law of the land, and in early June it stood at 83 cents. Domestic commodity prices meanwhile rose somewhat, and the farmers felt better. But the monetary authorities of Britain and France were shocked—the British fearing that a cheaper dollar would undermine the world trade on which they relied for survival, and the French that it would force them, too, to go off gold. Roosevelt, thinking above all of domestic problems, had chosen monetary nationalism over internationalism; yet even so, he allowed plans to go forward for United States participation in the International Monetary and Economic Conference, and between June 12 and July 23, at the Geological Museum at Kensington, London, the conference took place.

Attended by delegations from sixty-six nations along with platoons of staff and experts—more than one thousand persons, all told—it was structurally the greatest international assemblage since Versailles. All the more anticlimax, then, when it proved to be a memorable disaster and farce. As originally planned by Hoover and British Prime Minister Ramsay MacDonald, it had been intended to discuss world currency stabilization and the reduction of trade barriers, but now there were no clear limits to its agenda. The United States delegation was a magnificently ill-assorted lot. Its chairman was Secretary of State Hull, whose *idée fixe* was reciprocal reduction of tariffs, a matter that it was now not clear whether or not the conference would take up at all. Among its members were James M. Cox, former Governor of Ohio and Democratic Presidential candidate in 1920, a devotee of monetary orthodoxy and low tariffs; Senator Key Pittman of Nevada, a survival of the Old West, a silver fanatic, and a *high*-tariff man; Senator James Couzens of Michigan, onetime partner of Henry Ford and another high-tariff advocate, making the delegation score on that particular issue an even 2–2; Ralph W. Morrison, a Texan with no visible qualifications of any sort for membership; and Representative Samuel D. McReynolds of Tennessee, chairman of the House Foreign Affairs Committee but a monetary illiterate. No member of this motley crew had ever attended an international conference before, and, moreover, Roosevelt was keeping his intentions so secret that they apparently set out

157

for this one without specific instructions, each man free to ride his particular hobbyhorse to his heart's content. The delegation did have an expert staff—an able group of monetary conservatives including Warburg, Feis, Harrison for the Federal Reserve, and Oliver M. W. Sprague for the Treasury.

Even on shipboard on the way to London, the delegates fell to wrangling among themselves so constantly that reporters on board predicted disaster for the conference and called the vessel a "funeral ship." The conference had no sooner convened than an international dispute erupted between the gold-bloc countries, conspicuously led by France, which clung to gold with almost mystical fervor, and those who were off gold and favored greater flexibility, led by Britain and the United States. As the days went by without guidance from Washington, the American delegates became progressively more eccentric and unruly. Hull kept pleading doggedly for lower tariffs, but hardly anyone listened to him. Pittman, between set speeches in favor of silver coinage, was usually quarrelsome and often drunk; on one occasion he amused himself, Western style, by shooting out the street lamps on Upper Brook Street, and on another, informed that it was improper to wear a raincoat to meet royalty regardless of the inclemency of the weather, he nevertheless wore one to a Palace garden party, declaring loudly, "I ain't going to get soaked for no king and queen." (The King and Queen were delighted with him and his raincoat, or pretended to be.) McReynolds seldom attended conference sessions, concentrating instead on arranging to get his daughter presented at Court. At least one of the delegates was thought to be passing inside information obtained at the conference to associates in New York for purposes of speculation. The arrival of Moley, unexpectedly and dramatically dispatched to London by Roosevelt in mid-conference, led to a series of undignified rows between him and Hull, who had become bitter rivals and enemies, and to a comical competition between them to determine who could send the most sycophantic cables to Roosevelt. Behind the scenes, meanwhile, Warburg, Harrison, and Sprague, along with the monetary authorities of the European countries, were doing just about the only substantive business of the conference—trying to arrive at some sort of agreement to stabilize, even temporarily, the relationship between their currencies and thus end the state of chaos in the exchange markets.

Wall Street, knowing only what it read in the newspaper dispatches from London, was dismayed to the point of paralysis. On days when rumor said that a stabilization agreement was near, the dollar would go up and stocks would go down; on days when the stabilization talks were said to be going badly, the dollar would go down and stocks up; on days when there were no new rumors, everyone would hold his breath and wait. At the end of June, the word was that a joint declaration of the major powers on stabilization had been agreed upon and was being prepared for publication. At this moment, on the very verge of accomplishment, the conference suddenly exploded into fragments when Roosevelt, from aboard the cruiser *Indianapolis* off the Atlantic Coast, wrote out by hand and sent the conference what came to be called the bombshell message, in which he called the stabilization proposal "a purely artificial and temporary expedient" based on a "specious fallacy," denounced the "old fetishes of so-called international bankers," and made it clear that the United States was not prepared to enter into any stabilization agreement whatever. Although it would drag on for three more weeks, the conference was over in everything but name.

The representatives of the gold-bloc countries were dumfounded. Prime Minister MacDonald was so upset that the King was moved to comfort him by saying, apropos of Roosevelt, "I will not have these people worrying my Prime Minister this way." All members of the United States delegation were completely demoralized at seeing their work go up in smoke except for Pittman, who hadn't liked the idea of stabilization anyhow. The celebrated John Maynard Keynes, a veteran opponent of the gold standard, was almost alone among leading economists anywhere in pronouncing Roosevelt "magnificently right." To a stunned and disillusioned Warburg, the Roosevelt message seemed "one that could not possibly have come from the man whom I had learned to love and admire"; three days later, just before leaving London to sail for New York, he resigned as financial adviser to the delegation on the ground that "we are entering upon waters for which I have no charts and in which I therefore feel myself an utterly incompetent pilot." And in the exchange markets the gold value of the unstabilized dollar dropped in two days to 73.4 cents, its lowest point since the Civil War.

IV

The method in Roosevelt's madness, while it would remain opaque to Wall Street for three more months, began to reveal itself to his closest advisers during July. He had, it seemed, torpedoed the London conference on purpose; in fact, in retrospect it appears that he may have been considering such a move since before it had begun, inasmuch as his later moves make clear that he did not want the dollar tied to the pound and the franc any more than he wanted it tied to gold. (In mid-June, before the conference, he had privately offered to stabilize with sterling at $4.25 per pound, but had apparently been bluffing, and his bluff had not been called.) Roosevelt's opposition to stabilization was based on the fact that it would limit his freedom of action at home. It would restore order to the foreign-exchange markets at the cost of much of his power to bring about domestic inflation. Nowadays when we think instinctively of inflation as a prime bugaboo, it is hard to conceive of those days when *deflation* was the problem, and inflation—or, more delicately, reflation—was held a worthy and necessary objective by the majority. Roosevelt considered it an objective worth almost any price to attain.

His domestic plans, it began to appear, were intimately connected with the theories of Professor Warren of Cornell, who by the end of July had become one of his closest economic advisers. Warren was— or else played at being—the archetype of the American hayseed, down to earth in every sense. Born on a farm in Nebraska in 1874, he had graduated from the University of Nebraska with a degree in farm management, written a number of books and pamphlets with such earthy titles as *Alfalfa, An Apple Orchard Survey of Orleans County,* and *Some Suggestions for City Persons Who Desire to Farm,* and since 1920 had served as professor of agricultural economics and farm management at Cornell. In 1933 he was a stocky, smooth-faced man approaching sixty, who peered through round spectacles with narrow black rims with a steady, vacuous gaze slightly reminiscent of Calvin Coolidge's, and, invariably, carried a clutch of pencils with the ends sticking out of the breast pocket of his coat. He was given to careless dress, homely witticisms, and pithy, irrefutable sentences like "Here is a farm, here is a farmer, and here are the facts." He was a master of that classic kind of rural American apothegm that is portentously delivered, as if it were a scintillating epigram, and that is numbing to an urban listener precisely because it seems to him to be not *quite* pointless; it makes a sort of oblique approach to sense, then veers away again. For example: "You paint a barn roof to preserve it. You paint a house to sell it. And you paint the sides of a barn to look at—if you can afford it." (Smiles and wise, appreciative nods.) Warren himself had a large farm outside Ithaca on which he kept some four thousand chickens, and liked to characterize himself as a "dirt farmer."

The Warren theory that bewitched Roosevelt was contained in a book entitled *Prices*, which he had written in collaboration with a younger Cornell colleague, Frank A. Pearson. It had the alluring simplicity of a syllogism. The prices of commodities, Warren and Pearson postulated, went up and down automatically with the price of gold in terms of paper currency, and as evidence of this they adduced a bewildering array of historical statistics and charts going back beyond the California and Australia gold rushes of the middle nineteenth century to the Spanish Conquest, and even further. Therefore, they concluded, all one had to do to control the price of commodities was to control the price of gold. In the present situation, the theory logically concluded, this meant that the government should go into the market and buy gold at progressively higher prices, thus forcing the gold value of the dollar progressively down and—if the theory was right—achieving the objective: higher prices of commodities. The ultimate goal was a "commodity dollar"—one that, through government manipulation of the gold price, would be kept constant in terms of goods rather than in terms of gold as was the case under the gold standard.

To orthodox economists, most of Roosevelt's economic advisers included, the Warren theory's syllogism was a false one. Commodity prices *had* usually moved with gold prices, they conceded; but the catch was that commodity prices were the cause of this conjunction and gold prices the effect. To reverse the roles by trying to make gold prices affect commodity prices was like a man in a building lobby trying to move an elevator from floor to floor by pushing the indicator dial from place to place: it wouldn't work, and it could easily end up ruining the whole mechanism. Warren, then, was to the orthodox economists just another example of a hardy, perennial, and surprisingly numerous American species, the monetary nut. Of course, the orthodox economists could not prove their point empirically, since nothing like the Warren theory had ever been put into practice. Or not quite. In 1869 Jay Gould—the Mephistopheles of Wall Street, as Matthew Josephson called him—in attempting to bribe President Grant's brother-in-law to help him corner the nation's gold supply, had piously argued that market operations to force up the gold price would undoubtedly bring about great public benefit by inflating the price of Western grain. But Gould's real concern had been not the welfare of farmers but his own illegal enrichment, and the chief effect of his plot had been not public benefit but the worst money panic in American history up to that time.

Moreover, Gould's maneuver had been a matter of private manipulation rather than government action, and his premature adoption of the Warren theory had been an excuse rather than a reason. As to government policy, nations had often before 1933, and have often since then, intervened in the markets to *defend* the value of their currencies; conversely, over the years they have often deliberately lowered the relative value of their currencies in order to gain competitive advantage. But no nation had ever mounted a systematic and concerted attack on its currency, in a time when its gold stocks were ample, for the sole purpose of creating domestic inflation and thus helping debtors. They had not done so because the idea was so outlandish it had never occurred to them. If it had, it would have appeared to their economic ministers as about as sensible as repeatedly hitting oneself on the head with a hammer so it would feel good when one stopped.

Roosevelt's fascination with Warren (whose sincerity no one doubted, or could possibly doubt) had begun before the inauguration, and continued during the first month after it. When Moley

162

wrote later that during that March Washington had become a Mecca for "goo-goos of all types" who took the New Deal to be "a kind of crusade which the discontented of every variety were invited to join," he did not mention Warren as one of the goo-goos, but no doubt had him in mind. During April and May Warren's star appeared to wane—only to wax again. In mid-June, Fred I. Kent, foreign-exchange head of the Federal Reserve Bank of New York, felt called upon to warn in a speech that the idea of raising farm prices by reducing the gold content of the dollar was fallacious in principle and would lead the nation to disaster if attempted. It is illogical to suppose that Kent would thus go out of his way to attack a theory that was not current in government circles at the time. By midsummer Warren, although holding no official post, was unmistakably occupying a prominent place in the Presidential picture. On vacation from Cornell, he had his own office in the Department of Commerce building in Washington, where he pored over his charts and behaved like a hermit, refusing to answer his telephone, and responding to knocks on the door with a firm if self-refuting "Not in!" Some said he entered and left the White House by levitation; at all events, he was never seen doing so.

As the market value of the dollar eroded of its own accord during May and June, the prices of farm commodities rose sharply. Roosevelt let a few of his aides know that he was delighted with this combination of events. He did not say precisely why he was so delighted, but the aides were afraid that they could guess. Here was practical evidence that his new pet theory was working out just as it was supposed to—or at least the first half of it was. But in mid-July came a disconcerting reversal. Suddenly, for no very discernible reason except the collapse of the London conference, the New York stock market suffered its biggest setback in more than a year, bringing the "Roosevelt market" to an end; the dollar rallied slightly against gold; and, worst of all, commodity prices abruptly changed direction. Between July 18 and 21, wheat went down from $1.24 a bushel to 90 cents, its sharpest slump in years, and cotton from 11¾ cents a pound to 8 cents. Seditious mutterings were heard again from the West. And at this point, it seems clear, Roosevelt's resolve to tinker with the dollar stiffened. The free market could not be trusted to continue depressing the gold value of the dollar. It would be necessary to put the second, activist part of the Warren theory into practice; it would be necessary, that is, for the United States Treasury to stage a bear raid on the dollar.

No one had more than an inkling of Roosevelt's plans at the time. Warburg, although through with the conference, was still anxious to make his banking expertise available to the government; he was, after all, the only man with practical banking experience among Roosevelt's economic advisers, and he thought he might at least serve as a sort of ballast to the high-flying theorists. On shipboard en route home from the conference, he read Warren's writings for the first time. (They had been sent to him not by Roosevelt but by the Committee for the Nation, a rabidly inflationist organization with which Warren had been loosely associated for about a year.) Warburg was not surprised to find that his opinion of the Warren theory coincided with that of the great Keynes, who had told him just before his departure from London that he considered it "rubbish." (This despite the fact that Keynes was known for certain inflationist leanings of his own.) Warburg, on going to lunch at the White House late in July, received confirmation of his worst fears about the company the President was now keeping when, on being ushered into the President's office, he found him in conversation with Warren and Professor James Harvey Rogers of Yale, the proponent of a slight variant of the Warren theory. After Roosevelt had gaily introduced Warburg to the two theorists, they left, whereupon Warburg began remonstrating with the President about his message to London. Roosevelt reacted first angrily, then airily. "He takes the whole currency question very lightly," Warburg wrote in a pained diary entry.

Roosevelt's parting instructions to Warburg were to get together with Warren and Rogers during the next week, and then report back to him at Hyde Park early in August. Accordingly, Warburg gritted his teeth and spent the following evening with the professors in New York. For the son of the "father of the Federal System"—a family situation that seemed to make him a blood brother of the Federal Reserve System—the evening was a matter of finding oneself in Hell and taking some comfort in discovering that the Devil wasn't as bad as he had been painted. Warren and Rogers didn't seem to be as radical as he had feared, Warburg found; moreover, as he wrote afterward, he found Warren "earnest and well-intentioned," "anxious to help," and "not dogmatic or bumptious." Arriving at Hyde Park ten days later, according to instructions, who did Warburg—no doubt wincing slightly—find there with the President but Warren and Rogers? Despite their presence, to Warburg the occasion was an entertaining one; Warren, to Roosevelt's evident beguilement, produced "countless scrolls of tissue paper on which [he] had traced all sorts of curves and diagrams," while Rogers kept smiling enigmatically and nodding his head. The three economists argued their conflicting ideas back and forth; the upshot was that the President said he wanted Warren and Rogers to go to Europe for a month or so to sound out opinion there on American monetary policies, while Warburg was to become a key member of a special, high-level Presidential monetary study group that was being formed. Was this exile for Warren and Rogers? Or the runaround for Warburg? None of them knew. Afterward, Warburg and Warren shared a taxi to the railroad station—epitomes, to a degree, of the two antagonistic forces that had always dominated American economic life up to then, the financier and the farmer. Warren said ruefully to Warburg, "Well, I guess you ruined my plan." "On the contrary," Warburg replied, "you have won." On Wall Street, the innocent stock market, quite unaware that gods up the Hudson were trifling with its fate, held steady.

Meanwhile, farm prices went on dropping. In the first half of September, as rumors spread more and more insistently that Roosevelt was planning to do *something* of an inflationary nature, the dollar sank sharply—on the eighteenth it stood at a new low of 63¾ cents relative to gold—and farm prices turned up again, but not enough to satisfy the President. Late in the month Warburg visited him at the White House to plead with him for the last time not to try out the Warren theory. Roosevelt responded to his protests by saying, "If we don't keep the price of wheat and cotton moving up, we shall have marching farmers," and then challenged Warburg to say what *he* would do to raise prices. Warburg had to admit that he had no panacea; general recovery, which could be started only by removing this nerve-racking uncertainty about the currency, was the only way. This left Roosevelt cold. Well, Warburg then asked, would the President have any objection if Warburg were to take steps to stir up public sentiment against further inflation, through the agency of the big banks and life-insurance companies? That is—in effect, though not in Warburg's words— how would Roosevelt like to have a well-financed public attack launched against his favorite economic policies? The President replied emphatically, but not without delicacy, that such action "would only create complications." Warburg left the White House believing that he would never see the President again; although not yet an opponent of the New Deal *in toto,* he was now the prototype, the advance drummer boy, of the splenetic Wall Street Roosevelt-hater who was to become a folk figure of the decade. Warburg's departure from Roosevelt's office that day has a symbolic impact something like that of Ibsen's Nora slamming the door.

From then on there was no restraining Roosevelt from his purpose. As early as mid-August, a week or so after the Hyde Park meeting, he had mentioned to his friend Morgenthau, by that time Farm Credit Administrator, that he would like to have the Treasury buy gold in the open market to force its price upward. (Morgenthau had demanded whose idea that was, and Roosevelt had replied, blandly, "Mine"—an answer that suggests both defensiveness and sheepishness about his adherence to the economically disreputable Warren theory, since both men knew perfectly well whose idea it was.) Now he pressed forward, brushing aside some formidable legal obstacles to the prosecution of the plan by arranging for the gold purchases to be made not directly by the Treasury but on its behalf by the Reconstruction Finance Corporation. When the dollar turned bullish again in October, rising obstinately to around 72 cents, matters came to a head. Over the grim objections of Acting Secretary of the Treasury Dean Acheson, who was to resign in a rage less than a month later, Roosevelt on October 19 told his aides that the RFC gold-buying was about to begin; and three days later, in a "fireside chat" on radio briefly expounding the Warren theory (although the shadowy professor went unmentioned), he announced the program to the public. To the end of depressing the dollar and raising commodity prices, he said, the RFC would buy all gold newly mined in the United States at "prices to be determined from time to time," and, when necessary, would also buy it in the world markets through the Federal Reserve

Bank of New York. "This is a policy, not an expedient," he added, as if to deprive the flinty international bankers and their hard-money allies of any crumb of comfort. And thus the stage was set for the whole national economy to become Professor Warren's test tube, in a period that Keynes would describe as "a gold standard on the booze," and of which the *New York Times* would say contemporaneously that it was characterized by "a sense of unreality," and five years later would add as a postscript, "There is probably no instance in history of so bold an economic experiment."

V

The first national reaction to the announcement was general bewilderment. Those closely involved in the events leading up to it reacted predictably; the archinflationist Senator Thomas, for example, was overjoyed, and Warburg, listening to the "fireside chat" at a friend's home in Chicago, felt as if he had been dealt a body blow. But the lay public and the newspapers were hopelessly divided and confused. Even Wall Street itself seemed to be puzzled rather than outraged—stunned, indeed, into a momentary trance. Many leading bankers, according to the *Times*, "confessed themselves unable to understand the full import" of the plan. If the bankers couldn't understand it, who could? One of them said that he "saw in the President's announcement nothing which departed in any way from orthodox financial principles"—a comment that has a certain Zen quality, as if the banker had searched for, and found, a response that had a flabbergasting illogicality commensurate with the challenge. The House of Morgan was silent now; indeed, not one of the celebrated spokesmen of New York finance, Thomas Lamont or Richard Whitney or Otto Kahn, could find his tongue—an extraordinary and enlightening historical anomaly, since in reality the Roosevelt program was not all that confusing; perfectly clearly, it represented a direct assault on the very thing that Wall Street held most sacred, sound money. True, there was a practical reason for caution: Wall Street and the New Deal were already moving fast toward a head-on confrontation on the matter of federal regulation of the stock market, and it may not have seemed the politic moment to open up a second front. Washington was learning something, then: depression-riddled Wall Street, for all of its famously crusty old lions, could be taken by storm.

On October 25 the great experiment began. That morning and on each subsequent weekday morning, Roosevelt, Morgenthau, Jesse Jones, head of the RFC, and sometimes Warren, met in the President's bedroom and, while the President ate breakfast, decided on the price at which gold would be bought that day. At first, operations were only domestic, and the world gold market was left to its own devices, in the hope that it would tend to conform to the U.S. government price without intervention. The little group in Roosevelt's bedroom would simply decide, more or less arbitrarily, a gold price a few cents above the previous day's free-market price, and upon concluding their deliberations would announce to the world the sum the RFC was now prepared to pay for all newly mined gold in the United States—that is to say, presumably all of the gold available for sale in the country now that private hoarding was illegal.

On the first morning, the price was set at $31.36 an ounce, 27 cents above that day's world price. (The old gold-standard price had been $20.67; the difference represented the amount that the dollar had depreciated in the markets since April.) Obedient to the theory, commodity prices rose. On the second day, the gold price was edged up 18 cents more, but commodity prices *declined*. What was this? Surely a disconcerting reaction in the test tube? Or perhaps only some sort of temporary aberration; government officials let it be known that they were not downhearted. Next day the gold price was upped 22 cents. Commodities rose again. But another disturbing phenomenon was beginning to appear: the world exchange market was showing a tendency to disregard the RFC price and to arrive at a separate daily valuation for gold in terms of the dollar, suggesting all too plainly that the RFC price of domestic gold was of no great importance and could not have any permanent effect on anything. There were really two dollars now, the Warren dollar and the foreign-exchange dollar. This *was* alarming, in that it raised the prospect that the RFC might have to abandon its strict confinement to domestic operations and go directly into the world market, an act that might be interpreted by Britain and France as outright economic warfare. On the following day, a Saturday, the gold price was advanced 6 cents more, and commodities declined again. Professor Warren's actions, and even his location, are unknown, but it stands to reason that he was scratching his head. Meanwhile in Wall Street, confusion still reigned. The general feeling was based on negatives: the latest earnings reports of industry were dreadful, but the prospects for the stability of the dollar, all things considered, looked even worse, and consequently the stock market rose somewhat. Everybody in the Street was spending his odd moments trying to guess exactly how the amount of the daily gold price rise was being determined. Those engaging in this interesting activity could hardly have been reassured if they had known the truth. As they learned it years later from Morgenthau's diary, one day he came into the daily breakfast meeting and suggested an increase of somewhere between 19 and 22 cents. Roosevelt proposed 21 cents. "It's a lucky number," he explained, cheerfully, "because it's three times seven." A touch of numerology was perhaps all the program needed.

In his private counsels with Warren, however, Roosevelt seems to have been less cocky; indeed, it appears that he demanded of Warren exactly why the theory wasn't working. Warren appears to have replied doggedly that all that was needed to make it effective was to extend the gold-buying into the world markets. On October 29, five days after the campaign had begun, Roosevelt announced his intention to do just this, with the RFC to make its purchases daily in London and Paris through the normal agent of the Treasury in foreign-exchange dealings, the Federal Reserve Bank of New York. This would amount to introducing a far more volatile chemical into the test tube—perhaps even an explosive one. Immediately there was an anguished outcry from the British and French, whose own currencies would now beyond any question be competitively disadvantaged. "If it went far, it would be necessary for us, from a trading point of view, to do something also," Sir Robert Horne, Britain's former Chancellor of the Exchequer, warned the Bond Club of New York, adding, "Believe me, it would not be done in any respect in the shape of retaliation. You must not think of that. But we have got to defend our trading position." What the tactful ex-chancellor was saying, in effect, was that Britain might be forced in self-defense to mount a similar bear raid on *its* own currency. Hitting oneself on the head with a hammer was a game that two could play.

So began the agony of George Harrison, the man in the middle. As a good bureaucrat, he had the duty to carry out the outlandish policy. Meanwhile, he found himself simultaneously trying to explain and justify it to the outraged European bankers, damp down insofar as possible the protests of the bewildered Wall Street bankers in whose midst he lived, and use whatever influence he had to get the President to cease and desist from it. At least he had his heart in the last role; sound and conventional banker that he was, he personally loathed the policy. Moreover, with Warburg out of the picture he remained as almost the lone sound-money man among those who had Roosevelt's ear.

On November 2 the first world-market orders for gold were placed. The price and amount of the order were kept secret, in order to achieve maximum effect and not tip off speculators; and, as planned, the dollar weakened in the foreign markets. From Liberty Street, Harrison kept the international telephone wires humming as he tried to calm down the French and British to abstain from retaliation. Robert Lacour-Gayet of the Bank of France told Harrison on the phone that the French simply couldn't grasp what was going on in Washington; he had, he said aggrievedly, been called upon to explain the new American policy to the French press, and had found himself at a loss since he couldn't make head or tail of it himself. The most comfort Harrison could offer was to say that the gold purchases would be made in as orderly a manner as possible. As for Governor Norman of the Bank of England, when he had first heard of the plan four days earlier he had, as Harrison confided to his office diary, "hit the ceiling"; today he was back on the floor, but still deeply worried. And so all through November, with only a day's surcease now and again, the government's assault on the dollar continued, with gold purchases made regularly on both the domestic and world markets at ever-higher prices. After a week of world-market operations, the dollar in terms of gold was down to 63.4 cents, another new low since Civil War days; Paris and London were jittery, and as a result of the uncertainty international trade was virtually paralyzed; the stock markets, both European and

American, were still too confused to know which way to jump; and Alexander Dana Noyes, the venerable and judicious *Times* financial editor, was keening about what he called the "plainly needless intrusion" of the United States into world markets that had served to "reduce to despair the effort of serious home and foreign bankers to understand what Washington is driving at." Meanwhile, farm prices had not risen significantly, and in Iowa farm strikers had burned a railroad bridge and shot at a passing train. Professor Warren was not answering his phone.

Matters came to a crisis on the ninth. The dollar on the world market suddenly plunged to under 62 cents as the speculators joined the United States government in trouncing it. Domestic grain prices rose substantially, but Governor Norman, seeing the pound against the dollar now at an all-time record high of well over five dollars, hit the ceiling again, and although his country still patiently refrained from retaliation, British commercial and merchant bankers began telephoning, cabling, or writing their American counterparts to beg pathetically for some intelligible explanation of what was going on and how far it was going. Since the American bankers were equally in the dark, they could offer no help. By that weekend it was statistically clear that the Warren theory was not working very well even with the foreign interventions; while the world price of the dollar had by then been forced down about 7 percent since the gold-buying had begun, domestic wheat prices had risen slightly less than 2 percent and cotton prices only 1.55 percent.

Still Roosevelt was not discouraged. (Certainly he seems to have been little moved by the moans from across the ocean; when he heard from Morgenthau of the frantic protests of the stately Governor Norman, whom he liked to call "old pink whiskers," both men roared with mischievous laughter.) On Sunday the twelfth, he called a monetary meeting at the White House at which Morgenthau, Harrison, and Warren were present. After Roosevelt had said that he believed a farm revolt had now been averted and announced himself satisfied with the results of the gold-buying program so far, Harrison spoke up to predict that further depreciation of the dollar would result in a breakdown of the government's credit, and urged, at the least, a slowdown. Well, replied Roosevelt, there were two sides to the question; and anyway, if at any time the dollar should get too weak, the RFC could always reverse itself and *sell* some gold to the world markets. Seizing on this idea, Harrison praised it enthusiastically. By all means, he said, let's start selling some gold, and the sooner the better. The meeting broke up without any substantive decisions having been taken. During the following week, between sessions of fending off the continuing protests of the Banks of England and France, Harrison became Roosevelt's almost hour-to-hour counselor—hardly a rewarding role, since little of his counsel was accepted, but still a highly anomalous one for a Wall Street banker, where the New Deal was concerned.

Back on Liberty Street the next morning, Harrison got a phone call from Roosevelt. How were things going in the foreign-exchange markets? the President wanted to know. Harrison, surely gratified by this evidence of a new convert to the ranks of students of foreign exchange, answered the question, and seized the opportunity to put in another plug for the gold-selling idea. Roosevelt was evasive on that point, but told Harrison that for the present he wanted a daily report on what was happening in the markets. Accordingly, early the following afternoon Harrison called the White House to make his report: the dollar was down sharply against the pound and the franc, and how about selling some gold *now*—or, rather, since the European trading day was already over, the following morning? Roosevelt surprisingly replied that that was a good idea, and suggested $200,000 worth. Such a sum would be only a drop in the bucket, Harrison replied, and suggested half a million dollars' worth each in the Paris and London markets. Roosevelt agreed, and Harrison hung up feeling much better; it seemed that a vestige of sanity was about to return to the monetary scene.

But at four-twenty that afternoon Harrison got a call from Jesse Jones, who said the President wanted him to know that the United States would neither buy nor sell gold the next day, since more time was needed to look up the matter of whether selling gold abroad was legal. With characteristic conservatism, Harrison noted in his office diary that he was "surprised." For one thing, a recision of the President's verbal order of three hours earlier might be expected to come from the President himself; for another, the legal question had been thrashed out, and presumably disposed of, before the overseas program had begun, and no one wished more than Harrison that it had been decided the other way. After simmering for three hours, Harrison called Roosevelt at seven-fifteen. The White House operator explained to the Federal Reserve operator that Harrison would have to wait, because Mr. Jones wanted to talk to the President before Mr. Harrison did, and, in fact, was with him at the moment. Finally connected with Roosevelt some minutes later, Harrison encountered, as usual, a soft answer to turn away wrath. Jones, Roosevelt reported, was all up in the air about the legal questions involved in United States gold sales abroad. In reply Harrison could only point out the obvious—that such dealing had already been going on for almost two weeks without objections on legal grounds, and that presumably the same laws applied to selling gold as to buying it. Roosevelt said he would call back. In fact, though, it was Jones who called Harrison back a few minutes later, to say that his call was to be considered an oral and temporary revocation of the authorization to sell gold, and to add—a bit gratuitously, one can hardly help noting—that he didn't see why Harrison wanted to sell gold, anyhow.

After what well may have been a restless night at his apartment on East End Avenue, Harrison tried to call the White House the next morning to learn what the latest instructions were. But Roosevelt proved to be a hard man to reach just then. After being shuffled from one aide to another for a while, toward noon Harrison was finally connected with Morgenthau, who informed him that the President was dressing and was therefore unavailable for the moment. But meanwhile, the foreign-exchange markets were approaching the point of panic again, with the dollar below 60 cents and in a state of violent collapse, and Norman and Lacour-Gayet were on the transatlantic phone again. After concluding his conversation with Morgenthau, Harrison, switching quickly to his role of mollifier, explained to the Europeans in turn that the situation in the U.S. farm belt was still bad, and calmed them somewhat by hinting that he had some evidence that Roosevelt's inflation drive was about to level off. (The evidence, presumably, consisted of the rising confusion and indecision that he sensed from the White House; Harrison had no other.) Finally at noon, Jones called to tell Harrison that he had won their tiff—the legal problems were brushed aside again—and the authorization to sell a million dollars' worth of gold in Paris and London. (Again, it was too late for European trading that day.) That afternoon, connected with Roosevelt at last, Harrison got still further cause for elation, and further material to use in tranquilizing Norman and Lacour-Gayet, when the President went so far as to *ask* him how Wall Street brokers felt about his program at this point. Well, Harrison said, he had explained it as best he could to six or seven of them, and after he had finished "they seemed a little more comforted." "Fine," said the President, heartily. "Keep up the good work."

Harrison's victory was equivocal. The next day, November 16, the gold was sold as agreed, and the dollar obediently strengthened. Roosevelt agreed to Harrison's request that, in order to calm the markets, he state publicly that he was now fairly well satisfied with the results of his program, but when Harrison asked for authorization to sell at least a million dollars' worth more of gold the next day in London and Paris, it was denied. Indeed, on the eighteenth gold-*buying* was resumed. But Roosevelt's attitude was now showing unmistakable signs of change. Partly as a result of the cautious but constant pressure from Harrison, partly from seeing the foreign-exchange chaos that he had created, and perhaps most of all because massive and well-organized protests were at last being mounted by United States business groups, he was coming to see matters in a new light—to see that he was engaged in a cosmic juggling feat in which too much concentration on one ball, the plight of the domestic farmers, would result in his dropping the others, the nation's economic relations with Europe and his own relations with American business, small as well as big. On November 21 he left Washington with Morgenthau for a stay in Warm Springs, Georgia. Distance only seemed to lend enchantment to Harrison, on whom Roosevelt was coming almost to rely. A kind of long-distance intimacy sprang up between these two very different men, with such conflicting temperaments and interests, who seemed to have nothing in common but two far from inconsiderable factors—genteel upbringing and physical disability.

On the twenty-first Harrison succeeded in persuading Morgenthau to urge Roosevelt not to buy any more gold abroad for a few

days, on the ground that the franc's competitive position had now
been damaged so much that France was on the verge of being forced
off the gold standard, an eventuality that would leave no major
currency tied to gold, and the world monetary outlook uncertain
indeed. The plea worked. Harrison found to his relief that no order
to sell gold reached him from the RFC that day. Very early the next
morning, Roosevelt called Harrison, rousing him at home on East
End Avenue. Morgenthau had relayed the message, the President
said, and added that he was very glad he had followed the advice, in
view of the uncertainty about the franc. Here, surely, was a new
Roosevelt. When Harrison called Warm Springs from Liberty Street
that afternoon to make his daily market report, he found the
President in a thoughtful mood, and the two men fell to debating
the question of exactly how well the Warren theory was proving
out.

Despite all the dollar depreciation, Harrison pointed out, domestic wheat and cotton prices stood at about the same levels as they
had at the start of November. Yes, countered Roosevelt, but look at
rubber and tin—*their* prices were up. Harrison explained that this
proved nothing, since rubber and tin, being largely imported
commodities in the United States, had fixed world prices in terms of
gold, and therefore a rise in the gold price *automatically* meant a
rise in their prices. Apparently impressed by this logic, Roosevelt
agreed to leave the exchange markets alone for the remaining three
business days that week.

There were more such conversations. "It's funny how [prices]
sometimes seem to go against all the rules," the President mused, in
evident perplexity, in the course of one of them. The long-distance
talks were becoming an economics seminar—which is to say that
Harrison, as the tutor, was gaining the upper hand. On the twenty-
third, even though the dollar strengthened and the price of wheat
fell 3 cents a bushel, Roosevelt stuck to his pledge not to buy more
gold that week. They returned to sparring, Roosevelt saying he had
charts to prove that prices were improving as planned, Harrison
reiterating his point of the previous day that the higher prices,
being mostly those of imported commodities, didn't count. Harrison
noted in his office diary that he now felt Roosevelt was coming to

understand the principle of stabilization. "On the whole, I considered it an encouraging conversation," he wrote. His exalted pupil might finally grasp the basic concepts after all.

VI

While the seminar went on, the protests from across the country were mounting to a crescendo. On November 18 the United States Chamber of Commerce issued a blast calling for an early return of the country to the gold standard. On the twentieth Bernard Baruch, a vintage F.D.R. supporter, came out with an article in the *Saturday Evening Post* saying that the inflation resulting from the gold-buying might nullify the other accomplishments of the New Deal. On the twenty-first Oliver Sprague resigned his Treasury job to be free to attack the program. ("Sprague is a nuisance," Roosevelt had just told one of his aides.) The same day, a leading commercial trade journal denounced Warren, who up to then had somehow remained almost entirely out of public view and even public discussion, as the "financial dictator of the United States." On the twenty-third the chiefs of Du Pont, General Motors, and Macy's joined the dissenters, and on the twenty-fourth Alfred E. Smith—the "happy warrior" himself, as Roosevelt had called him on a more harmonious occasion—joined the battle by announcing that he was "for gold dollars as against baloney dollars," and attacking the "crackpots and quarterbacks" in Washington who were using all Americans for guinea pigs. Wall Street itself, encouraged and perhaps shamed by its outspoken allies, still stayed prudently mum in public, but began systematically whipping up the opposition behind the scenes, and silently manifested its changed attitude toward the New Deal it had welcomed so warmly eight months earlier. Although every bank and brokerage house in New York had endorsed an NRA code, a newspaper reporter who toured the whole Wall Street area on November 24 found only three blue eagles displayed in windows. And high in the councils of the protestors was the partially repatriated Wall Street renegade Jimmy Warburg. Following his disagreement with Roosevelt in September he had quietly begun laying the groundwork for a

176

national anti-inflation campaign. "Here and there, little groups of businessmen foregathered to see if they could help each other understand what was going on," Warburg wrote later. "I took part in organizing a protest by a group of Chicago businessmen and economists and urged various friends to take action. Bob Lovett helped the New York newspapers to understand the situation. John Schiff alerted the New York Chamber of Commerce. . . . I myself talked to some of the important life-insurance company presidents." On November 22, before the American Academy of Political and Social Science in Philadelphia, Warburg came out in the open. Avoiding, out of sentiment or diplomacy, a personal attack on his erstwhile idol the President, he lashed out at the Warren theory and those in Congress and the Administration who had urged it on Roosevelt. Thus when Wall Street finally found its public voice, it was, ironically, an ex–New Deal voice.

Now groups and committees to protest the gold-buying were springing up almost hour by hour; they culminated in a huge "sound money" rally held on the evening of the twenty-seventh in Carnegie Hall, and cosponsored by, of all organizations, the American Federation of Labor. True enough, thirteen blocks south at the Hippodrome that same evening an even bigger rally (fifteen thousand persons, including those milling around in the streets outside) was being conducted in *support* of the gold-buying program, with Morgenthau, Senator Thomas, and the radio-preaching priest Father Charles Coughlin, at that time a rabid Roosevelt fan, as its stars. But here Roosevelt was unlucky in his backing, and the rally backfired badly. The rabble-rousing, anti-Semitic Coughlin, ranting intemperately against "British propaganda from these Tory bankers of lower Manhattan," and dismissing inflation as "a trick word to scare us," went too far. Even though it was not until several months later that Coughlin's integrity would come into question with the revelation that his organization, the Radio League of the Little Flower, had all the while been speculating for private profit against gold and in favor of silver (which he rather arbitrarily pronounced to be a "gentile" metal), Coughlin's bad showing at the Hippodrome, Warburg concluded later, was the single factor that turned the tide of public opinion against the Warren program. At all events, after raising the gold price 9 cents on November 28 and

177

another 8 cents on November 29 in what seemed to be a last gesture of defiance, Roosevelt all but gave up. Repeal of Prohibition, effective on December 5, tended to crowd money out of people's minds and off the front pages. On the ninth Roosevelt confided to Harrison that he now hoped "to maintain a period of relative quiet in all fields," and Harrison, hardly able to believe his ears, knew that could only mean the experiment was essentially over. It was. Through the rest of December the gold price was raised only once, and then very slightly.

In his State of the Union message in mid-January, 1934, Roosevelt formally repudiated the Warren theory by proposing dollar stabilization in terms of gold at a relationship near the present open-market one, and on the last day of that month, following Congressional passage of enabling legislation, he put the stabilization into effect, decreeing a return to a modified gold standard at a dollar valuation of 59.06 percent of the old one. This odd figure was chosen to permit the round sum of $35 an ounce to become the official price of gold. And thus, what for a strange month had been changed daily and haphazardly over the President's breakfast was now to be fixed, perhaps permanently. Just how permanently, no one could foresee. More than a generation later, in 1968, heads of state would travel halfway round the world to meet, a queen would confer with her ministers into the small hours, and the whole world of central banking would labor mightily, to hold the dollar price of gold at—$35 an ounce.

VII

The boldest of economic experiments was over, and the gold standard was off the booze, just as the country went back on it. The stock market, its sky some 40 percent lower than before but firmly back in place, leaped upward in relief. Professor Warren slipped inconspicuously back to Cornell to tend to his student farmers and his four thousand chickens. That October, he returned to Washington for a day and had lunch with Roosevelt, setting off a flurry of rumors of further dollar devaluation. Asked on this occasion if his unofficial connection with the government might be about to be resumed, Warren replied, "The place where I worked in the Department of Commerce has never been closed, so far as I know." The world exchange markets plummeted at this news, but neither further devaluation nor Warren's return to government materialized. Over the remaining three and a half years of his life he was little heard from, enduring in comparative silence the galling experience of seeing his theory, now that it had been discredited in practice, solemnly dissected and derided by just about every living economic pundit. But the Ithaca dirt farmer, if he had hardly been a success as a financial dictator, had surely been the most unlikely one in history.

Wall Street had won, but at its cost. Its honeymoon with the New Deal had ended with the bride's committing the fatal gaffe of demonstrating that the groom's favorite theory was wrong. In reality, both sides had lost. The New Deal, which had started out with Wall Street's almost abject subservience and dependence, was now faced with a Wall Street that, confirmed in its worst suspicions about wild-eyed crackpots in Washington, had totally reversed itself in a year and now presented a practically solid phalanx of opposition; while Wall Street, for its part, now faced a New Deal fairly spoiling to return hostility in kind.

What can be said in retrospective summary about Roosevelt's tinkering with the dollar during his first year in office? Certainly his understanding of the whole matter was ludicrously superficial and his attitude toward it scandalously offhand; certainly he disregarded the advice of all the learned and accredited money doctors of the land, and accepted that of a virtual quack. Yet somehow or other, the farmers neither starved nor made a revolution, and out of the episode, incredibly, came a stable dollar that would endure for a generation and more. Essentially, the wise but frightened Wall Streeters offered *no* program; the Warren program, unsound as it was, did no permanent harm and at least offered action and motion, bringing hope.

Through dumb luck or genius, Roosevelt pulled the country through; could Wall Street have done the same?

Chapter Eight

Ordeal in Washington

I

Almost everyone remembers the picture of a midget sitting on
J. P. Morgan's knee, but few recall, or ever knew, the end of that
story. It is so near to being unbearably sad that it will be told
first.

The thing happened in the Senate Caucus Room on the morning
of June 1, 1933, while Morgan, surrounded by a cortege of partners
and lawyers and assistants, was sitting in a leather-upholstered chair
waiting to testify before the Senate Banking and Currency Committee. Reporters, photographers, and spectators were milling around,
and suddenly, in the confusion, too quickly for official intervention,
a press agent for the Ringling Brothers, Barnum & Bailey Circus,
apparently with the connivance of a Scripps-Howard reporter
named Ray Tucker, popped the midget, a member of the circus
troupe, into Morgan's lap. Instantly the photographers were climb-
ing onto chairs and pushing people aside to get into position for
pictures.

Morgan at the time was a dignified, avuncular-looking man in his
middle sixties. The circus lady, whose name was Lya Graf and who

180

was twenty-seven inches tall, was a plump, well-proportioned bru-
nette with sparkling dark eyes and a fresh peasant prettiness, and
she was decked out in a flounced blue satin dress and a red straw
hat of fishnet weave. Morgan's cortege stiffened as if frozen; but
Morgan himself did not. His face, previously set into hard lines by a
week of hostile questioning by the committee, relaxed, became
disturbed, then turned kindly, and a small, warm smile crossed it,
under the bushy black eyebrows and the neat white mustache.

"I have a grandson bigger than you," he said.

"But I'm older," Miss Graf replied.

"How old are you?"

The press agent said she was thirty-two, but Miss Graf corrected
him: "I am not—only twenty."

"Well, you certainly don't look it," Morgan said.

The photographers clamored for one more shot, and the press
agent told Miss Graf to take off her hat. "Don't take it off, it's
pretty," Morgan said; then he lifted her from his lap and set her
carefully on the floor. The partners, who had been looking on in
rigid dismay, exhaled and collapsed in their chairs; Richard Whitney, ever the man to take charge of situations, brusquely shooed the
press agent and Miss Graf away; and Morgan went on smiling, more
feebly now. Next day the picture was famous almost everywhere in
the world where newspapers are published.

Morgan, and even Wall Street as a whole, profited adventitiously
from the encounter. From that day forward until his death a decade
later, he was in the public mind no longer a grasping devil whose
greed and ruthlessness had helped bring the nation to near-ruin,
but rather a benign old dodderer. The change in attitude was
instantaneous, and Morgan took advantage of it, seizing, whether
by calculation or instinct, on further chances to "humanize" himself. The following day, asked by reporters possessed of a new
interest in his personality to comment on the incident, he replied
unaffectedly that it had been "very unusual and somewhat un-
pleasant," but that he didn't blame the photographers, who had
merely been doing their job. Asked about a bloodstone set in a gold
crescent that he was wearing as a watch charm, he became positively
garrulous: "Oh, that. Well, now, I'll tell you about it. My father's
mother was J. Pierpont's daughter. She had that made. It has the

Pierpont coat of arms on one side. She gave it to her father. He wore it day in and day out. I don't think I would have known him without it. My father gave it to me. Does that tell the story?"

"Your father's father gave it to your mother's brother . . ." a reporter began in a puzzled tone.

"No, no," Morgan said, with a chuckle, and launched into another round of ancestral rigamarole. "I still don't—" the reporter began again, but Morgan had waved and swept grandly out. Could anyone hate such a man?

But Lya Graf did not benefit from the encounter. She was shy and sensitive, and where the role of ordinary circus freak, a kind of craft requiring skill, had been supportable to her, the role of celebrity freak was not. Two years later, hounded by fame, she left the United States and returned to her native Germany. She was half-Jewish. In 1937 she was arrested as a "useless person" and eventually she was shipped to Auschwitz, never to be heard of again. There had been no place for her anywhere: as the New World had exploited her, the Old had obliterated her. Her gift to a rich and famous old man had cost her first her peace of mind and then her life.

The story would be a cozy and manageable fable except for the picture, in which Miss Graf is smiling proudly, and has a plump hand splayed out on Morgan's coat sleeve to steady herself. They both look happy and at ease; that is the almost unbearable part.

II

As early as that March, word had reached the Street that the new counsel to the Senate committee continuing its investigation of the stock market—a remarkable young New York City assistant district attorney named Ferdinand Pecora—intended to focus the spotlight on J. P. Morgan & Company. Thomas Lamont and another celebrated Morgan partner, J. Parker Gilbert, walked up to Liberty Street one day and called on George Harrison at the Federal Reserve Bank. Perhaps there was something a bit furtive, and un-Morgan-like, in their demeanor; in any case, it soon became clear that their mission was an anomalous one. The House of Morgan no longer had an open wire to the White House, and certainly none to Capitol Hill; Lamont and Gilbert were calling on Harrison in his capacity as the uneasy link between Wall Street and the new Administration. Pecora had been to 23 Wall the previous week and had wanted to see various private papers; there had been talk of subpoenas. That could mean only one thing. Now, Lamont said, J. P. Morgan & Company, following a normal routine, had recently filed its most recent balance sheet with the Federal Reserve Bank. Would the Federal Reserve Bank please be cooperative and refrain, if requested, from releasing the balance sheet to Pecora or anyone else connected with the Senate investigating committee?

Harrison replied that he did not feel he could give any such assurance.

There is a certain aura of shock about Harrison's office diary entry for that day, and no wonder. The House of Morgan pleading with another bank—and a bank, after all, in whose establishment two decades earlier the House of Morgan had had a large hand—to keep its affairs from coming to public view! How the mighty were fallen! At all events, at the end of the inconclusive conversation Harrison felt called upon to volunteer a promise not to speak loosely of what had been said. Lamont smiled a small Morgan smile. "Of course," he said.

The committee got the balance sheet; the plans for the investigation went forward. By the time it began, late in May, J. P. Morgan & Company had fully regained its aplomb and its lordliness. Scorning any show of frugality that might have smacked of defensiveness or even of guilt, the partners and their entourage moved into Washington to be investigated as if they were a Renaissance court taking over a conquered country, spending two thousand dollars a day on hotel bills alone. At the hearings they disdained to be furtive or secretive. They had moved on to a new phase now; they managed to be lordly in their very openness, their willingness to answer the most embarrassing questions or submit the most compromising documents candidly, without stint, and with no trace of remorse. In an extraordinary moral feat, they made candor under inquisition into a kind of arrogance, a form of *noblesse oblige*.

Morgan himself was the first witness, and the confrontation

between him and Pecora, extending on and off over more than a week, was a thing of simplicity and beauty. The great man took the witness stand in an atmosphere of the most intense public interest—after all, no Morgan had been on public show since 1912 when J. Pierpont had been grilled by the Pujo Committee—and the character of the interest was curiously ambivalent; Morgan seemed to be thought of variously or in combination as a king and as a master thief. He presented himself as neither, but as a gentleman and a businessman, with the gentleman coming first in a pinch. Pecora, an immigrant in childhood from Sicily, was the other face of American life, short and squarish where Morgan was tall and commanding, swarthy where Morgan was fair-skinned, energetic and ambitious where Morgan was languid, all conscience and earnest intellect where Morgan was all style. Neither was afraid of the other. It was a confrontation out of Kipling.

Coolly, under questioning, Morgan described the autocratic articles of partnership under which his firm was governed. Any disputes among the partners must be submitted to the decision of the senior partner—Morgan himself—"which shall be final." The senior partner might at any time compel any partner to withdraw, or he might dissolve the partnership. Annually, the profits were divided on a fifty-fifty basis—that is to say, half to Morgan, half to all the other partners. No capital contributions were required of new partners.

As to the firm's methods of doing business, Morgan clearly relished the questions from Pecora and the Senators, and took satisfaction in answering them. Did the firm ever advertise or announce itself to the public or the banking trade? "We have our name on the door, that is all." And nothing but the name—nothing, perhaps, to suggest the firm's line of business? "Nothing but the name."

MR. PECORA: Mr. Morgan, is the name of the firm on any outer door of the firm's office?

MR. MORGAN: It is not on the outer door. It is on the inner door.

MR. PECORA: Not visible from the street to any passer-by?

MR. MORGAN: No. Most of them know the address.

MR. PECORA: You do not think the firm suffers any lack of prestige in the banking world because it does not advertise itself to the bankers, do you?

MR. MORGAN: It does not seem to.

Were statements of the firm's financial condition ever submitted to depositors? No. "They never asked for it." Would the bank lend money to anyone who could provide acceptable collateral? No—only to its own clients, and the same applied to the acceptance of deposits.

THE CHAIRMAN [Senator Duncan U. Fletcher, a seventy-five-year-old Floridian]: But you do not turn a man down; you do not select your clients? . . .

MR. MORGAN: Yes; we do.

THE CHAIRMAN: You do.

MR. MORGAN: Yes, indeed; we do.

THE CHAIRMAN: I suppose if I went there, even though I had never seen any member of the firm, and had $10,000 I wanted to leave with the bank, you would take it, wouldn't you?

MR. MORGAN: No; we should not do it.

THE CHAIRMAN: You would not?

MR. MORGAN: No . . . Not unless you came in with some introduction, Senator . . . That has been the rule for many, many years.

THE CHAIRMAN: Then I am quite sure I could not *borrow* any $10,000.

MR. MORGAN: Not without an introduction.

Later he amplified this granitic regulation: "We do make . . . loans, and we make them because we believe the people should have the money; that we should loan money if these gentlemen [the firm's clients] want it. They are friends of ours, and we know that they are good, straight fellows."

This classic statement of the philosophy of old-fashioned hierarchical private banking, its reliance on economic trust enforced by social sanction, marked the watershed between Morgan and Pecora.

Hereditary economic aristocrat and democratic son of Mediterranean peasantry, they could exchange views and even feel interest in each other's views, but could not really communicate because their moral assumptions conflicted. But afterward, commenting on Pecora to his friends, Morgan dropped his majestic air and permitted himself scorn and a little petulance: "Pecora has the manner and the manners of a prosecuting attorney"; while Pecora, in a book published in 1939, spoke of Morgan on the stand as having been "courteous to a degree and cooperative in his attitude," with the air of "a man who, far from having any guilty secrets to hide, manifested a pride in his firm and its works which was obvious and deeply genuine." In this exchange, at least, who can deny that the peasant's son comes off the aristocrat?

The Pecora-Morgan exchanges were a kind of entr'acte, of chiefly symbolic importance. The main attack on J. P. Morgan & Company centered on a single episode—the 1929 stock issue of the Alleghany Corporation—and the answers to Pecora's questions were given mostly not by Morgan but by his partners, and most of all by George Whitney. Slim, immaculate, chain-smoking as usual, and handsome as ever, Whitney was the Morgan firm's perfect prompter, ever ready with the facts and figures. Time and again one or another of the partners on the stand found himself at a loss to supply some detail; time and again the solution was to "ask George," who always seemed to know, to have the documents in his briefcase or the figures in his head, and who poured forth the information with endless patience and with no hint of grudging—even when the information, more or less imperfectly understood by a committee and a public weary of depression and hungry for scapegoats, could give rise to a kind of Roman holiday of gloating over the discomfiture of these most patrician of custodians of private wealth.

III

In January, 1929—that far-distant time, to the Wall Street of 1933—the Van Sweringen brothers of Cleveland had set up the Alleghany Corporation as a holding company to consolidate their vast railroad empire in the East and Midwest. Of the 3,500,000 shares of common stock that they issued, the Van Sweringens had kept 2,250,000 for themselves, and issued the remaining 1,250,000 to J. P. Morgan & Company at $20 a share, for its own account and for distribution to the public. It had been unquestionably a highly speculative stock issue—emphatically not the sort Morgan's normally handled—but for one reason or another the firm had taken it on, and the manner of distribution decided upon represented a curious compromise. Rejecting the idea of selling the stock directly to the public on the grounds that it would be wrong to subject the public to such great risk, the Morgan partners had taken most of the stock themselves and offered the rest, about 575,000 shares, to 170 of their well-to-do friends and clients—all men of sufficient substance, it was judged, to be able to "afford the risk." It was the extent and nature of this "risk" that intensely interested Pecora, the Senators, and the country in 1933. Immediately upon announcement of the new issue on February 1, 1929, the stock, which would not become physically available for almost three weeks, had begun being traded over the counter on what was called a "when issued" basis (that is, for delivery when it became available), and, in the manic speculative atmosphere of the time, it had immediately gone to a price of around $35 a share. What Morgan's had to offer its friends and clients, then, was stock priced at $20 that could instantly and readily be sold for $35. Put more crudely, what it had to hand out was the equivalent of money, and the amount of money it had to hand out, on the basis of those prices, totaled over eight million dollars.

The list of Morgan friends and clients who were offered shares in this windfall reads like a compendium of the American establishment of the time. The great names of Wall Street had been there: Baker of the First National Bank, Mitchell of the National City, Wiggin of the Chase, each offered 10,000 shares convertible at will into a risk-free profit of $150,000. Morgan had personally kept 40,000 shares ($600,000 potential profit), and his partners various lesser amounts ranging up to Thomas Lamont's 18,000 shares; Dick Whitney, as the Morgan broker, had been cut in for 1,000, and John W. Davis, as Morgan's personal counsel and the acknowledged leader of the Wall Street bar, for 400. The chief executives of the country's leading corporations had been there. So had the powers in both political parties, John J. Raskob, chairman of the Democratic National Committee, coming in for 2,000 shares, and Joseph R. Nutt, treasurer of the *Republican* National Committee, for 3,000. So had cabinet officers past and future: former Secretary of the Treasury William Gibbs McAdoo (500 shares), former Secretary of War Newton D. Baker (2,000 shares), soon-to-be Secretary of the Navy Charles Francis Adams (1,000 shares), and later-to-be Secretary of the Treasury William Woodin (1,000 shares). (In explaining the presence of Adams to the committee, George Whitney said indignantly—and, by the Morgan code as previously set forth, righteously—that Adams had been included not because he was about to assume a powerful post in Hoover's Cabinet but because he was J. P. Morgan's son's father-in-law.) And just plain national heroes, too: Charles A. Lindbergh and General John J. Pershing, 500 shares each, the former presumably because he was married to Dwight Morrow's daughter, the latter presumably for old remembrance's sake.

The letters and telegrams of notification that the Morgan partners had sent out to the elect during the early part of February, 1929, were read into the committee record in the quite different America of summer 1933. The passage of time had changed these communications into little masterpieces of unconscious irony—truly an investigator's dream. For example:

MY DEAR MR. WOODIN:

. . . Although we are making no offering of [Alleghany] stock, as it is not the class of security we wish to offer publicly, we are asking some of our close friends if they would like some of this stock at the same price it is costing us, namely, $20 a share.

I believe the stock is selling in the market around $35 to $37 a share, which means very little, except that people wish to speculate.

We are reserving for you 1,000 shares at $20 a share, if you would like to have it.

There are no strings tied to this stock, so you can sell it whenever you wish. . . . We just want you to know that we were thinking of you in this connection. . . .

Sincerely yours,
WILLIAM EWING [a Morgan partner]

Whether Woodin found any "meaning" in the market price of Alleghany apart from an interesting instance of the human urge to speculate is unrecorded; at all events, he accepted the offer and sent in a $20,000 check for his 1,000 shares. Thomas Lamont's telegram to Albert Wiggin (aboard the Golden State Limited, car No. 27, Room A, approaching Douglas, Arizona) was briefer and more informal in tone than Ewing's letter to Woodin, and it omitted to explicate the Morgan firm's scruples about the public risk; but it did not neglect to emphasize the happy situation obtaining in the market:

THE VAN ESS BOYS OF CLEVELAND HAVE JUST ORGANIZED ALLEGHANY CORPORATION. . . . WE ARE MAKING NO OFFERING OF COMMON STOCK, BUT HAVE SET ASIDE FOR YOU AND IMMEDIATE ASSOCIATES 10,000 SHARES AT COST TO US, NAMELY $20. THE . . . MARKET IS QUOTED AT $35. PLEASE WIRE PROMPTLY YOUR WISHES. I AM SAILING FOR PARIS TONIGHT. WITH BEST REGARDS, TOM.

Wiggin did not delay about wiring back that he would gladly take the stock; indeed, all 170 of the selected recipients accepted the offer with more or less alacrity. Nearly all of them, in their replies, accepted either explicitly or implicitly, and always with a straight face, the proposition that what they were doing was assuming a business risk inappropriate for less substantial investors; but one, Raskob—a man perhaps more accustomed to the blunt ways of politics than the more delicate ones of finance—failed to grasp this idea at all, and made it clear that he understood the matter quite differently. He wrote George Whitney from Palm Beach:

DEAR GEORGE:

Many thanks for your trouble and for so kindly remembering me. My check for $40,000 is enclosed herewith in payment for the Alleghany stock. . . . I appreciate deeply the many courtesies shown me by you and your partners, and I sincerely hope the future holds opportunities for me to reciprocate. The weather is fine. . . .

Best regards and good luck,
JOHN

"Everybody Ought to Be Rich," Raskob would entitle his article in the *Ladies' Home Journal* that summer; he, at least, evidently had little enough reason not to be.

The public stir caused by the Pecora committee's revelation of the Alleghany preferred list was enormous; the House of Morgan would never thereafter entirely recover from it. Here was something everyone could understand. That the toploftiest of Wall Street dukedoms had dispensed patronage, presumably in the hope of future favors in return, just like the lowest and most cynical ward heeler, was lost on nobody; jokes about the list swept the country, and even solidly Republican newspapers had fun clucking and gloating. But they, and Pecora himself, went too far. In sober truth, the Morgan handling of the Alleghany issue had not really been as reprehensible as it was now being made to appear. For one thing, there really was an element of risk to the purchasers of the stock, as was to be amply demonstrated in practice. After soaring up to a peak price of 57 in the summer of 1929, Alleghany collapsed, and at the nadir of the depression was selling at one dollar a share; so those on the preferred list who had bought at $20 and then held on rather than selling immediately—Wiggin claimed to be among them—were left with a stinging loss. However, since the tone of the offering letters made it plain enough that the House of Morgan was not just permitting but actually suggesting that the recipients cash in their profits at once, this must be accounted a rather feeble argument for the defense. A far stronger one is that there had been nothing in the least exceptional about the whole operation. It was the sort of thing investment houses in 1929 did all the time, and had been doing regularly since large public distributions of stock had begun, during and immediately after the First World War. True enough, the House of Morgan was supposed to live not by the *Zeitgeist* but rather by its own more stringent ethical standards; it was also true enough that the firm traditionally never sold the public speculative common stocks, or for that matter *any* common stocks, and had no reason to break tradition in the Alleghany case. What it had done was to use its friends and clients as middlemen in the process of achieving the public distribution of the stock necessary to qualify it for listing on the Stock Exchange. Assuming that the distribution was to be undertaken in the first place by a firm that did not sell stock directly to the public, the method used had been a reasonably equitable method. To have distributed the bonanza among widows and orphans would scarcely have been practicable.

Pecora knew this, of course. But, brilliant, single-minded, crusading, politically ambitious as he was, he was in the role of advocate rather than that of judge; he painted his adversary as black as he could, and as black as the angry and frustrated country wanted him to. In this matter and in others, he overstated the case. In the different context of the Morgan partners' absurdly, scandalously low, but still not fraudulent, income-tax payments during the early depression years, Pecora pilloried them mercilessly, and explained later that "the country in 1933 was in no mood for nice distinctions between tax 'evasion' and tax 'avoidance.'" Which, of course, is to say that it was in no mood for nice distinctions between lawbreaking and law-abiding. The coin was turned; the irrational business worship of 1929 had become its equally irrational opposite; and Pecora, three-quarters righteous tribune of the people, was one-quarter demagogic inquisitor.

IV

Apart from the Morgan investigation, Pecora and the committee through that summer turned up all sorts of stones to reveal all sorts of repulsive things—the past pools, manipulations, and sundry deceptions of the Mitchells, the Wiggins, the Insulls, the Van Sweringens. On and on the revelations went, until there seemed to be no bottom to the sinkhole in lower Manhattan. But the mood of the hearings was not always heavy with squalid vice; often it was lightened by the comedy of turned tables, of the elephant tortured by the mouse, and never more so than in the attitude of some of the witnesses toward certain words—words like "manipulation" and "pool," which by 1933 had become the slogans of the country's effort to pin the depression on Wall Street, and which the Wall Streeters on the grill were understandably anxious to avoid.

The word that proved to be a problem for Murray Dodge, vice president of Chase Securities Corporation, was neither "pool" nor "manipulation" but the more universally understood jargon term "gravy." In April, 1931, Dodge had written his boss, Wiggin, a confidential memo that had eventually found its way into Pecora's hands. Speaking of a certain motion-picture company underwriting that had been under negotiation, Dodge had written: "With Halsey, Stuart out, it is possible for me to discuss the whole financing with Kuhn Loeb again, a thing that I am loath to do unless necessary, as the split-up of the gravy would hurt my feelings." Now what, exactly, Pecora asked blandly, had Mr. Dodge meant by "gravy"?

"What I really meant," replied Dodge, fighting for time, "was that I anticipated that going to Kuhn, Loeb and Company after Halsey, Stuart had withdrawn that we would be on the defensive, and that therefore what I called 'gravy' was a certain amount of—"

The witness hesitated desperately; unable to avoid confronting the barrier of definition any longer, he shied. "It is a difficult explanation, isn't it?" put in Senator Couzens, a compassionate man.

"It is a difficult explanation," Mr. Dodge agreed. Sweating, he stumbled on a bit more, plunged desperately into his vocabulary, and at last came up, triumphant, with "prestige." "I would say that it was the prestige—that was the word I was trying to think of . . . I meant *prestige*."

"I think you are not making it any better," Senator Couzens said. "You had better stop." It may be presumed that Mr. Dodge was glad to do so.

Wiggin himself, among others, had trouble with, or at least qualms about, the word "pool." When Pecora was questioning him about the pools he had participated in, Wiggin, while not denying the deeds, all but pleaded with Pecora that the precise word for them be avoided; wouldn't something like "investment account" do as well? But why not "pool"? Pecora wanted to know. "Just the reputation of the word," Wiggin begged. Well, Pecora pursued, did it connote something reprehensible, then? "I don't know," Wiggin said, "but there is that feeling against the word 'pool.'" Pecora courteously avoided it as much as possible during the rest of his examination of Wiggin, but could not resist putting into the record a 1928 letter to one of Wiggin's private corporations, from the brokerage firm of W. E. Hutton & Company, which read in full:

"Enclosed please find a check of $105,467.29, being the amount of your subscription and profit on the Hudson Motor Car Company pool account." Wiggin did not claim that either the check or the language of the covering letter had offended him at the time he had received them.

Even so, the curiousness of his attitude to the word "pool" was as nothing compared to that of another witness, a Stock Exchange specialist named Charles Wright, who had conducted many gaudy pools in his time, including one in behalf of a White Russian prince. Asked by Pecora to define "pool" and "pool account," Wright replied unequivocally enough, "I do not understand those terms, Mr. Pecora. I have never been able to understand them." Yet in almost his next breath he found himself not only explaining in detail how pools worked, but even learnedly distinguishing between different kinds of pools:

> MR. WRIGHT: Some pool accounts operate on options . . . some by way of direct purchase of stock and redistribution of it, and others may be accumulation pools where they accumulate stock that somebody desires. . . .

> MR. PECORA: And frequently, if not invariably, a pool has an option covering the stock in which it trades?

> MR. WRIGHT: That is right.

> MR. PECORA: And it gets that option as a rule from what kind of persons?

> MR. WRIGHT: Sometimes from individuals, and sometimes from officers of the company, and sometimes from large stockholders, and sometimes from the corporation, which might hold a good block of stock and which wanted to get rid of it. . . .

To Pecora's credit as a showman, he refrained from pedantically reminding Wright of what he had said at the outset, and thus avoided running this veritable vaudeville routine into the ground. A country sorely in need of laughs was getting some at Wall Street's expense; if Wall Street with its sinister maneuvers had taken away people's bread in the past, now it was generously, if inadvertently, giving them a circus.

But the last laugh that summer was Wall Street's. In the very weeks when Pecora was patiently drawing out the stories of the pools and manipulations, exposing Wall Street's misdeeds of the past to public indignation and derision; in the very days when Otto H. Kahn was appearing as a witness and declaring, on behalf of Wall Street's most responsible and public-spirited element, that manipulation through pools was an "artificial, antisocial, illegitimate practice which thrives on the gullibility of the public"—in such days, one of the most picturesque and egregious stock-market pools of all time was in full cry, under the noses, so to speak, of Pecora's staff of earnest investigators and the responsible Wall Streeters alike. It was a tour de force of social misbehavior that a Willie Sutton might have admired, and its chief initiator and benefactor was an obscure businessman named Russell R. Brown, chairman of the board of the American Commercial Alcohol Company, a Maryland corporation with executive offices in New York City. With repeal of the Eighteenth Amendment waiting only on ratification by the states, the star of the alcohol stocks was shining brightly that summer, and with the prospect that his firm would soon be able to add substantial sales of potable alcohol to its line of antifreeze, Brown and some of his associates saw the chance for a major coup in the stock of their own company. They first obtained control of 25,000 shares of it, then selling at around $20 a share, through a Byzantine series of maneuvers involving an exchange of stock with two dummy corporations created especially for the purpose—Maister Laboratories, Inc., headed by a Mr. Phagan, and Noxon, Inc., headed by a Mr. Capdevielle. (Unlikely as it may seem, there really was a K. B. Phagan, an accountant friend of Brown's, and a C. C. Capdevielle, a molasses broker; indeed, there was even a Dr. Maister, a German-born fermentologist employed by American Commercial Alcohol who was supposed to have invented a secret process for making vitamins. Noxon apparently had no corporeal existence.) Brown and his associates formed an eight-man pool to manipulate the stock of ACA, and to make its operation possible they gave options on the 25,000 shares to the notorious market operator Tom Bragg. And whom did Bragg engage as manager of the pool? None other than Sell 'em Ben Smith, the famous, boisterous, rags-to-riches bear operator who had been the public's favorite Wall Street villain in the first months after the 1929 crash—and who had testified with admirable candor and less than admirable lack of repentance to the Senate committee about the past pools he had managed, back in the spring of 1932.

Using techniques that by this time must have been second nature to him—and about which, in any case, his memory would have been refreshed if he had been reading the Pecora committee testimony in the newspapers or the *Congressional Record*—Smith began his market operations on May 3, 1933, to draw the gullible public into ACA stock by causing it to rise and to appear constantly on the ticker. The record of his transactions, which came to light later, is nothing short of dizzying. On May 4, for example, he sold 3,700 shares. The following day he bought 600. On May 8 he bought 500 and sold 1,000; then after three days of buying more than he sold, on the twelfth he suddenly sold 1,100, and topped this on the sixteenth and seventeenth, respectively, when he sold 1,600 and 3,300. Then back to buying, building up to a climax on May 29, when he kept the ticker racing by buying 8,200 and selling 4,800. By the end of the month he had bought, all told, 13,300 shares and sold 22,100, and in spite of the fact that he had lived up to his nickname by keeping sales in a solid preponderance, so successful had been his advertising of ACA on the ticker that the public under his guidance had forced the price upward from 20 to above 30. But this was only the beginning. Joined now by Bragg, Brown, and others in the pool who began operating in ACA on their own, through June Smith kept the stock churning around and gradually rising to just above 40; then in the first half of July, like a violin virtuoso building a passage to crescendo, he brought the public to the classic frenzy of buying that climaxes a well-run pool operation, and on July 18 ACA went completely wild and hit 89⅞. That was the day Smith chose to pull out the plug. Coincidentally, it was the day of the big general market break precipitated by the disintegration of the London Conference. The combination of circumstances caused matters to get a bit out of hand, and ACA, having risen strictly according to plan, now sank a bit faster than Smith or the pool participants found convenient. Charles Wright, who was the ACA specialist and was in on the pool, said later, "I shiver every time I think of it, of the price at which the stock was distributed and the price it went to. . . . That got to be a nightmare with me." With the pool no longer buying, the public suddenly disillusioned, and the market as a whole in a state of collapse, in the three days following July 18 ACA plunged from 89⅞ to under 30, and the pool account was closed. The nightmare-ridden specialist Wright had a personal profit of $138,000; Bragg and Sell 'em Ben had their liberal commissions as managers and their trading profits; and the eight pool participants—including Phagan and Capdevielle, since even dummies get rewards for their availability—had *their* profit, which probably ran into millions. Eventually, Pecora got wind of the whole thing and tried to subpoena Bragg and Smith, but they had anticipated him; by that time, it turned out, Bragg was in Honolulu and Smith, even more prudent, in Melbourne, Australia.

As stock-market manipulation the ACA pool was fairly small-time stuff, a sort of last fling before the cops came and broke up the party. But, timed as it was, it retains a certain interest for two reasons. It shows more eloquently than any speeches or statements the response of Wall Street's more raffish, speculative element to the Pecora committee and its mood of high moral indignation. And it is a small mine of a substance always in short supply, low comedy.

V

To be an outlet for public frustration wasn't the investigation's only point; in the background, and then later in the foreground, was the question of Congressional action in the form of a law to regulate the stock markets. Early in 1933, back in the hundred days, Roosevelt had quietly put the venerable Samuel Untermyer, hero of the Pujo investigation more than two decades earlier, to work writing a bill. But the Untermyer draft had not pleased Roosevelt and had never been introduced. Now in December, with the Pecora committee's most lurid revelations in the public record and the public mind, work on a new bill began in good earnest. The drafters this time were men of a new generation: James M. Landis of the Harvard Law School faculty, Telford Taylor of the Department of the Interior, the blue-blooded Brain Truster Isaac Newton Phelps Stokes II, the New York lawyer Benjamin V. Cohen, and Thomas G. Corcoran of the RFC—all men in their twenties and thirties bursting with brains and energy, central members of the group of young intellectuals drawn to Washington by the excitement and high promise of the New Deal. In strictest secrecy, in an inconspicuous downtown Washington apartment that had been rented for the purpose, the group labored through the winter months, often consulting Pecora and his chief investigator, the energetic and talented crusading journalist John T. Flynn. Eventually, the writing of a final draft devolved chiefly on Cohen and Corcoran. In early February, 1934, with Congress back in session, Senator Fletcher suddenly demanded a bill, forthwith. The bright young men had not finished their work, but, as bright young men can do with an ideal to drive them, they worked without sleep until they did. Forty-eight hours and countless cups of coffee later, they had a draft ready. On February 9 Roosevelt, who up to then had been publicly noncommittal on the Pecora committee findings and had not expressed himself in favor of Stock Exchange regulation, sent a message to Congress demanding it at once. Immediately afterward, the fruits of the bright young men's hectic and heroic labors—an intricate technical document fifty pages long outlawing all forms of stock manipulation, putting federal controls over stock-market credit, and giving the Federal Trade Commission wide powers to act as Wall Street's policeman—was introduced in Congress as the Fletcher-Rayburn bill. So at last the federal intentions toward the stock market were out in the open.

Richard Whitney was ready. His attitude was simple: he was flatly opposed to any federal regulation of the Stock Exchange whatever. His always rigid personality and iron will had been forged to a new degree of hardness by a series of incidents in October. Pecora had written Whitney asking him to send out to all Exchange members a questionnaire designed to elicit various sorts of embarrassing information. Whitney had stalled. Pressing the matter, Pecora had sought a personal interview with Whitney. But somehow or other the Stock Exchange president always seemed to be engaged when Pecora wanted to see him. Seeking an appointment on a Saturday or Sunday, Pecora was told that it was impossible because of social engagements; asking about Monday, he learned that that was impossible because of *business* engagements. Eventually, Whitney, arming himself with the presence of his close and loyal friend

Roland Redmond, a senior partner of the Exchange's law firm, had received two Pecora emissaries, one of whom was John Flynn.

It was the same John Flynn who a year and a half before had characterized Whitney in *Collier's* as "the highest type of Wall Street broker." Just possibly that year and a half, during which Flynn had become the shrewdest and most aggressive of Pecora's investigators, had revealed to Whitney a different man from the one who had described him thus. Just possibly, too, he felt at all times only contempt for personal flattery from journalists. In any case, the sight of Flynn in his office now had caused Whitney to flush purple, mutter something incomprehensible, and leave the room. Several minutes later he had composed himself sufficiently to return—but not sufficiently to speak prudently. Drawing himself up, Whitney in his iciest and haughtiest tone delivered a sentence that his enemies would never thereafter allow him to forget. "You gentlemen are making a great mistake," he said. "The Exchange is a perfect institution."

"We thought we would get the cooperation of the Stock Exchange," Pecora commented in the committee hearings a few days later. "Apparently we cannot get it." Indeed they could not; on October 16 Whitney wrote Pecora formally, refusing to distribute the questionnaire, citing in explanation Redmond's legal opinion that "the information sought by the proposed questionnaire has no direct bearing on market practices or on the conduct of members of the Exchange." Publicly, he insisted that the Exchange had not failed to cooperate with the committee. "Mr. Pecora sought to have the Exchange compel its members to answer the questionnaire," he charged, adding that such a procedure deprived the members of their constitutional right to silence. Pecora countered by issuing subpoenas to the heads of a number of leading Stock Exchange member firms, with the intention of asking them directly the questions he could not get Whitney to ask them for him.

And now the first crack appeared in Wall Street's façade. Among those subpoenaed was E. A. Pierce, proprietor of E. A. Pierce & Company, a prominent brokerage house that had recently absorbed the highly successful Charles E. Merrill Company, and would later add the New Orleans firm of Fenner and Beane. Pierce, as will later become clear, had a close business relationship with Whitney, but not really a close personal one. The two men were very different, and went very different ways; both were clubmen, but in different spheres; they seldom met at a club unless it was the Stock Exchange Luncheon Club. A son of Maine and of Maine's beloved Bowdoin College, Pierce had grown up in modest circumstances, spent five years in his youth as a lumberjack, and started in Wall Street at the bottom. He had no pretensions to blue blood or influence in what the world still called "society." On the other hand, he and Whitney shared several qualities—a nostalgic flamboyance manifested in a taste for wearing formal clothes to work, a desire to be Wall Street statesmen, and an imposing physical bearing; where Whitney radiated an athlete's ruthless decisiveness, Pierce, fourteen years Whitney's senior, with his crisp Maine speech and his mane of white hair, suggested experience and mellow wisdom. Hearing about the Flynn-Whitney confrontation from another member of Pecora's staff, Pierce decided that Whitney was being unreasonable. The course of mature wisdom lay somewhere between the two; he resolved to assume the role of mediator between the committee and the Exchange, the voice of reason from Wall Street.

Pierce's standard once set up, others rallied to it. Doubtless in some cases this was a matter of personal dislike of Whitney, whose charm did not affect everybody; but much more, it reflected a functional split in Wall Street that had grown up during the 1920s as a result of the entry of the mass public into the stock market. On the one hand was the Old Guard—the specialists and floor traders, the men who actually traded stocks face to face and knew the men they beat or were beaten by; heirs in role, if seldom in either daring or rapaciousness, of the Goulds and Fisks and Drews, the bulls and bears whose nineteenth-century battles had both built and corrupted the nation. They still controlled the Stock Exchange, and Whitney was their leader. But now there were also the far-flung many-branched brokerage firms serving the general public, most of whose members never saw the Exchange floor or made a stock trade face to face; firms whose business consisted of making trades for others, many of them in distant cities or towns tied to Wall Street by the thin strands of telegraph wires, and who, because their livings depended on the public, could not afford to turn their back on the public interest as the Old Guard could. It is neatly symbolic that the leader of this new Wall Street element, spawned by social change, should have been a future founder of the Wall Street colossus to come, the celebrated firm of Merrill Lynch.

Pierce testified to Pecora that he believed a certain amount of regulation of stock-trading was desirable and feasible. Whitney, for his part, sought and obtained an appointment at the White House. After the two Groton-and-Harvard men—the President of the United States six years senior to the president of the New York Stock Exchange—had conferred for forty-five minutes, Whitney emerged and told the press laconically that they had discussed Stock Exchange speculation, "each giving the other his ideas." In mid-December, when rumors were circulating that a stock-exchange-regulation bill was being drafted, Whitney felt called upon to issue a denial that the Exchange was planning a huge publicity campaign to fight it.

No doubt his denial was in good faith, because Roosevelt's February 9 message calling for legislation and the subsequent introduction of the Fletcher-Rayburn bill clearly took him by surprise. But he was not long in recovering. Instantly the Stock Exchange, at Whitney's instigation, attempted to forestall federal action by passing a few speculation-control rules of its own. Immediately after that, Whitney called together the heads of thirty leading member firms for what amounted to a council of war, at which plans were laid for organized campaigns against the bill in New York, Chicago, Philadelphia, San Francisco, and Boston. At about the same time, in his capacity as head man of the Exchange he sent out circular letters to all member firms, and to the presidents of eighty leading corporations whose shares were listed on the Exchange. The Fletcher-Rayburn bill, he asserted, was "the most important legislation affecting the Stock Exchange and its listed corporations which has ever been introduced in Congress." It would have "very disastrous consequences" for member firms and their clients alike.

To the corporation heads he addressed the warning, "The powers [granted in the bill] are so extensive that the Federal Trade Commission might dominate and actually control the management of each listed corporation." Without suggesting what specific action the member firms and corporation heads might want to take, he ended by saying that additional copies of the letter and the bill were available to them on request. Meanwhile, in Washington, Tommy Corcoran, on behalf of the bill-drafting team of Cohen and Corcoran, was explicating the bewildering complexities of the bill to the Pecora committee.

The letters were only the beginning of the Whitney-led campaign of opposition, which soon became so intense that Roosevelt himself was moved to protest that "a more definite and highly organized drive is being made against effective legislation [for Stock Exchange regulation] than against any similar recommendation made by me." Committees were formed and rallies held; special trains carrying anti-Fletcher-Rayburn delegations converged on Washington; a special drive was made to get the support of university professors. Follow-up messages went out from the Stock Exchange to member-firm offices in forty-three different cities, this time striking a more urgent, even a threatening note. "Will you please ascertain and advise," one such message went,

> what is being done by concerted action of savings banks, corporations listed or unlisted, insurance companies, in your territory in the way of organized effort for the fight . . . ? Are your employees alive to the fact that with the passage of the bill a great many of them will be out of employment? Are they writing their Senators and Representatives? If not, they should do so at once, using their own note paper, not firm paper, and writing in their own way. . . . Please advise.

The letters to Washington poured in.

Meanwhile, with the battle fairly joined, Whitney's turn came to testify publicly in rebuttal of Corcoran. Like the House of Morgan the previous year, the Stock Exchange moved into Washington in state; Whitney brought his whole general staff with him and set up headquarters in a handsome house. Pierce and his band of Wall Street moderates established a separate command post at the Carlton. Publicly the moderates maintained a reasonably solid front with Whitney. One Pierce ally told the press that the bill would give the government the power to destroy corporations, and another, a lawyer, chimed in that he doubted its constitutionality. Pierce himself allowed that he agreed with Whitney's objectives, "since I'm quite sure Mr. Whitney and his associates are honest." But behind the scenes the Carlton group was cooperating with the government on a revision of the bill—working day after day and week after week with Rayburn, helping to redraft it in terms of greater financial sophistication, and at the same time working for the elimination of those provisions that they found harsh or unfair to Wall Street. Finding out about these negotiations, Whitney became so enraged that he had one of his lawyers telephone Pierce at three o'clock one morning to give him a tongue-lashing. The rebuke had muscle behind it; Whitney, after all, was the dictator of the Stock Exchange, with a board of governors entirely obedient to his bidding, and thus he had in his hands the power to deprive Pierce of his livelihood by arranging to have him expelled from membership. The lawyer did not explicitly make that threat. Even so, to grasp the almost awe-inspiring arrogance of the postmidnight reprimand we must anticipate our story a step. At that moment Whitney personally owed Pierce's firm the round sum of $100,000.

VI

But in the witness chair Whitney was magnificent, cool and forceful and persuasive and almost always reasonable. "Any attempt to regulate by statute in minute detail the operation of security markets is impossible of accomplishment," he said, introducing his case. The Fletcher-Rayburn bill gave the government "an absolute power to manage and operate" stock exchanges. Patiently he refuted each provision of the bill, showing why he believed it would do more harm than good. Time and again he emphasized the telling fact of Wall Street competence and Washington inexperience in the technical aspects of finance: "The bill as drawn presumes that the drafters have the supreme knowledge of the subject, and grants us no knowledge." He suggested that he was not opposed in principle to liberal ideas: "I do not believe that liberalism requires the federal government to operate our exchanges. . . . Reform should be limited to the correction of abuses and should not retard recovery by unwise restrictions." He conceded that the "perfect institution" was not composed of perfect men: "I do not want to give an impression that our members have been . . . or are pure white lilies." He skirted demagoguery: the bill "goes against human nature" and "is almost a full brother to the dead and unlamented Prohibition law." To want regulation, then, was to be almost like a teetotaling bluenose. At last, in mid-March, he was done. "I thank you gentlemen," he said courteously to Pecora and the Senators. "We are all at your disposal at any time."

"Those old Wall Street boys are putting up an awful fight to keep the government from putting a cop on their corner," Will Rogers said shortly after the end of Whitney's testimony, pretty well hitting, as Rogers so often did, the precise temper as well as the language of the national majority. Indeed they were putting up an awful fight, and, largely because they had succeeded in enlisting a huge segment of big business, not without good effect. The government retreated under the attack; the draft of the Fletcher-Rayburn bill was abandoned, and Cohen and Corcoran submitted to the House a new and apparently much milder one that took into account not only the objections of the moderate Pierce group but even some of those of the intransigent Whitney group as well. Compromise that it was, the new bill outraged the fire-eating reformers like Flynn, who saw it as a sellout to Wall Street. But neither did it please Whitney; he promptly pronounced it no more workable and even more complicated than the previous version. "Of course," Pecora commented, "if all Mr. Whitney's objections were met, there would be no bill at all."

The Stock Exchange campaign went on full blast. Committees to attack the bill, much of their voluminous prose suspiciously resembling that of Richard Whitney, kept on popping up here and there. Even the telephone clerks of Wall Street, several hundred strong, met on March 23 to organize themselves in opposition, the rationale being that if the bill were passed grass would grow in the streets of the financial district and they would be thrown out of work. Similarly, on March 25 word went out to the newspapers that two days later there was to be a mass protest meeting at the corner of Broad and Wall of thousands of brokerage-house employees, and that simultaneous mass meetings were to be held in dozens of commuting towns in New Jersey, Connecticut, Long Island, and Westchester County where the Wall Street employees lived. Mysteriously, none of the meetings materialized. The implication was unmistakable that the Stock Exchange had put out the announcement in a last-ditch bluff, and that the bluff had been called. The little people of Wall Street were no longer on the Stock Exchange's side. It was the seal of defeat: the troops were in sullen revolt against the generals.

So Whitney was beaten at last. On May 5 the House passed the bill by a huge majority; a week or so later the Senate passed a somewhat different version of it. By the beginning of June the two versions were reconciled, and on June 6 Roosevelt signed the Securities Exchange Act of 1934 into law; whereupon Whitney, acceding to defeat with an alacrity that might have been laid to either grace or expediency, but in a vein that certainly seemed uncharacteristic, announced that the Stock Exchange "intends to do everything in its power to cooperate . . . in the administration of the act," and added, "I am truly hopeful that if wisely and judiciously administered, the act will be a constructive measure." But after all, he had some reason to be in a cheerful frame of mind. On May 14, during the last stages of the downfall of his campaign, he and his Old Guard cronies had been re-elected by acclamation to another term in charge of the Stock Exchange. If the war was lost, the beaten army was still not routed or dispersed.

The essence of the compromise embodied in the law that had been passed consisted of creating an entirely new administrative body and passing the buck to it. The hated notion of having the Federal Trade Commission administer the law had been eliminated; instead, a new five-man Securities and Exchange Commission, to be appointed by the President subject to confirmation by Congress, was to do the job. Gone, too, were most of the earlier version's specific and detailed antispeculation and antimanipulative provisions; these were replaced by more general directives giving no more than guidance to the new SEC, which was charged with making up its specific regulations as it went along. Flynn commented soon after its passage, "The law as it stands forbids and requires so little that we may truthfully say there is no body of laws as yet governing the securities markets until the commission considers, adopts and promulgates them." But the point—and for Wall

Street's whole future, a crucial point—was that the commission existed, and had broad powers to do just that. An historic moment had passed almost unrecognized. The cops were on Wall Street's corner, and they were well armed.

In these circumstances, everything turned on who the cops would be. Nominally bipartisan, Roosevelt appointed as commissioners two New Dealers, Pecora and Landis, and two liberal Republicans who as far as Wall Street was concerned might as well have been New Dealers, George C. Mathews of Wisconsin and Robert Healy of Vermont. His bombshell was the chairman he named. There had been speculation that it would be Pecora, or Landis, or even Moley; at any rate, the general assumption went, it would be someone without Wall Street connections and with unquestioned loyalty to the New Deal. And whom did the mercurial Roosevelt appoint but Joseph P. Kennedy—not just a Wall Streeter, but a speculator and manipulator hardly less notorious than Sell 'em Ben himself? The faithful were appalled. Here was a man who seemed to be better equipped, not to say more inclined, to participate in pools than to regulate them—who, in point of fact, was known to have participated profitably in a particularly gaudy pool in the stock of Libby-Owens-Ford only the previous summer, and whose sole basis for appointment to any federal job, let alone that of regulating the stock market, seemed to be his substantial contributions to Roosevelt's Presidential campaign in 1932. It all looked like ward politics at its least attractive. "I say it isn't true. It is impossible," wrote a dazed Flynn. Not only intransigents like Flynn but New Dealers almost to a man were outraged. *The New Republic* wailed that the President had "exceeded the expectations of his most ardent ill-wishers," and the Washington *News* commented that Roosevelt could not "with impunity administer such a slap in the face to his most loyal and effective supporters." Yet such was the insight that went along with Roosevelt's cool pragmatism that the Kennedy appointment was to turn out to be a good one; if the President had paid off a political debt, and appeared to placate Wall Street, in what seemed to be the most cynical and disillusioning manner possible, he had also, most improbably, brought to birth a vigorous and effective public servant who would start Wall Street on a new path from which there would be no turning back.

The Securities Exchange Act began functioning on July 1, and a few days later the cops arrived bodily on Wall Street's corner when the five new commissioners came for their first visit to the Stock Exchange. A tight-lipped Dick Whitney led them on a formal tour of inspection, having first taken the precaution of surrounding the floor with guards to restrain any brokers who might seek to do the visitors physical harm. The brokers stared coldly at the commissioners; trading came almost to a standstill; and in this atmosphere of suppressed hostility the new era dawned.

VII

It will be recalled that we left Whitney's private financial affairs in parlous condition, as he entered 1932 still living like the millionaire that, as the national symbol of Wall Street, he was universally assumed to be, but actually a negative millionaire, owing some two million dollars that he could not pay. The next couple of years were somewhat better for him. All but giving up hope of a miraculous recovery of his disastrous Florida fertilizer interests, he now undertook a new and at first more fruitful investment plunge. All through the years of Prohibition, the favorite bootleg drink in the New Jersey hills where he had his country estate was "Jersey Lightning," a harsh but authoritative applejack that had been distilled locally for generations before Prohibition and, of course, had continued to be produced massively though inconspicuously in those well-wooded hills and valleys—then still remarkably remote and unpopulated—without the blessing of law. Incredibly (or so we can say in hindsight), this urbane and sophisticated man came to believe that after repeal Jersey Lightning would capture the fancy of the whole country, and become a standard national drink like Scotch or bourbon; and to make it a still more attractive investment prospect, the stuff had the great commercial advantage of requiring very little aging to be potable, or as potable as it would ever be. Accordingly, early in 1933, with repeal clearly on the horizon at last, Whitney and one of his brokerage associates took over a chain of old New Jersey and southern New York State distilleries and organized Distilled Liquors Corporation for the purpose of producing and marketing alcoholic beverages as soon as repeal should become effective. The firm's principal product was, of course, to be applejack. Whitney himself, and the firm of Richard Whitney & Company, initially subscribed for between ten and fifteen thousand shares of Distilled Liquors stock at $15 a share.

This, of course, meant the need for new money. There was still the now-familiar nightmare of old loans continually coming due and needing to be either extended or replaced with new loans; and now this fresh capital outlay. On September 22, 1933, Whitney went to his old and trusted friend, and long-time henchman in the administration of the Stock Exchange, Herbert G. ("Duke") Wellington, proprietor of a brokerage firm much like Whitney's. "Duke," said Whitney—as Wellington recalled years later—"this is one of the hardest things I've ever had to say to anyone. I have given my word that I would repay a loan today, and it's not convenient for me. The money I thought was coming to me, was promised to me, has at the last moment turned me down. I pledged my word that I would repay this money, and I wonder if you would help me?" Then Whitney asked Wellington to lend him $250,000 for thirty days, without security.

In the ensuing discussion, the matter of Whitney's Florida ventures was mentioned, although not, apparently, that of his new applejack firm; presumably the fact that he was embarking on a new flyer in the market would not be well calculated to reassure his friend. Also mentioned was the fact that Whitney had a rich, successful, and indulgent brother. Dick Whitney explained to Wellington, "George has been lovely to me, and I just can't go over there and ask him to give me any more money." Nevertheless, Wellington was to relate later that always in his mind was the feeling that as a last resort, if worse came to worst, Dick Whitney would swallow his pride and go to 23 Wall to see his brother. No doubt, then, it was with that in mind that Wellington, although he did not meet the request for $250,000, agreed to lend Whitney $110,000, unsecured—nominally for a month as requested, but actually, by tacit mutual understanding, until Whitney should be able to repay. (As a footnote on Wall Street mores it may be noted that the matter of interest on the loan was not even mentioned in the conversation during which the loan was arranged, yet in the subsequent accountings of it, interest at 2 percent—the nominal going rate at the time, more or less—was added with no objection from either party. The subject, then, had been too trifling to *need* discussion, since all that was at stake was $2,200 a year.)

A week and a half later, on October 2, Whitney borrowed $100,000 unsecured from Roger D. Mellick, not only a downtown friend of long standing but a New Jersey country neighbor, too; Mellick explained much later that he had made the loan because of "knowing Dick Whitney so many years and admiring him and thinking that he was such a good fellow." (Morgan had said to Pecora, "We do make . . . loans, and we make them because we believe the people should have the money . . . they are friends of ours, and we know that they are good, straight fellows.") And not quite two weeks later came the most astonishing of Whitney's feats of borrowing for that year. On October 14, the same week that Whitney formally refused to distribute Pecora's questionnaire and E. A. Pierce came out decisively as a Whitney opponent, E. A. Pierce & Company extended Whitney a loan of $100,000, fully secured by an assignment of one New York Stock Exchange seat and one New York Curb Exchange seat belonging to Whitney and his firm. Why, then, did Pierce—who just then could hardly have thought that Whitney was a particularly good fellow—do it? Perhaps, the collateral being so sound, it was a case of "business is business and politics is politics"; Pierce was a practical man. Or perhaps—though not likely in the case of the straightforward former lumberjack—Pierce wanted the power over Whitney that the debt and the possession of the collateral might give him. Or perhaps it was one more case of the operation of the famous Whitney charm.

At all events, the deal went through, and it marked an ominous turning point in Whitney's borrowings: now he was taking money from men outside his circle of relatives and close friends, from people who might conceivably want to harm him. But he had the money, and he put it to work. Repeal became effective in December; Distilled Liquors leaped into business like a racehorse leaving the starting gate, and, as the great boom in liquor stocks continued, by the spring of 1934 its price on the over-the-counter market was being quoted at 45. Meanwhile, Whitney had continued to accumulate shares of it for himself and for his brokerage firm, and at that boom price his holdings were worth far more than a million dollars.

Right there, if he had been another man, he might have sold out wholly or in part, paid off all his debts except those to his brother and the Morgan firm—the debts that were, literally or figuratively, in the family—and made a fresh start. But he had a gambler's faith in Distilled Liquors, not to mention in his own judgment; so he went on carrying the stock and owing the money, looking forward confidently to a glorious day when Jersey Lightning would be drunk everywhere, eagerly ordered by the harried commuter with five minutes between office and train and suavely served in fashionable houses and country clubs, and Whitney would at last have the money to live as he had always lived. In that same spring when he was suffering his great public defeat in Washington on the Securities Exchange Act, he was close to the business miracle that alone could salvage his tangled private affairs—as close, that is, as he would ever come.

Chapter Nine

The White Knight Unhorsed

I

In 1934 Wall Street was almost a ghost town; customers' men drowsed in the empty board rooms, and brokers idled and joked the days away on the floor of the Stock Exchange, where trading volume was running at less than half the pace of 1933. The first fine rapture of the "Roosevelt market" had vanished with the failure of the early New Deal measures to bring about significant recovery, and apathy had settled over the market. When stocks were traded at all, they were traded listlessly, desultorily, with little price movement. The professional speculators were on the sidelines waiting to see what would happen next, and the public had little money to invest and less interest in investing. Brokerage firms were laying people off again, and giving them "apple weeks"—one week off without pay out of every four weeks, during which they could, and some did, sell apples. Investment bankers were no better off, since with scarcely any new money available the capital market was all but dead.

Whole months would go by when new corporate issues of industrial stocks and bonds for the whole country totaled only one or two million dollars. The Banking Act of 1933 compelled firms that had previously engaged in both commercial and investment banking to choose one or the other, thereby forcing the Chase and the National City to get rid of their notorious "security affiliates," and—far more significant from the standpoint of the Wall Street social structure—breaking in two even the House of Morgan. Grimly obedient, it chose commercial banking, and emerged with its prestige intact but its power and influence much reduced, especially, and perhaps most painfully, in relation to that of Kuhn, Loeb, which lost nothing because it had never gone in for commercial banking anyhow.

In this time of dissolution and stagnation there was talk of the end of finance capitalism.

Even the mighty of Wall Street felt the direct economic pinch to a degree—to a greater degree, at any rate, than the mighty of business, many of whom found themselves able to continue drawing annual salaries of $300,000 or $400,000 a year right through the depression, while their employees often endured pay cuts and their stockholders did without dividends. In 1934 J. P. Morgan, sixty-seven years old and increasingly embittered by events in spite of his refurbished public image, began to withdraw from active participation in his firm's affairs. That winter he took his *Corsair*, the largest private yacht in the world, on an extended cruise of the British West Indies and the Galápagos Islands; the following spring he laid her up permanently as too expensive to maintain, and sold the cream of his famous art collection, including paintings by Fra Angelico, Fra Filippo Lippi, Rubens, Hals, and Holbein. It was in 1934 or 1935 that a du Pont is supposed to have rejected the proposal that his company sponsor a Sunday-afternoon radio program on the grounds that "at three o'clock Sunday afternoons everybody is playing polo"; but it was during the same period that Wall Streeters who were members of the Union League Club allowed themselves an unaccustomed kind of luxury, that of self-pity, by gloomily frequenting a room at the club that was wallpapered with securities, contributed for the purpose by members, that had once been worth millions and were now presumed to be worth nothing. (In 1936, when things looked brighter and some of the securities had regained some of their former value, the club would steam them off the walls and return them to their former owners.)

Indeed, one of the liveliest spots downtown in 1934 was a place called the "securities graveyard"—a room on Vesey Street where the auctioneering firm of Adrian H. Muller & Son regularly conducted public sales of huge blocks of worthless stock in bankrupt companies. A band of seedy bargain-hunters—the flotsam of wild optimism floating on the dark sea of depression—frequented the place, bidding minuscule sums for hundreds of thousands of shares that they hoped might somehow, sometime, be miraculously recalled to life. One of the band, an Englishman named Harold Deighton, always ritually bid one dollar for every lot offered, a hundred shares of this ruined company, a thousand shares of that. Sometimes his was the winning bid; but he never got rich.

II

Investigated, ridiculed, reviled, scorned, and even, relatively speaking, impoverished, Wall Street grew sullen, and its rancor focused on its chief tormentor, the New Deal. Joe Kennedy's appointment was only momentarily comforting. Far from acting as a Wall Street agent in the New Deal camp, the old speculator turned out to fill just the opposite role. Moving deliberately but firmly, he first tackled the huge administrative job of registering the nation's 24 stock exchanges, their 2,400 members, and their 5,000 listed securities; then, concentrating his attention on the one incomparably biggest and most powerful stock exchange, he used his knowledge of Wall Street to set up a system of Trojan horse listening posts there and was soon coolly putting their findings to work by initiating the SEC's first legal actions against unreformed stock manipulators. Meanwhile, he was efficiently presiding over enforcement of the law's new provisions requiring the issuers of new securities to tell the public the truth about them. Wall Street had called the new law unworkable; Kennedy was making it work. In the process he was not surprisingly losing the approbation of his victims and their allies. "Sane and sound," Dick Whitney had said cozily, of Kennedy's initial cautious, and apparently ineffectual, approach to Stock Exchange regulation; but in the weeks and months following, as it gradually developed that Kennedy was not only serious about his job but also downright good at it, Whitney's cooperative attitude gradually gave way to one of surly obstruction to every SEC move.

Who did Joe Kennedy think he was? Back in the days when he was running pools for John Hertz he hadn't given himself any high-minded airs! Talk about That Man in the White House being a traitor to his class—well, by God, Joe Kennedy was a traitor to *his* class, too! Or so they were saying in the clubs and pubs where bankers and brokers withdrew to lick their wounds.

There was a moment, in the fall of 1934, when relations between Wall Street and Washington might have turned decisively for the better—and then the moment passed and things went the other way. The occasion was the annual meeting of the American Bankers Association, held the third week of October in (of all places) Washington, D.C., with the chosen theme of cooperation between government and business and the chosen speaker—of all people— Roosevelt himself. Thus grasping the nettle, the bankers were nevertheless in a wary mood. Only a few months earlier the Senate investigation had been exposing the Mitchells and Wiggins and pillorying even the sacred Morgans; and at its convention in Chicago the previous year the bankers had invited Jesse Jones of the RFC to speak, only to hear him tongue-lash them as if they were miscreant children ("Be smart for once—take government into partnership with you") and point out, with brutal lack of tact, that they were failures even in their own terms. Half the banks represented at the gathering, Jones had reminded them, were insolvent at that very moment.

Now, to tell the truth, the bankers were at bay and knew it; terrified of further government regulation and restrictive measures, they had chosen Washington as their 1934 site and Roosevelt as their chief speaker as a deliberate, if perhaps painful, show of propitiation toward the government. As if to emphasize the point by honoring the occasion, the bankers turned out in unprecedented numbers. Some four thousand came to Washington, from the presi-

dents of the tiniest, most down-at-heel holders of defaulted mortgages and deposits in dimes and quarters—the kind of bank Bonnie
and Clyde had lately been ravishing—to the elegant heads of
practically every major banking institution in Wall Street. Rarest of
all among the delegates were Lamont and Gilbert of Morgan's. No
Morgan partner had ever before honored an ABA convention with
his presence.

On the surface, the convention was a love feast as planned.
Dominated by the big men of Wall Street, who had decided that for
the moment meekness and humility were the watchwords, the
bankers, all but an unruly few from the boondocks, kept their
rancor against government well in check. The ABA's president
declared that the organization was "wholeheartedly for any program of recovery that does no violence to sound banking principles
and does not place in jeopardy the interests of [bank] depositors."
Jackson E. Reynolds, the gentlemanly, venerable president of the
First National Bank of New York, in his speech introducing Roosevelt, went much further. "I do not mean to suggest any surrender,"
he was careful to say in prelude—yet in the minutes following he
was confessing the shortcomings of bankers in the precrash years,
conceding that it was unreasonable to expect a balanced national
budget immediately in a time of general poverty, describing the
banking community as being now in a "chastened and understanding mood," and finally making the ultimate self-abasement of
thanking Roosevelt for all he had done to "rescue and rehabilitate
our shattered banking structure." It sounded like surrender, all
right, and Roosevelt, responding magnanimously though lightheart-
edly with remarks about how banking and government in cooperation could make an "all-American team," was actually greeted with
an ovation. Next day the bankers salvaged some of their pride by
voting a resolution calling for a balanced budget as soon as possible,
and everybody went home glowing with goodwill and good intentions.

Or so it seemed. But many of the bankers privately had other
feelings; in the corridors and hotel suites they were muttering that
Reynolds had gone too far, that peace had been bought at the cost
of honor. And then it gradually came to be known that there had
been a secret sellout. Reynolds had indeed surrendered, privately

and in advance. Roosevelt, it emerged, had insisted on seeing a transcript of Reynolds' proposed introduction as a condition of his appearance. The draft Reynolds had submitted had included a slyly pointed comparison of Roosevelt to the Roman commander Scipio, who as a result of having rejected a laurel branch extended by his enemy Hannibal "died in exile." It had also included a mildly needling reference to the time long past when Jackson Reynolds had been a young professor at Columbia Law School and Franklin Roosevelt had been one of his pupils—not a particularly apt pupil, Reynolds had planned to say, with a smile. The inclusion of these two paragraphs would have entirely changed the tone of Reynolds' remarks; but Roosevelt had flatly and adamantly insisted on their deletion as the price of his acceptance of the bankers' laurel branch.

It was the ultimate, gratuitous humiliation—denial to the conquered of the right to irony. When they found out about it, the bankers hardened their hearts, and the era of Roosevelt-hating in Wall Street was fairly launched.

III

But organized Roosevelt-hating in the nation did not begin in Wall Street. Precisely, it began two months before the bankers' convention, in August of 1934, with the formation of the American Liberty League, a coalition of rich, conservative Democrats and top-level Republican businessmen chartered to "teach the necessity of respect for the rights of persons and property." Nominally nonpartisan, the Liberty League at first proclaimed itself "definitely not anti-Roosevelt," and Roosevelt, tongue firmly in cheek, declared himself in full agreement with its announced principles and suggested that perhaps he might be able to use a Liberty League advisory committee in the preparation of the next national budget. All this was political comedy of the sort Roosevelt relished; he, and the public too, realized from the start that the Liberty League had been formed for the specific purpose of doing away with the New Deal and restoring the Old Deal. As time passed and the League's membership grew—to 36,000 by mid-1935, and finally to a peak of 125,000 during the 1936 Presidential campaign—it came to be the very focus and instrument of Roosevelt-hating by the rich and the well-to-do, a national symbol of selfish greed. Politically, its efforts were almost certainly counterproductive because of its undisguised sponsorship by the rich; as its historian, George Wolfskill, wrote later, "New Deal spokesmen did not have to refute the views of the League; they had only to call the roll." Yet it struck a note sympathetic to a significant minority of Americans, not all of them rich. The orators its speakers' bureau dispatched to business and service organizations throughout the country were the hard core of anti–New Deal political and ideological invective; and its individual members (although not, or not provably, its official management) were the conduits for the spreading of the always vicious, often scurrilous, and usually ludicrous anti-Roosevelt gossip that was a lamentable feature of the middle 1930s. Roosevelt was secretly Jewish (an entire faked genealogy was worked out for him, stemming back to a Colonel van Rosenfelt) ; his smile had been grafted on his face by a plastic surgeon; he was insane, as evidenced by his maniac laughter; he and his family were drunk all the time; he was having an affair with Frances Perkins; Mrs. Roosevelt was a Communist, and it was arranged that she would succeed him in the Presidency and turn the country over to Russia—such were the preposterous, and indeed pathetic, stories that Liberty Leaguers fell into the habit of telling each other, and anyone else who would listen. Some of the stories actually came to be widely believed. A national news service once distributed to its subscribers as *news*—or at least, as a "confidential background report" to the news—an item hinting at evidence that the President was afflicted with syphilis. Meanness of the spirit had become an epidemic sickness among the rich, and the contagion had spread beyond them.

Wall Street caught more than a touch of the sickness. It was saved from the worst public excesses of businessmen by its chronic tendency to pussyfooting on national issues—the same tendency that had caused it to stay mute until the last minute on the Warren gold-buying scheme. But in the privacy of their clubs and board rooms, where they could safely indulge their deeper feelings without jeopardizing their relations with either customers or the government, Wall Streeters conducted their own soul-satisfying orgies of Roosevelt-hating. The Liberty League, for example, started out confidently expecting to enlist practically all leading bankers and brokers; it ended up with many Wall Street–based anonymous contributors and secret sympathizers, but only a handful of open members. Yet in the unrefined purlieus of the marginal brokerage houses the lowest anti-Roosevelt stories catering to sexual prurience and religious prejudice were freely repeated (and were repeated on occasion, too, in the elegant and sporty Protestant clubs of the Wall Street mighty) ; the head of one of the largest Wall Street banks confided in deadly earnest to Elliott V. Bell of the *New York Times* that he believed Roosevelt to be literally "a pathological case"; and newspapers containing photographs of Roosevelt were said to be kept from the sight of J. P. Morgan by acolytes fearful for his aging heart.

Morgan was old, and the story itself is no better substantiated than those that were circulated about Roosevelt. What, on firmer evidence, can be said about the quality of guidance provided by the House of Morgan—still at the time Wall Street's moral and intellectual authority—during the Roosevelt-hating era? The record is curiously mixed. No Morgan partner joined the Liberty League, though Morgan himself openly contributed to its activities on occasion. Thomas Lamont, by then effectively the firm's top man, told Harry Hopkins in October, 1934, that he considered Roosevelt to be "the only hope" and "a bulwark for sane policies" and went on to say that he did not consider the New Deal's relief expenditures excessive. But Lamont was the firm's diplomatist. Russell Leffingwell, a lifelong Democrat, went on doggedly sending Roosevelt letters of encouragement and what he hoped was helpful advice, even though Roosevelt always rejected the advice and reacted to the letters with growing coolness. In 1936 Leffingwell and Gilbert, the other Morgan Democrat, dutifully contributed substantial sums to Roosevelt's campaign for a second term (along with virtually no other Wall Streeters, by the way, except W. Averell Harriman and Paul Shields) , but their offers were far more than balanced by the contributions to the Republican cause of the Morgan family and George Whitney. Humanly enough, Leffingwell himself came to be less than a Roosevelt enthusiast. "Russell was a very tolerant man, with a good word for everybody," one of his fellow Democrats in Wall Street has since said. "But I never remotely heard anyone call him a New Dealer."

Suppressed rage, smooth diplomacy, cautiously offered advice, pained silence—these were the elements of Morgan leadership, and, while better than gutter invective and men's room scurrility, they were too negative to keep the Street from doing itself discredit in the form and style of its predestined opposition to Roosevelt. Yet the irrationality of the personal hatred to which the Morgans never publicly gave way, and others did, would seem to have been rooted firmly enough in human psychology. On the one hand, bankers and brokers, far more specifically than businessmen, had indeed been saved from ruin by Roosevelt in 1933, and they knew it. On the other hand, whenever Roosevelt spoke of them or dealt with them, it was invariably with either condescension or contempt. To have a condescending, contemptuous savior is too much for all but the most secure egos, and outside of 23 Wall Street there were few secure egos in Wall Street in those days.

One Wall Street Roosevelt-hater, perhaps the most outspoken and surely the most endearing of them, deserves a niche of his own.

Brooding over his disillusionment with the monetary policies of his former idol the President, James P. Warburg, newly resigned from his Washington duties, persuaded his Wall Street banking associates to extend his leave of absence and spent the early months of 1934 on a long Caribbean cruise, writing a book giving his version of the London Conference and the Warren program. Entitled *The Money Muddle,* and of enough topical interest to be an instant national best seller, it was intended as friendly criticism of Roosevelt's policies, and was accepted as such; Warburg sent the President a prepublication copy "with every good wish" and many protestations of his continued affection and admiration, and got back a "dear Jimmy" letter in which Roosevelt allowed with airy good nature that he had been reading the book "with plenty of interest," and cordially invited his former adviser to "run down and see me some day" to talk it all over. But Warburg never accepted the invitation. Still brooding, and perhaps a bit carried away by his sudden public acceptance as an author—it has happened, after all,

218

to other authors—he wrote in rapid succession two more books extending and enlarging upon the theme of his original smash hit. The first of them, *It's Up to Us,* openly called for modification of three key New Deal measures, the Banking Act, the National Recovery Act, and the Gold Reserve Act; again the author sent the President an advance copy and again he got back a cordial reply, although this time the cordiality had a certain air of coming from between clenched teeth.

The other book—*Hell Bent for Election,* really an extended pamphlet, first serialized in the New York *Herald-Tribune* and then issued in book form in the summer of 1935—was another matter. This time no advance copy went to the White House, and no wonder. As his disillusionment had deepened, Warburg had found himself consorting more and more with the unrestrained Roosevelt-haters; without quite realizing it, he had edged almost into their ranks himself. *Hell Bent for Election* was emphatically not friendly criticism, despite its author's elaborate protestations to the contrary. "It is much as if I had a brother who was a locomotive engineer and developed color blindness," Warburg wrote. "I should continue to love my brother, but I should certainly not feel justified in urging his employers to continue entrusting him with the lives of others." Specifically, he accused Roosevelt of having fulfilled not his own campaign promises but rather those of the Socialist candidate, Norman Thomas, and sweepingly dismissed the whole NRA as a "gigantic fiasco." Far more unforgivable and less brotherly, he attacked Roosevelt's character and motives, accusing the President of having "a rather pronounced flair for the dramatic," of going in for "showmanship rather than statesmanship," and of being irrationally driven by a desire "to be a hero" and "to be liked and admired by the greatest possible number of people." Warburg's conclusion was that "the present administration is doing more harm than good," and that as to Roosevelt himself, "the sooner we have done with him the better."

Hell Bent for Election sold almost a million copies, became the key piece of anti-Roosevelt propaganda, and made its author the darling of Roosevelt-haters of every stripe. And Warburg, as if swept along by his own rhetoric and the howls of delight it elicited, was carried toward the far shore, the Liberty League itself. When the League held its famous January, 1936, dinner launching its campaign against Roosevelt's re-election, at which Al Smith said that the New Deal smelled of "the foul breath of communistic Russia," the agonized brother of the color-blind locomotive engineer was on hand to lend his support to the occasion. So his apostasy was complete at last; he was one with the sullen carpers in the celebrated Peter Arno cartoon who went to the newsreel just to hiss Roosevelt.

But wait. All the while he had been edging toward apostasy, Warburg had been nourishing secret, half-conscious misgivings; and now that he had reached it, the misgivings took over. When the Republicans nominated Landon and Knox, Warburg's support of the ticket was halfhearted. He spent a painful, conscience-stricken summer; then at last in October, seizing as a pretext a Landon speech against reciprocal tariff reductions, he wrote an open letter to Secretary of State Hull announcing that he was reversing himself and now intended to vote for Roosevelt.

Thus ended James P. Warburg's political *Wanderjahr*. After the election he left both banking and active participation in party politics, to devote most of the rest of his life to writing and the cause of world peace. What makes his meteoric career as a Wall Street Roosevelt-hater such an engaging detail in an otherwise most unengaging chapter in American life is his own subsequent explanation of how it all came about. "A most illuminating psychoanalysis," he wrote in his autobiography, eventually opened his eyes to his own motivations. His beloved father's death in 1932 had been swiftly followed by his adoption of Roosevelt as a surrogate father-figure; but then, "unfortunately, Roosevelt proceeded to attack precisely those psychological symbols for which my father had stood: the traditional banking structure . . . and the general concept of 'sound money.' . . . President Roosevelt's actions . . . aroused not only rational misgivings but an irrational unconscious feeling that my substitute father had betrayed the beloved parent whose place he had to a certain extent taken." And so he had violently rejected the false father only to discover his mistake too late.

A handsome apology, to be sure! one perhaps unique in the annals of political confession, and certainly unique in those of Wall Street Roosevelt-hating. Would those other crusty old clubmen, the

splutterers and newsreel-hissers of legend, have been similarly reformed if only they had submitted to the couch? At least no one can
prove the contrary, and it's fun to think so.

IV

The endemic Wall Street insecurity was felt at the Stock Exchange, and one expression of it was a revolt against Richard
Whitney and his stubborn Bourbon regime. But it was a feeble
revolt, and its backers, taken as a whole, must be accounted among
the most reluctant rebels on record.

The issue, simple enough, was whether the Stock Exchange would
continue to be run as a private club as it always had been, or would
become the public-oriented institution its function by that time
clearly called for. As of the end of 1934 the Old Guard, private-club
faction was still firmly enough in the saddle; in that year's elections
Whitney had been smoothly returned for his fifth successive one-
year term as president, and the slate of governors elected with him
had, as usual, been his hand-picked men. Commission brokers—the
potential opposition because they dealt with the public and therefore had a direct financial stake in the public's interest—owned
more than half of all Stock Exchange seats, but occupied only about
one-third of the seats on the Governing Committee, and the per-
petuation of the "ins" on that body from year to year was assured
by a carefully stacked system of nominations and elections.

Still, the commission brokers—the men, after all, who had defied
Whitney by cooperating with the government in the writing of the
Securities Exchange Act—were restive. Their leadership had long
since formed itself into a little group called the Elders, a sort of
Stock Exchange shadow cabinet that met regularly for lunch to
grumble about the arbitrariness of the Whitney faction and discuss
strategy. Despite the presence among them of a real Wall Street
maverick, E. A. Pierce, the Elders were scarcely a flaming liberal
group. Indeed not! One of their number, Grayson M.-P. Murphy,
was soon to become the active and enthusiastic treasurer of the
American Liberty League, and their lawyer, Raoul E. Desvernine,
to become chairman of the Liberty League's legal division. These

were the Wall Street reformers of 1934 and 1935—but when it comes to reformers, Wall Street can hardly ever pick and choose.

In truth, the Elders were caught between fear of Dick Whitney and fear of Joe Kennedy. Above all, they lacked leadership—one man with the personality and drive to stand up to Whitney and beat him and his system in an election. Pierce or Paul Shields wouldn't do, because they were already too well known as rebels to stand a chance of election. A candidate for the assignment finally emerged, more or less by accident, early in 1935. All through the second half of 1934 Kennedy had been hammering away at the Stock Exchange to start reforming itself before the government was forced to step in and do the job, but Whitney had rebuffed him again and again, and when Kennedy had turned to the Elders, he had encountered mainly foot-dragging. At last, out of patience, Kennedy issued a flat ultimatum calling on the Exchange to enact an eleven-point reform program without delay, and, after Whitney had contemptuously ignored it as usual, Kennedy laid the matter on the line to the Elders: "You people say you're friends of mine. Now I want you to endorse the program." Thus goaded, the Elders passed a resolution endorsing the Kennedy program and urging quick action on it. When, at their next meeting, the members of the Governing Committee indignantly denounced this rebellious action, it at first appeared that no one would speak in defense of the Elders since none of them were there—understandably, since Whitney had taken pains to see that none of them were on the Governing Committee. Or almost none. One Elder, a rather junior one at the age of forty-two, was present; he was John Wesley Hanes, senior partner of Charles W. Barney & Company, who had recently slipped into a temporary appointment to the Governing Committee to fill a vacancy. Hanes rose and, in a soft North Carolina accent, vigorously defended the resolution and dared to attack the Exchange Old Guard—right under Richard Whitney's nose. When he sat down, there was a stunned silence. Later, the word the governors applied to Hanes' outburst was "heresy."

So the reformers had a hero—but what a hero! what a reformer! John Wesley Hanes, although by no means a Liberty Leaguer, was hardly out of the revolutionary mold. His family, major textile

222

manufacturers in Winston-Salem, had been the original owners of the Reynolds Tobacco Company and had retained into his time a large enough interest in it to put them among the unassailably rich. After Yale, he had gone into investment banking and, hardly against odds, made a success of it. In the middle 1930s he was one of those gentle, courtly Southerners who used to bring a touch of languid grace to Northern business and professional life, with an air of genuine kindness and a florid, rather pious and sentimental manner; among his pieties was an almost worshipful attitude toward the House of Morgan, which in his canon stood for all that was right and proper, and it was his proudest boast that he could count Lamont, Leffingwell, and George Whitney among his dear friends. His philosophy was pure free-enterprise: that the one thing that makes men go forward on this distracted globe is the hope of reward. Although a good Southern Democrat, a close friend of the Democratic mighty who had attended the 1932 convention in the company of Harry Byrd himself, he had never voted for Roosevelt—not even in 1932, not even for Governor of New York State. In later life he would become a horse-breeder and co-owner of the great Nashua, and would keep a Bible on his desk along with his racing trophies. A model tobacco princeling, then, a fine Southern gentleman of the old school, John Wesley Hanes—but a radical reformer? Only in the Wall Street of 1935.

Hanes and Richard Whitney, the latter the older by four years, had had relations of various sorts for years, but they were scarcely friends. Their families were in contact because their daughters were roommates at Foxcroft, but Hanes opposed Whitney's administration of the Stock Exchange, and, moreover—by some accounts, though not that of Hanes himself—the two men just didn't hit it off. As early as 1932 Hanes had come to the conclusion that Whitney's policies were too unresponsive to public opinion and were consequently doing serious damage to Wall Street's public image. The following year he had gone to the House of Morgan and expressed this view to his friends and idols Lamont and George Whitney. George Whitney had said, "Don't tell me—go over and tell it to Dick." Hanes had done so, and Dick Whitney had given him the same short shrift he habitually gave all his critics. Then in 1934 straight business rivalry, and the suspicion of business vindictiveness, had come between them. Like so many other investment firms that year, Barney & Company had been going through a solvency crisis, and when speculators had launched a campaign of rumor and manipulation to push it over the brink into bankruptcy, Whitney had coolly declined Hanes' plea that he intervene in his capacity as president of the Exchange. The raid failed, and in later years Hanes with Southern gallantry insisted that Whitney's aloofness had not been a reprisal. But can the incident have been entirely out of Hanes' mind when he stood before the august Governing Committee and its bull-necked president early in 1935 and, with fire in his soft voice, spoke the heresy that made him Wall Street's radical champion?

V

Once again, Whitney rallied his forces for a fight. On February 7, immediately after the Elders had come out in the open in opposition to him, he said bitterly at a public dinner at the Plaza, "We have today a new boss. It is the Securities and Exchange Commission. They can do almost anything to us. . . . We are accused, and I in particular, of being arbitrary, antagonistic, noncooperative. Yet the only thing the Stock Exchange and its executives are trying to do is cooperate. . . ." Perhaps; but meanwhile Whitney and his cohorts did not bother to make even a show of cooperation with their opponents within the Stock Exchange. Just as in any private club, nominations for officers were handled by a nominating committee, which annually presented a single, unopposed slate of candidates who could then be smoothly elected by acclamation. This system is, of course, the traditional one by which oligarchies of many kinds perpetuate themselves. But Whitney was in danger of being hoist by his own petard; the nominating committee that had slipped into office in the confusing months following passage of the Securities Exchange Act the previous year was cautiously liberal and anti-Whitney, concerned above all about the Stock Exchange's public reputation. During the two months between the Plaza dinner and the time when the nominating committee was due to present its 1935 slate, the Whitney forces conducted an all-out campaign of power politicking on the Exchange floor and attempting to influence the members of the committee directly. Arms were twisted, deals suggested, threats made; at one point cards were openly circulated on the floor calling for pledges of Whitney votes in the forthcoming election. Eager to drop Whitney as presidential nominee, but not quite daring to, the nominating committee in March planned to duck the issue by naming not one but three nominees for president and letting the membership decide between them in an open election. The nominees were to be Whitney, Hanes, and Charles R. Gay, a mild, likable broker who seemed to be able to get along with both sides in the controversy and was therefore the perfect compromise candidate. But this arrangement quickly came unstuck. Hanes, the putative firebrand, had by this time decided that on thinking it over he would prefer not to be president of the Stock Exchange, or to engage in a public campaign against Whitney, or both; whatever the case, he abruptly and definitively withdrew as a presidential possibility, agreeing only to run for membership on the Governing Committee. As for Gay, the putative compromise candidate, he muddied matters still further by amiably telling Whitney that if Whitney wanted to succeed himself in office—something that he knew very well Whitney wanted to do badly enough to taste it—then he, Gay, would be delighted to vote for him. So the radical tiger had declined to fight, and the moderate tiger had come out in favor of his supposed enemy the lion. Surely a sad situation for the antilion movement at the Stock Exchange.

For a while it looked as if Whitney would remain in office by default. But now the nominating committee, bolstered by the continued prodding of Kennedy and the Elders, mustered its courage and came to the firm decision that Whitney as president had to go; as a sop to him and his supporters he would be nominated for a place on the Governing Committee. The next problem was to persuade Gay to accept the presidential nomination he had been so cheerfully ready to renounce. "Charley, the job's yours," Gay was told heartily by R. Lawrence Oakley, chairman of the nominating committee. "You've got to take it." When the matter was put that way, Gay nervously consented; later he apologized to Whitney for having done so, adding placatingly, "I don't care who wins. But I've told Larry Oakley that I was in this thing for good." The nominating committee, too, had its troubles explaining things to Whitney. Oakley tackled the job, not without qualms; this time it was *his* turn to be nervous. "There's nothing personal in this, Dick," he pleaded, after informing Whitney of the decision to drop him. "It's a matter of public relations." As Whitney's neck flushed crimson, he coldly replied that he might well decide to run for president as an independent, and that, moreover, he had the votes to win. So the fat was in the fire.

Early in April, a month before the election as required by the by-laws, the nominating committee bravely announced its slate: Gay for president, Benjamin H. Brinton, a neutral, for treasurer, and to fill the eleven vacancies on the Governing Committee a list containing eight anti-Whitney men of various stripes—among them Hanes, as well as a little-known twenty-eight-year-old St. Louis broker named William McChesney Martin, Jr.—and only two hard-core Whitney men in addition to Whitney himself. Now Whitney faced the alternatives of giving in gracefully or carrying out his threat to run for president as an independent. He took his problem, as he had so often taken other problems, across Broad Street to his brother George at No. 23. George, with the concurrence of Thomas Lamont, told him in no uncertain terms that an independent candidacy would be far too disruptive and divisive at a time when Wall Street's national reputation was at rock bottom. It was a judgment from which there was no appeal. While he might endlessly defy, snub, and affront his enemies at the Stock Exchange and in Washington, for reasons certainly practical and no doubt psychological Dick Whitney could do none of those things to his elder brother. But if he slunk back from his visit to No. 23 in a self-pitying, et-tu-Brute mood, he was quick in recovering. Whitney was not through yet. He could salvage something from his chagrin. George and Lamont had forbidden only an independent candidacy for *president;* he was still free to sponsor some of his faithful followers as independent candidates for the vacant governorships, and thus bring about a test of strength with the reformers. Perhaps these followers might score smashing victories over the official nominees; perhaps one of those slaughtered in the carnage might be the willy-nilly symbol of reform, John Hanes; and perhaps, yes, perhaps Dick Whitney himself might still show who was the real boss by getting more votes for governor than Gay got for president. In sum, perhaps he could turn the semblance of defeat into the substance of victory.

So back to the floor with their arm-twisting and their pledge cards went the Whitney cohorts. Publicly giving pious assurances of support for Gay as the next president, they privately urged members to withhold their votes from him and thus indicate lack of confidence. They put up three independents, all reliable Whitney men, to oppose the official slate for the vacant governorships. The contest began to attract national attention. The gallant struggle of the Old Guard and its White Knight to hold its ground against progress came to engage financial-page readers almost as much as the prices of stocks. It was Wall Street drama of a new sort.

The election, held on May 13 with twice the usual number of Exchange members voting and with voting booths to ensure secrecy set up on the trading floor for the first time ever, resulted in precisely the smashing, symbolic victory Whitney had hoped for. The three independent candidates for the Governing Committee were swept into office with resounding votes of 844, 898, and 918. Gay got 1,131 votes for president; Whitney, just as he had hoped, topped that with 1,146 for governor. Possibly sweetest of all, the candidate most crushingly defeated for the Governing Committee was John Wesley Hanes; his 371 votes represented by a wide margin the lowest total given anyone running in the election.

VI

The new president of the Stock Exchange was a stout, bespectacled, Methodist, self-made man of sixty, with no special animus against anyone. Born in Brooklyn, Charley Gay had been educated there, too—at P.S. 35 and then at Brooklyn Polytechnic Institute. He had started in Wall Street as a three-dollar-a-week runner back in the 1890s, worked and saved like an Alger hero, at last bought himself a Stock Exchange seat in 1911, become senior partner of Whitehouse & Company in 1919, and served as a governor of the Exchange continuously since 1923. In background and social position he was far, far removed from Dick Whitney; on the other hand, as a floor member he fell naturally into the Whitney faction, and the

227

two men had been business friends for many years. The question now was, To what extent would Gay as president feel compelled to carry out the mandate of the liberals and change or reverse Whitney's policies? It was not long in being answered. The very day after the election the new Governing Committee, at Gay's suggestion, picked as vice president to serve with him E. H. H. ("Harry") Simmons, the man who had preceded Whitney as president—and a man who had never been known as anything but a steadfast Whitneyite. Step by step, in the days following, the Old Guard was allowed to consolidate its power in the supposedly new regime. The powerful Law Committee remained in their hands. The organizational reforms that the SEC and the Elders had called for showed no signs of coming about. And in dealing with the SEC, Gay, although a good deal more friendly and less arrogant than Whitney had been, turned out when the chips were down to be scarcely more cooperative than the old master of intransigence himself. Finally, Paul Shields—along with Pierce, one of the two most wholehearted backers of the reform movement—took Gay to dinner and accused him of having betrayed it.

"What else can I do?" Charley Gay pleaded. "My hands are tied."

He had a point. The Whitneyites, of course, still had a large holdover majority of the Governing Committee, since only a quarter of its seats had been at stake in that year's election. Moreover, by the end of the year they had managed to re-establish such an iron grip on the whole Exchange machinery that any liberal initiative by Gay could be quickly quashed. With the election setback the reform movement had lost its impetus, and Gay had been left a minority president, almost a puppet. It began to appear that Whitney's victory had been a good deal more than symbolic— to appear, indeed, that he was still boss of the Stock Exchange.

And he had another reason for satisfaction. His retirement, or pseudo retirement, had provided the occasion for public manifestations of the extraordinary respect and even devotion he commanded in Wall Street. A couple of weeks after the election he was handed a testimonial signed by almost two thousand employees at all levels of the Stock Exchange and the Stock Exchange Luncheon Club, declaring that "during the past five years Richard Whitney has gained the loyalty, friendship, and confidence of all those who have served under his leadership." Such a thing is not easily stage-managed. There is little reason to believe that the testimonial was not spontaneous or that what it said was not the literal truth.

Somewhat less surprising, everything considered, was the action of the Governing Committee that December 26, when it elected Whitney to a four-year term as one of the six trustees of the Stock Exchange Gratuity Fund. The Gratuity Fund was a mutual-benefit arrangement for the families of deceased members with a treasury running into millions, and its trusteeship, of all posts in the Exchange hierarchy, was perhaps the one calling most clearly for scrupulous and unassailable probity. This time the election was untroubled and the vote unanimous. Liberal or conservative, friend or foe, there was no one on the Governing Committee, or almost anywhere else for that matter, who so much as dreamed of questioning that Dick Whitney, whatever his other qualities, was anything but an exemplar of that one.

Chapter Ten

Rising Action

I

Whitney had fought so hard to hold power out of more than stubborn pride, or the love of power for itself; he needed the influence that power confers for urgent personal reasons. Jersey Lightning was still not sweeping the country, and the price of Distilled Liquors stock was sinking. From its early-1934 high of 45 it went into a long, inexorable decline that in a little more than two years would bring it down to 11.

In 1935, while the Stock Exchange fight was going on, he was feeling the vise of debt beginning to tighten. He had paid off his friend Mellick in full the previous July. But the $100,000 he owed Pierce—or, more accurately, owed E. A. Pierce & Company—was still very much outstanding. Open antagonists in public now, he and Pierce, for reasons that can only be guessed at, in private maintained with elaborate ceremony the relationship of debtor and creditor. Every ninety days, as the loan fell due, Whitney would decorously request an extension, and Pierce would decorously grant it. Eventually the renewals became so numerous that Whitney, possibly with a touch of deadpan humor, took to using a form letter to ask for them: "With sincerest thanks and appreciation, believe me, Dick Whitney." The man who was one of the twin spearheads of the drive to oust Whitney from the Exchange presidency was unfailingly willing to go along with the joke—or, at least, with the request.

The $110,000 debt to Herbert Wellington was still outstanding, and this was in a sense a more difficult matter just because the men were old and close friends. That borrowings between friends can strain or destroy friendships is, of course, notorious. The dynamic of the strain is less often noted. The trouble is that the relationship is entirely one-sided; on the lender falls not only the practical burden, but the moral one as well. The borrower is in the position of testing his friend's loyalty—entitled by the code of friendship to scrutinize the lender for the slightest sign of restlessness or unease that might signal a wavering of faith, and all the while holding the money, too. Let the lender venture to ask for repayment—a dun—and he runs the risk of being accused of impugning his friend's honor. Apart from nominal interest on his money, and the dubious reward of gratitude—pale counters when matched against trust in most relationships between men—there is nothing the lender can win.

Wellington did not ask for his money back from Whitney, or not in 1935. The original loan two years earlier had been for a term of thirty days; it was renewed on request a half-dozen or so times, and then, by mutual consent, made open-ended: Whitney would pay when he conveniently could. The two men met constantly at the Exchange and at their clubs, and from time to time Whitney would say casually, "Duke, I haven't forgotten about that loan and I hope to take care of it." Wellington would nod equally casually; meanwhile, with Spartan correctness he never initiated a single conversation on the subject. But by late 1935, Wellington said later, he had begun to wonder whether Whitney wasn't "imposing a little on my friendship." Moreover, Wellington's partners, who at least technically shared in the risk, were beginning to get openly nervous. Wellington soothed them by continuing to assume personal responsibility in the matter, and by invoking the sacredness of his friendship: Whitney, he told them, was a man of honor, his pledge was "as good as cash in the bank," and he might interpret an abrupt request for repayment as an unfriendly act.

At the same time, of course, Whitney still owed J. P. Morgan & Company half a million dollars and his brother George almost a million; but these debts were in the family, and—the Morgan and George Whitney families being morally and financially what they were—causing no strain. Much worse, Richard Whitney in 1935 was borrowing new money, and not from family or even friends.

That January, he approached Paul Adler, a Stock Exchange floor specialist. The two men's work had thrown them into close and generally harmonious association for over two decades, but their relationship scarcely extended beyond business hours; over the two decades they had dined together on just three occasions. Still, Adler admired Whitney extravagantly.

Whitney said to Adler, "Paul, I want you to do me a great personal favor."

"Boss, I will be happy to do so," Adler replied, without even waiting to hear what was to be asked of him.

Whitney asked for a loan of $100,000 for one week. Adler instantly consented, commenting, "I am glad you asked me." After a number of extensions, Whitney repaid the loan in full. But shortly before making the repayment, he borrowed the same sum, $100,000, from another Stock Exchange member, Otto Abraham, who explained later that he had been willing to make the loan—and also, incidentally, to keep the matter confidential, even from his own staff—out of respect for Whitney's "high honor and integrity." In due time, or rather overdue time, Abraham, too, was paid off.

Both Adler and Abraham happened to be Jewish, and from this it might be inferred that Whitney was suffering the legendary fate of the hard-pressed Western businessman, that of "falling into the hands of the Jews." Such was hardly the case. Interest on the loans, far from calling for a pound of the borrower's flesh, was an inconsequential part of the arrangements. The loans of Adler and Abraham were motivated by neither avarice nor the wish for revenge. Rather, they were favors granted to ease the presumably temporary embarrassment of a man looked up to—and, no doubt, feared a little; to a man, withal, who headed a regime that still systematically excluded Jews from membership in the Exchange power structure. In truth, the Jews were falling into Whitney's hands.

232

All the while, the Street knew nothing of Whitney's borrowings. By ancient Wall Street custom a rigid code of secrecy shrouded personal loans. Gossip about them might impair the borrower's future credit, and, moreover, today's lender knew well enough that he might be tomorrow's borrower. As Wellington once put the matter, "I have always considered that when I loan money to a friend, it was an act that one didn't discuss, even with mutually best friends." Even so, Wellington stretched the code a little once, in the cause of protecting precisely a mutually best friend. It was on Christmas Day, 1935, and Wellington, having slipped off in the afternoon from family doings to the Racquet Club, encountered there George H. Bull, president of the Saratoga Racing Association, and a former Stock Exchange member who had long been close to both Wellington and Whitney. When Bull mentioned that he was considering making a substantial loan to Whitney, Wellington reacted instantly. He strongly advised Bull not to do it without first consulting a lawyer and drawing up a formal note. He gave no elaboration, nor did Bull ask for it; the comment was sufficiently startling—at a club on a Christmas Day—and its implication sufficiently clear. Nevertheless, a week later Bull loaned Whitney $150,000.

II

Most of this money was going straight into Distilled Liquors stock, to which Whitney had by this time decided on a do-or-die commitment. If no one else would buy the sagging stock, he would. Whether or not he dreamed of getting a corner, like Ryan's in Stutz, is not known. Probably he didn't; there were no particular bear raiders to corner; the stock was sinking simply for lack of buyers. At any rate, Whitney, apart from all his unsecured borrowings, had huge bank loans outstanding that were secured by Distilled Liquors stock, and if its price were to drop too low, the banks would call for more collateral, which Whitney didn't have. His alternatives, then, were to support the stock's price by continuously buying it, thereby protecting his bank loans, or to allow the loans to be called and his insolvency exposed. He was in the classic debtor's

233

trap of needing to negotiate new loans to support old ones. Throughout 1936 and 1937 he bought Distilled Liquors by the bushel, effectively pegging its price at around 10—and, of course, constantly needing new money in enormous quantities for the purpose.

And in his quest for new money he soon slipped over the rather fine line between asking and taking.

For years he had been treasurer of the New York Yacht Club, as well as its stock and bond broker. In these capacities he had physical access to the club's securities, and the authorization of the club to dispose of them for its benefit; as a matter of routine, in fact, some of the club's holdings were usually, and properly, kept in the safe in his office. On February 14, 1936, having temporarily run out of Wellingtons, Adlers, and Abrahams willing to lend him short-term money without collateral, he withdrew from his safe $150,200 worth of bonds belonging to the New York Yacht Club, took them to the Public National Bank & Trust Company, and pledged them as part of the required collateral against a loan of $200,000 to Richard Whitney & Company.

This was criminal embezzlement—no more and no less criminal than the less esoteric form of grand larceny practiced by an ordinary bank robber, the chief difference being that Whitney's position of trust gave him the vast advantage of being able to work in secrecy and of not requiring violence or the threat of it. Yet the curious fact is that Whitney—who was no psychopath, but a man of exceptional rationality as well as exceptional intelligence—does not seem to have thought of it as wrong. Much later, a psychiatric report would say that he had "never given a thought to the ethical aspects of what he did." No doubt the psychiatrist was naïve—taken in by Whitney's arrogant stoicism, his refusal to whine. But it is equally probable that, at the time, Whitney did not think of himself as a thief. Rather, he thought of himself as one who would not be a thief no matter what he did; that is, as a moral superman.

He had done it, or something like it, before. As early as 1926, long before he had become the White Knight, long before his strong-man role in the crash had made him famous as well as powerful, he had misappropriated some bonds belonging to the estate of his wife's father, George R. Sheldon, and pledged them against a personal loan to himself. Lifetime income from the bonds went to the testator's daughter, Whitney's wife; and the residuary legatees of the estate were to be Harvard University and St. Paul's School. Three years later, Whitney had paid off the loan and replaced the bonds in the estate. Then in 1932, temporarily strapped again, he had again pledged some Sheldon estate bonds; again, he had later replaced them.

In both cases, no one had been the wiser, and no one had been hurt. The bank robber, having had the use of his loot, had figuratively re-entered the bank and replaced it. But it is impossible to imagine that Whitney saw the thing quite that way. He had only made temporary use of family money; he had merely caused his father-in-law's estate to make him what a wit among embezzlers has described as an "involuntary loan." It is even unlikely that Whitney ever felt the need to go through even such rationalizations as that. What he had done was, alas, very far from uncommon in the Wall Street of his time. Moreover, everything in his particular makeup and surroundings—his patrician background; his instinct for command; his natural hauteur; his antipathy to public authority; the incessant approbation of his peers, his inferiors, his schools, the great world itself—conspired to make him feel that what was placed in his trust was effectively given to him, as so much else in life had always been given to him. Would George Sheldon, if he were living, have loaned him the bonds? Emphatically so! Would Harvard and St. Paul's have minded? Certainly not! The world repeatedly pronounced him a financial wizard as well as a man of the highest integrity. "Your career in the world of finance has now become of nationwide significance," New York University had assured him, in conferring on him a Doctorate of Commercial Science in 1932, the year of the second Sheldon embezzlement. Was he not perhaps doing the family a favor in serving as a trustee of the estate—a favor for which the estate might well want to reciprocate?

In sum, the evidence suggests that his "borrowings" from the Sheldon estate prior to 1936 caused Whitney as many qualms as, and no more than, his unpaid loans from his brother George. One did not like to seek help from relatives, but when one did seek it, it went without saying that one intended to repay. Finely honed conscience may not have been Whitney's predominant trait, as it has seldom been that of men of power, but he was insulated from such conscience as he had by universal approval and the clannishness of the American ruling class in a time when it was under fire. In temporarily taking family funds—Whitney may well have put it to himself—he had taken only what was his own.

Taking New York Yacht Club funds was rather another matter; a man has a sense of owning a club where he feels at home, but not of owning its money. In resorting to this step in the extremity of his situation in 1936, he may have gone through a crisis of conscience, even though never, then or afterward, is he known to have admitted anything of the kind. At the least, he was far too rational and intelligent not to have grasped the practical risks of his action. Now he had crossed his Rubicon; he knew full well that the danger of exposure and scandal was great, and that exposure would bring crashing down in ignominy not just his own life, but with it the old Wall Street of gentlemen and class privilege and *noblesse oblige* whose ethical code, whose justification of its existence, rested squarely on the concept of sacred private honor. Richard Whitney in 1936 knew that he and the class he had come to symbolize were living with the bright sword of danger.

And all for Jersey Lightning!

Meanwhile he went on borrowing—rather, attempting to borrow—more furiously than ever. That May of 1936 he was back to Paul Adler asking for another $100,000. "Paul, can you lend me a hundred for a week or so?" was the way he put it, according to Adler's later recollection; Adler—stopping short, this time, of telling Whitney that he was pleased to have been asked—laconically said "O.K." and went back to his business. He got his money back— not in a week or so, to be sure, but within three months. In June, Whitney took time out to go to his twenty-fifth Harvard class reunion, where he was not surprised to be voted the class' No. 2 man in achievement, second only to Gluyas Williams, the cartoonist. Later that month Mellick came through with a second $100,000, unsecured. In July Whitney got a second $100,000 from Abraham. Sometime during the summer things took an ominous turn when his request for $200,000 from the firm of De Coppet & Doremus was refused for reasons unstated. It is the first recorded case of a flat turndown of a Whitney request for a loan, and it shows clearly enough that by that time the curtain of secrecy shrouding Whitney's promiscuous borrowings was at last beginning to fray. And then in the fall the curtain frayed further, and rumors of the borrowings got back to George Whitney.

Apart from the old debts from the previous decade, the Morgan partner had been largely out of his brother's financial life for years; Dick had come to him for money only twice since 1929. What George Whitney heard now via the grapevine was a good deal less than the whole story; indeed, as it happened, he did not hear about any of the cash borrowings just described. What he did hear about was a group of entirely separate borrowings by Richard Whitney, not of cash but of securities, which, having been borrowed, were promptly pledged as collateral for bank loans; he also got wind of one cash borrowing of $100,000 that was of particular interest in that it came from George F. Baker, Jr., chairman of the First National Bank, son of its renowned founder, and himself one of the most renowned bankers in the country. Wearily, perhaps, George Whitney called his younger brother on the carpet. Dick Whitney readily admitted to those loans—but volunteered no additional information. George Whitney explained that this situation would never do. With the rumors proliferating so wildly, and the facts behind them so blatant, Dick Whitney's credit and that of his firm would shortly be destroyed. Again, as in 1929, George Whitney did not hesitate. He decided that he would forthwith lend his brother whatever sum might be necessary to clear up all his unsecured debts to others, and enable him to make still another fresh start; and to relieve himself of the detail work of determining what that sum should be, George Whitney asked his brother to submit a balance sheet of his and his firm's affairs to a younger Morgan partner, Henry P. Davison.

The balance sheet that Richard Whitney accordingly submitted in December was far from complete or candid; for example, it omitted the fact that some of his customers' securities were improperly pledged. Davison sensed the lack, but not the nature of what was lacking. Why, indeed, should he have sensed it? Promiscuous borrower or not, Dick Whitney was still a member of the Morgan family, still a member of that select circle of "good fellows," the Morgan creditors, still the Morgan broker at the Stock

237

Exchange, still a member of the Porcellian and the Links and the Knickerbocker! That fraud or larceny should be in the picture was unthinkable. On the last day of 1936 Davison wrote Whitney: "Dear Dick: Sorry to ask you to go to this additional trouble, but it would be very helpful to have a detailed list of all collateral under each loan. Sincerely yours, Harry." Such a list, if truthfully submitted, would have laid bare Whitney's defalcations and, it is possible to imagine, changed the course of Wall Street history. But during the first week of 1937 Dick Whitney, in the course of conversation about the jam he had got himself into, succeeded in persuading both his brother and Davison that the additional information was not necessary. Davison, thus misled, came to the conclusion that the sum needed to put George's brother back on his feet was $650,000. Accordingly, on January 8 George Whitney wrote out to his brother a check for that sum—an additional, unsecured loan for an indeterminate period, on top of the huge sum that Dick already owed him and had owed him for years. And thus, as far as George Whitney knew, he had saved his brother from himself once more.

III

Of course, he hadn't. Because the younger brother had not dared, or at any rate had not chosen, to confess to the elder that he was now an embezzler as well as a bad investor, and that the new loan had merely improved his situation from critical to desperate. After the $650,000 had been used to settle the securities loans and the Baker loan, the rumors, for good reason, continued. Reacting to them—and also to word that the bottomless well of riches and good nature, George Whitney, was again firmly behind his brother— Duke Wellington in January, 1937, at last decided that, friendship notwithstanding, the time had come for him to ask Whitney point-blank for his money back. Cool, but correct, Whitney returned it in April—three years and three months after the original due date. In an attempt to raise the cash for this purpose, he went again to Abraham asking for $100,000. Abraham risked insulting Whitney by cutting his offer to $65,000, no more; Whitney snapped the offer up, and raised the rest of his debt to Wellington elsewhere. Shortly before this, he had embarked on the venture in larceny that was to prove his undoing.

On the third Monday of February, 1937, the trustees of the Stock Exchange Gratuity Fund, to which the Governing Committee had so gratifyingly named Whitney shortly after his deposition as president of the Exchange, held their regular monthly meeting. Such meetings were always pleasant social events. Trusteeship of the Gratuity Fund was very much an Old Guard preserve; the chairman of the trustees was good old Harry Simmons, and all the other trustees were old friends and allies of Whitney except President Gay, and he, of course, had been coming around more and more lately. No wild-eyed reformers like Pierce, Shields, or Hanes were present to upset the even tenor of things. The only nontrustee who sat in on the meetings was George W. Lutes, an Exchange employee assigned, as part of his job, to serve as clerk of the Gratuity Fund. Lutes, in short, was a minion. Whitney had another reason for feeling at home with the Fund; as with the Yacht Club, his firm was its broker. At the February meeting, along with amiable chitchat, the trustees as a routine matter directed Richard Whitney & Company to sell certain Fund-owned bonds having a face value of about $350,000, and use the proceeds to buy other, more promising bonds. Whitney subsequently carried out the letter of the instructions; that is, he sold the bonds he was directed to sell and bought those he was directed to buy. What he did not carry out was a part of the instructions so wholly taken for granted that it had been unstated. He did not deliver the newly purchased bonds to the Gratuity Fund.

The following month, the trustees authorized a further sale of bonds worth $225,000. This time, for technical reasons, the sale was not made, or not until many months later; meanwhile, Whitney simply took over the Fund's bonds and held them. So it went month after month. By that November somewhat more than a million dollars in bonds and cash belonging to the Gratuity Fund—almost half of its total assets—were missing from the Fund's treasury because they were in the custody of its broker.

What Whitney had been doing, as the reader will have no trouble deducing, was illegally pledging the Gratuity Fund assets against further bank loans to himself and his firm. It was, by all odds, his riskiest defalcation so far—a theft not from family or club but from an organ of the Stock Exchange itself. The Fund's trustees did not normally consult its books. But one man, in the line of normal duty, did. The man who quite inevitably knew, over the months between February and November, that assets of the Fund were missing because they were being held by Whitney, was the clerk George W. Lutes—a rather meek and trusting man by all evidence, who did not assume that Whitney was using the Fund's bonds for his own purposes; indeed, according to his later testimony he never dreamed of such a thing. Rather, he assumed that Whitney and his office staff were merely fashionably offhand about the paperwork of getting the Fund assets back where they belonged. As a meticulous clerk, however, Lutes did feel that for the bonds to remain so long in the broker's hands was less than the "orderly and proper way" to do business. Therefore on five separate occasions between March and late summer he reminded Whitney that the bonds had not yet been delivered to the Fund, and inquired when Whitney would find it convenient to bring them over. On each occasion, Whitney gave approximately the same answer: he was very busy, he had meant to do it but hadn't got around to it; he would make the delivery shortly; he would let Lutes know.

Lutes never doubted that Whitney meant what he said. (Presumably, in a sense, he *did* mean it; if only Distilled Liquors would suddenly get on its feet and its stock go rocketing up, he would pay off everybody!) Ostensibly for this reason, all summer Lutes never mentioned the continued absence of the bonds to any of the other trustees of the Gratuity Fund. But there seems to have been another reason for his silence. Commenting later on Whitney's personality as it appeared in his relations with Exchange employees, Lutes said that Whitney had been "sort of sharp. . . . He was a man of great importance. He kept to himself. He was friendly enough, but . . . you could not talk to him if he was busy. . . . I was under him as an employee of the Exchange and I am only a clerk. . . . Frankly, I was afraid of him." Which would seem to shed light on why Whitney was not particularly worried about exposure by George W. Lutes.

And others, not so lowly or humble, were getting sharp replies from him, too; it is interesting that through the summer of 1937, as his financial plight worsened and the web of his deceptions grew more tangled, his hauteur seems actually to have increased. No compromise with his Groton-Harvard accent and manner, his Bourbon political and social views, his patronizing air toward upstarts, accompanied his Gargantuan panhandling. He never tugged a forelock—because he couldn't. That his panhandling continued, and on a Gargantuan scale, is recorded. Distilled Liquors by autumn was down to 9, and Richard Whitney & Company was pegging it there virtually unassisted, by meeting all offers; during the whole of 1937 the firm was the buyer in over 80 percent of all transactions in the stock. Down this rathole dollars by the hundreds of thousands simply disappeared, and more were constantly needed. George Whitney, who had been taken seriously ill shortly after making his bail-out loan, was unavailable, convalescing in the South. Once Whitney asked Pierce, whom he still owed the $100,000 from 1933, for *half a million dollars* more; Pierce, of course, turned him down. (Later Pierce was asked if he didn't think that was a terribly large amount to be asked for; he replied that he didn't consider it especially large "in the Wall Street sense.") In mid-September Whitney asked Abraham for $100,000, and this time was offered only $30,000, which he eagerly accepted; the declining scale of Abraham's loans was barometrically charting Whitney's descent to disaster. That same month he mortgaged his New Jersey estate for $300,000.

IV

Public life was meanwhile still impinging on him, and he on it. More than ever now he was the power behind the scenes at the Stock Exchange; and now, after a marked lull in 1936, the war between the Stock Exchange and the SEC was moving toward a showdown confrontation. In midsummer 1937 William O. Douglas, a tough-minded professor of law with leftish ideas, was appointed to take over the reins of the SEC from James M. Landis, the man who had succeeded Kennedy in 1935. Landis, a practical man of legal training and legal turn of mind, had been generally conciliatory toward Wall Street, but Douglas, the product of a State of Washington sheep ranch with a Westerner's distrust of slick Easterners and their ways comparable to that of the Populist legislators who had denounced Wall Street a decade earlier, was expected to be another matter. And rightly. Even before taking office, Douglas had resolved to force the Exchange truly to reform its structure, to cease operating as a private club, or face the prospect of nationalization in everything but name.

Sensing that a showdown fight was at hand, Wall Street contrived to strike the first blow. It was Charley Gay, the backslid reformer, who did the striking. In his Stock Exchange annual report, published in mid-August, he bluntly accused the SEC of harassing the Exchange and its members, maintained that the SEC had already hamstrung the market to the verge of destroying it, and left the clear implication that the Exchange demanded nothing less than repeal of the Securities Exchange Act and abolition of the SEC. The Exchange's cards were on the table—and they were Whitney cards; the Gay report expressed the Whitney hard line precisely, and obviously signaled the return of the Whitney faction to effective control of Exchange policies after two years in limbo. In September Douglas took office with fire in his eye. But before he had time to master the routine of his job, much less prepare a riposte to Gay, the unexpected happened. Peace emissaries, perhaps even surrender negotiators from the enemy camp, appeared in his. They were Pierce and Shields, the indefatigable reformers and commission brokers, who, both morally outraged and materially damaged by the way things were going at the Exchange, presented themselves without prior introduction at Douglas' Washington office.

Pierce, speaking for the visitors, abruptly asked Douglas, "What would you think of reorganization of the Stock Exchange?"

What would he think of it? It was the one goal he had set for his administration of the SEC. Douglas is said to have slapped his knee in delight and incredulity. "Would you mind saying that again?" he asked.

Pierce and Shields would not mind; they repeated, and amplified, saying the very things Douglas had been thinking: that the Exchange was being run like a private club, that the Old Guard that still controlled it was hopelessly out of date, that the proper solution was an entirely new organization with an independent paid president put in charge. Thus the stage was set for Douglas to move toward his objective stealthily, through this doughty fifth column within the Exchange itself, rather than through head-on attack. The only question was whether the Pierce-Shields faction had enough power to be useful. But before he could do anything, further events intervened. Two days after the Pierce-Shields visit—on October 18—the stock market, which had been declining since August, suddenly collapsed in panic. All summer the clouds of national recession had been gathering. The boomlet of the preceding two years had been based on government spending pure and simple; now Secretary of the Treasury Morgenthau finally prevailed on President Roosevelt to make a real effort to balance the national budget. The resulting cutbacks in federal spending did not balance the budget, but they all but ended the New Deal and emphatically ended the boomlet. Commodity prices, at a seven-year high early in 1937, went into a nosedive as buying power dried up in response to decreased government spending; strikes became epidemic; corporate dividends were cut; the familiar deflation spiral took over. On top of all that, the Gay report in August unsettled stock investors with its portents of Stock Exchange intransigence like that of 1934, and another long, tedious Wall Street–Washington bloodletting. What was most surprising was that the market collapse had not come sooner.

When it came, it was most frightening for the memories it aroused. Here it all was again—that nervous hum of talk outdoors in Wall Street every day, the worried crowds in the board rooms and outside them, and on the Exchange floor the constant appearance of huge blocks of stock for which no one would bid at any price, the sense of bottomlessness—a reprise of 1929, a sickening déjà vu, and, with panic feeding itself as usual, the market by the end of 1937 would have lost nearly all of its painful gains since 1934. The Stock Exchange and the SEC were not drawn closer together by the disaster. On the contrary, each blamed it on the other, the Exchange maintaining that the new crash merely bore out what Gay had said, and the SEC countering with the charge that it was a direct consequence of the Exchange's backward-looking and self-seeking mismanagement.

In this atmosphere of rancor and crisis, negotiations looking toward Stock Exchange reorganization hobbled forward—with

Whitney, simultaneously working so frantically toward the reorganization of his private affairs, doing all he could to cause the hobble. On October 20 Shields in Washington saw Joe Kennedy—out of office now, but still in official favor and acting as a personal emissary of the President. In picturesque language Kennedy made it clear that the President was unequivocally behind Douglas' determination that the Exchange reform itself or be taken over. Back in Wall Street the next day, Shields passed along this information to a grim-faced group representing the Exchange power structure—Gay, Simmons, the lawyer Roland Redmond, Gayer Dominick, and, of course, Dick Whitney. Impressed, and a bit intimidated perhaps, the majority of the Old Guardsmen were willing to concede that the politic moment had come to surrender gracefully, to agree in principle to reorganization. But one man held out, and held out so forcefully that the memorandum to Roosevelt that finally came out of the meeting tersely and arrogantly informed the President of the United States that the Stock Exchange had reorganization "under consideration." No more—the Exchange would decide what was best. The holdout, and principal author of the memorandum, was Richard Whitney, who, it was later reported by some of the participants, had been the most commanding and assured man in the room. Moralists who believe that secret debt and long-pursued wrongdoing undermine the character may well take note.

There followed, over the ensuing month while the market plunged on down, a confused series of skirmishes leading to stalemate. In the last week of October Shields took the Stock Exchange's highhanded memorandum to Hyde Park and there apologetically presented it to Roosevelt, who, logically enough, was merely confirmed in his conviction that the Exchange was hopeless and must be dealt with ruthlessly. But soon afterward Pierce and Shields, still gamely fighting for compromise, rounded up a coalition Wall Street delegation—Simmons and Shields included so as to give representation to both factions, Whitney excluded as too infuriating to everybody but his friends—to go to Washington for one last try at an accommodation with the SEC. They went, and were greeted with harsh words from Douglas: "The job of regulation's got to be done. It isn't being done now and, damn it, you're going to do it or we are. . . . If you just go on horse-trading, I'll step in and run the Exchange myself."

On a November Saturday a couple of weeks later, Gay, Shields, and Douglas, among others, spent some twelve hours in a private room in the Yale Club of New York, wrangling acrimoniously and unproductively. The only outcome of this session was that the matter of reorganization was referred to the Exchange's Law Committee—in other words, to Richard Whitney; the Law Committee was just as much a Whitney preserve as the Gratuity Fund. The fate it suffered there was what might have been expected. After due deliberation, the Law Committee concluded that reorganization with a paid president was inpracticable, and that negotiations with the SEC should therefore be broken off. It drafted a harsh letter to Douglas saying so.

That was on Friday, November 19. The following Monday, Richard Whitney's public and private careers came simultaneously to the point of crisis.

That morning his Law Committee formally approved the harsh letter; when an Exchange lawyer delivered it to Douglas in Washington a few hours later, the SEC chairman merely nodded and said grimly, "All right, then, we'll take the Exchange over."

Early that afternoon, when the Gratuity Fund trustees held their regular monthly meeting, Whitney, who was having a busy day with affairs of state, passed it up. This proved to be a costly slip. The clerk Lutes, emboldened by the absence of the man he found so formidable a presence, mustered his courage at last to inform the other trustees that Whitney had now been holding cash and bonds belonging to the Fund for months on end.

The interesting reaction to this bombshell on the part of the trustees, and in particular of their chairman, Simmons, was one of surprise and annoyance—the surprise occasioned by the fact that none of them could imagine Whitney doing such a thing, and the annoyance curiously directed chiefly not at the absent Whitney but at the present Lutes. What Simmons criticized the clerk for was not having mentioned the matter sooner; is it possible, too, that Lutes found in Simmons' tone some hint of rebuke for his presumptuousness in implying—in merely raising the possibility—that Richard

Whitney was guilty of wrongdoing rather than merely of careless-
ness? Whatever the case, Lutes felt that he had been thoroughly,
and unjustly, chastised. "He spoke quite sharply. He seemed to be a
little peeved," the clerk later complained of Simmons. The lot of
spear-carrier in the wars of the gods is not a happy one.

Immediately after the meeting, Simmons telephoned Whitney's
office. Whitney was out, and Simmons talked to F. Kingsley Rodewald, one of Whitney's nominal partners, who, like all of them, had
no personal investment in the firm and was for practical purposes
really not so much a partner as an employee. Simmons told Rodewald (who, it later appeared, had known nothing of the whole
matter) that his firm was holding Gratuity Fund cash and bonds
that were long overdue; and the mystified Rodewald assured Simmons that they would be returned the next day.

At around noon the next day, Whitney called on Simmons at his
office. We may imagine the complex moods of the two old friends
and allies at this encounter—Simmons suspicious, and feeling dis-
loyal for his suspicions, and desperately seeking reassurance that they
were wrong; Whitney forcing himself to be calm and casual, guard-
ing against the wrong word or gesture that would give him away;
both thinking of the enormous implications, for Wall Street and
even perhaps the nation as well as themselves, of what was at stake
between them. Whitney, in any case, asked for a one-day delay in
making the deliveries; his office was temporarily short-handed, he
explained, and it was not convenient for him to get the paperwork
involved in the restoration of the assets done that day. Simmons
replied, carefully and regretfully, that as chairman of the Fund
trustees he did not feel he had the right to grant such a request, and
asked Whitney to make every effort to return the assets that same
afternoon. Whitney said he would do the best he could.

His back was to the wall at last. At that moment he had $657,000
worth of Gratuity Fund bonds pledged as collateral on loans from
the Corn Exchange Bank, and, in addition, he owed the Fund in
cash $221,508.18. Yet the total cash he and his firm had on hand was
just under $75,000. He could neither release the bonds nor repay
the cash. From Simmons' office he went the only place he could
go—to his brother at 23 Wall. This time he did not evade. He had,
he told his appalled brother, pledged as collateral a sum of secu-

246

rities belonging to a customer, and was unable to meet a demand for their return. The customer, he went on, was the Stock Exchange Gratuity Fund, and the sum was substantial.

Richard Whitney later described his brother's reaction to this information: "He was terribly disturbed and aghast that it could have been done and asked me many, many times why I had done it, and just couldn't understand it—thunderstruck, as he had reason to be."

(George Whitney said later: "I asked him how he could have done it . . . and he said he had no explanation to offer.")

The thunderstruck one asked what sum would be required to make possible proper delivery. The younger brother, after some calculating, replied that he regretted to say it came to $1,082,000. George Whitney apparently did not blanch. He saw his duty. But he did not have that sum in his pocket—or, at the moment, in his bank account either. Accordingly, he immediately went to his senior partner Lamont. To Lamont he explained that his brother had misappropriated from "some customer"—he was no more specific than that—and asked Lamont to lend him the money to bail Dick out.

Lamont said: "Well, this is a devil of a note, George. Why, Dick Whitney is all right—how could he mishandle securities, even for a moment, no matter what the jam?"

George Whitney said, "I don't know, it is an inexplicable thing; it is an isolated instance; but he has got to deliver them tomorrow, and I am going to help him out; I have got to help him out, of course."

Lamont said, "I think you are dead right. Certainly I will help you to help your brother; certainly." Told the sum required, Lamont said, "Well, count on me. I am going South for some golf immediately after Thanksgiving. Put it in whatever shape you like and I will O.K. the ticket."

The following morning—November 24, the day before Thanksgiving—Thomas Lamont wrote George Whitney a check for $1,082,000 representing a personal loan at 4 percent annual interest, and George Whitney immediately in effect endorsed it over to Richard Whitney. Using this money to repay the Corn Exchange Bank, Richard Whitney that morning released the Gratuity Fund bonds. Between twelve-thirty and one he delivered them and the cash, without comment, to Simmons, whereupon Lutes, in the presence of Whitney and Simmons, put the bonds in the Gratuity Fund's vault and deposited the cash in its bank account. Whitney had missed Simmons' deadline by a day, but he had met the extension he had asked for; above all, he had delivered, and now all was in order.

So far as Simmons, the other trustees, and even Lutes were concerned, the incident was closed: Whitney's office short-handedness was the true reason for the delay in delivery, and his languid way of doing business the only occasion for the whole episode. For the present, then, no one knew for certain that Richard Whitney was an embezzler except George Whitney and Thomas Lamont. One other man, a couple of weeks later, was vouchsafed partial knowledge of the affair. George Whitney, in order to repay part of Lamont's million-dollar loan to him, needed permission to withdraw funds from his capital account with J. P. Morgan & Company, and so went to the only man who was empowered to grant such permission. The man was J. P. Morgan. George Whitney said, "Dick got into an awful jam in November, and I went to Tom Lamont when you were not here and he loaned me the money. And so I want to pay him, and will you let me take it out?"

Morgan said, "Certainly." And it was done.

"An awful jam"—horses? women? No, Morgan (who knew Richard Whitney only slightly) said later, he had realized it must be a business matter—"The sum was too big for anything else." He had delicately refrained from inquiring further into the affairs of his partner's brother.

Three men, then: Morgan knew of a million-dollar "jam," Lamont knew it was a criminal misappropriation, George Whitney knew it was a criminal misappropriation from the Stock Exchange Gratuity Fund. And these three men, figures of legend in their own time, by instinct kept silence—without even verbally agreeing to do so. Thus the rich wine of friendship and class loyalty, of brothers and partners and wives and schools and clubs, outmatched the paler, watery moral vintage of social conscience.

Chapter Eleven

Catastrophe

I

George Whitney devoted Thanksgiving Day to trying to salvage his brother's shattered affairs, and perhaps, too, his shattered opinion of his brother's character. That morning, at his insistence, Richard Whitney came to his house and laid before him a hastily assembled set of figures purporting to show the condition of Richard Whitney & Company as of that moment. The figures, which Richard Whitney would later admit were false, showed the firm to be in the black to the extent of about one million dollars. The elder brother, however, did not question the *bona fides* of the accounting—only Dick's high valuation of the enormous amount of Distilled Liquors stock that by this time had come to constitute most of the assets of Whitney & Company. After marking the stock down to a more realistic valuation, George Whitney concluded that the firm was still in the black by perhaps half a million—provided the stock could somehow be sold. He also concluded that the Distilled Liquors debacle demonstrated that Dick's business judgment had gone to pieces, and that the best course now would be for Dick to get out of the brokerage business as quickly as possible, before other debacles ensued. Someone ought to be found who would want to take over a firm with such a fine reputation extending over two decades—some wealthy man, say, might want to put his son into it. Shocking as the notion of giving up his very foothold in the world he had lately ruled must have been to Richard Whitney, he responded like a younger brother whose elder brother had just saved him from a desperate jam by lending him a million dollars; he agreed.

The next step was taken even without waiting for the holiday to be over. George Whitney telephoned his brother's old friend Harry Simmons and asked him to come over and join the brothers that afternoon. Simmons, taken aback, pleaded that he was committed to church and then a family dinner. Nevertheless, late that afternoon he came to George Whitney's house to confer with the two brothers, the elder of whom outlined the situation and explained the plan. Nobody quite came out and said so, but it was clear enough why Simmons had been so hurriedly and urgently invited, if not summoned. Obviously the thought was that *he* might be the man to take over Richard Whitney & Company. Simmons was not having any of that. Without even looking at Richard Whitney's sheet of figures, he volunteered the information that he knew nothing about bonds—ostensibly the principal business of Whitney & Company—and therefore wasn't in the market.

A mood of disappointment settled over the conference. The conversation trailed off in discussion of various possible methods of disposing of the business; it was agreed among the three, for one thing, that a sale of the firm would be preferable to outright liquidation because of the value of its celebrated name. It was agreed that in the days following, Richard Whitney would devote himself energetically to the related matters of finding a buyer for his firm and finding a way—*some* way—of converting all that Distilled Liquors stock, delicately referred to by the conferees as the "slow assets," into cash.

No one at any time mentioned the incident of the Gratuity Fund.

The day after Thanksgiving, George Whitney mentioned to his partner Lamont that he had decided Dick was no longer "capable of handling a business properly and adequately," and that accordingly he was "going to get him to wind up his business." "Well,"

Lamont replied, with Morgan understatement, "I should think that was a good thing." That same weekend, both George Whitney and Lamont left New York for their long-planned vacations in the South. As for Simmons—who, it will be remembered, had no firm evidence that Whitney had embezzled from the Gratuity Fund, and who, indeed, stated later that at this time he had not the faintest doubts as to Richard Whitney's integrity—he had several meetings with Whitney during December at the Stock Exchange Luncheon Club, in the course of which he inquired how the plans for liquidation were coming along. Slowly, Whitney replied, mentioning one group or another that he thought might be interested in taking over the Distilled Liquors account or even the whole firm. In fact, the plans were not proceeding at all; nobody wanted the stock or the firm, and Whitney was continuing his frantic efforts to support the market price of Distilled Liquors and for this purpose, of course, to borrow more money. Just before Christmas Adler let him have another $100,000, which this time was repaid on the button a week later; but the harder-boiled Abraham, asked for the same sum, this time came through with only $15,000—almost an insult, but Whitney nevertheless took it. On January 3, 1938, Whitney had to report to George, back from the South, that his liquidation negotiations had "fallen through."

Meanwhile Richard Whitney's career as the White Knight was in its appropriately quixotic last phase. Privately defeated and dishonored, he played to the hilt the last act of his public role as man of iron principle. Gay had decided by Thanksgiving Day that there was nothing for the Stock Exchange to do but give in gracefully to Douglas and the SEC, and reform itself from top to bottom. The alternative, he understood clearly now, was just what Douglas had warned of—a "takeover" by Washington. Early in December, with the reluctant approval of the Stock Exchange governors, Gay put together a new group, composed partly of outsiders to the Stock Exchange and headed by Carle C. Conway, chairman of the board of Continental Can, and notably including the New Dealer A. A. Berle, Jr., to make recommendations as to reorganization of the Stock Exchange. Here was an all-but-formal concession of defeat; everyone understood that the Conway committee would recommend reorganization of the Exchange along the lines proposed by the

251

SEC, and presumed that the Exchange would have to accept the recommendation. Whitney's Law Committee stubbornly objected to both the existence of the Conway committee and its generally liberal makeup, but in vain. Majority sentiment in the Exchange leadership, while probably still privately on Whitney's side, had opted for expediency; Whitney almost alone continued to stand on principle. By the first of January the Conway committee was writing its report; on the twenty-seventh, when the report was published, it was found to recommend everything—the paid president, the technical staff, the nonmember governors, the provisions for increased influence of liberals within the Exchange—that Douglas had wanted in the first place. Gay instantly endorsed the report in full, and Douglas warmly commended it. To emphasize the new mood of peace and harmony between Wall Street and Washington, the newest appointee to a seat on the SEC was the Morgan-worshiping North Carolinian John Wesley Hanes, who, interestingly enough, thereby became the first deep-dyed Wall Streeter since Joe Kennedy to join the New Deal in any top-level domestic capacity.

The long war was all but over at last; a stage had been reached when hostages were being exchanged. But Whitney was not done standing on principle. On January 31 the Governing Committee met to consider the Conway report. Overwhelming sentiment was for immediate and unconditional acceptance. Only Whitney and his cohorts, their ranks thinned to a pathetic few, held out, insisting that the report be accepted only in a general way, leaving leeway for rear-guard struggles on each individual provision, along the lines of the famous fight against the Securities Exchange Act. So great was Whitney's eloquence that for a moment it appeared he might still win the day. But Gay, stepping down from the presidential rostrum into the well of the governors' chamber to emphasize the gravity of what he had to say, replied with an impassioned exhortation that the Exchange at last stop maneuvering and temporizing and accept the inevitable with good grace.

Acceptance was unanimous—but for a single vote. It was, as a matter of fact, to be Whitney's last vote as a Stock Exchange governor.

II

During January George Whitney applied himself one last time to his brother's affairs, this time taking over the thankless task of personally trying to manage a liquidation of Richard Whitney & Company. Had he succeeded, he would later have been in trouble himself, since the firm, as his brother had not told him, was insolvent. But he did not succeed. His chief thought now was that the rescuer might be his own firm—that Morgan's itself "might conceivably in some way" arrange to take over the Distilled Liquors stock as collateral for a new loan giving Whitney & Company the cash that would make it more appetizing to a prospective buyer. If the matter were viewed as strictly a business proposition, one formidable obstacle to this course of action was that Whitney & Company still owed Morgan's all but $26,000 of the half-million dollars Whitney had borrowed back in the dark ages of 1931. Nevertheless, George Whitney doggedly, and maybe by this time a little sheepishly, asked Francis Bartow, the Morgan partner most versed in common stocks, to look over the Whitney Distilled Liquors portfolio with a view to seeing whether it might somehow meet his firm's standards for collateral on a new loan.

Bartow had his troubles. Digging into the affairs of Distilled Liquors, he found that the company's assets consisted mainly of about 550,000 gallons of Jersey Lightning ("brandy," Bartow called it elegantly) and one million gallons of cider. As he recounted later, he asked himself, "How can any man living determine that such a volume of liquor can be sold within six months or within a year?" Perhaps some man living could have determined it, but Bartow could not, and neither could the two of his other partners whom he consulted. Thus the matter of the new loan remained in abeyance, and the crisis of Whitney & Company dragged on.

But meanwhile something else had happened. Rumors of financial stringency at Whitney & Company had at last reached the place where they could do the most harm—the Stock Exchange—and set in motion an inexorable chain of events. Simmons, right after

Thanksgiving, had tortured himself with the notion that it was his duty to repeat the tale of Whitney's slowness in producing the Gratuity Fund assets to the Stock Exchange's Business Conduct Committee, its disciplinary body. On reflection, though, he had decided that since Whitney had come across with the assets and everything was now square, there was no call for such talebearing on his part. And now there re-enters our story a character who has been missing from it for a long time: Sell 'em Ben Smith, the bull-necked, bellowing speculator and pool operator and the public villain in the bear market of 1930 and 1931. In mid-December President Gay invited Smith, now a solid, respected member of the Exchange community, to lunch privately in his office. During the lunch Gay asked Smith what he thought could be done to create better public feeling toward the Stock Exchange.

The two men later differed on precisely how Smith had replied. Smith said, "I told him I didn't think he would ever be able to do it as long as he had the Old Guard in there. . . . I cited Mr. Whitney, and I told him that the quicker he got rid of him the better off the Exchange would be; that I felt that he was in a large measure responsible for the discredit in which the Exchange stood today. He wanted to know what I had against him, and I . . . said that he was broke and owed money all over the Street and I didn't think it was befitting for him to be one of the leading governors of the Exchange." Gay later corroborated all of this except that he vehemently denied that Smith had said that Whitney was "broke." He further commented that Smith's attitude toward Whitney, as expressed by his manner during the lunch, had been antagonistic, bitter, and angry.

Perhaps so; the self-made Irishman and the haughty Brahmin were set against each other by almost every *casus belli* that the harsh little society of Wall Street and the harsh big society of the United States could offer them. What had come between them since 1931 and 1932, when Whitney's fervent defense of short selling in Washington had been, after all—in general if not in particular—a defense of Smith? We do not know; but it is easy enough to imagine some offhand slight by the Brahmin or some tactless crudity by the Irishman, at one time or another, on the Exchange floor or some-where else in the little world they both inhabited. At all events, because of Smith's evident hostility toward Whitney, Gay discounted much of what he had heard. In the month following the lunch he made no effort to inquire into the financial affairs of Whitney & Company. But he was, inevitably, put on the alert for such news when it came.

By the kind of irony that life contrives with ease where art wouldn't dare, the rumor that did start action was a wholly false one. One day in mid-January, John B. Shetlar, Stock Exchange specialist in the stock of Greyhound Corporation, noticed what he called "distress selling" in Greyhound. "It came in five-hundred-share lots," Shetlar would recall later, "but was continuous"; moreover, the lots, coming from many different brokers, "were thrown in for sale at the market regardless of price." Somehow or other—without evidence, but relying on the sixth sense about market operations without which no floor specialist could survive—Shetlar came to the conclusion that the distress selling originated with Richard Whitney & Company (in spite of the blind provided by the multiplicity of brokers) and was the tip-off that that firm was in dire trouble. As a matter of fact, later investigation showed that during mid-January not a single share of Greyhound was offered for sale by Whitney & Company on behalf of either itself or its customers.

If he knew that a member firm was in bad trouble, it was Shetlar's clear-cut duty as a member to notify the authorities. Conscientiously acting on his hunch, he went to Duke Wellington, in his capacities as an Exchange governor and close friend of Whitney. He told Wellington of the distress selling and of his belief as to its source, whereupon Wellington nodded and replied, "I'll take care of the matter." Wellington immediately went to the proper Exchange authority—Howland S. Davis, chairman of the Business Conduct Committee—and passed along what he had heard, pleading with Davis that, in any action that Davis might see fit to take, Wellington's name as the informant be kept out in consideration of his personal relations with Whitney. Davis agreed to that. And then a strange thing happened. Wellington had scarcely moved from the spot on the Exchange floor where he had the conversation with Davis when he was given a message that Whitney wanted to see him. Upon his meeting Whitney, the latter asked for a loan of

$25,000, unsecured. Wellington, remembering the years he had waited to get back his original loan, had already turned down one request by his old friend for $100,000, the previous November. Now, with Shetlar's report to add to what he knew already, he had no doubt what he had to say. His answer was no.

The chairman of the Committee on Business Conduct went into action. Howland Davis was by background and inheritance a potential Old Guardsman; son of an old-school gentleman broker, he had grown up in a house in Murray Hill across Madison Avenue from J. P. Morgan's and had gone to the Morgan daughters' coming-out parties; as a broker himself, he was often thought to be a "Morgan man" because he had social relations with several of the Morgan partners, but in fact his firm was never a house pet of No. 23 in a business way. Davis had met both George and Dick Whitney in their boyhood and his, and had taken an instant dislike to them—as he put it years later, he found the two boys "perfect snobs" and "pains in the neck." Still, long after that, when Davis had become a Stock Exchange governor and had thus found himself often in Dick Whitney's company, he had modified his opinion as to that brother, and even become cautiously fond of him, though never close. As to Wall Street politics, for all his connections Davis had never been an Old Guardsman, but neither was he a reformer; as an independent he had remained aloof in the 1935 Stock Exchange fight. Now, when he heard Shetlar's report via Wellington, he saw his duty. One of the reforms that the Stock Exchange had lately adopted under SEC pressure was to institute the practice of sending questionnaires about current financial condition at intervals to all member firms. As it happened, the first of the forms under the new procedure were to be mailed out in just a few days, on January 20; in the normal course, Whitney & Company was not scheduled to receive its first form until mid-May, for reply by the end of May. But Davis now directed that Whitney & Company be advanced to the top of the list, and be sent its questionnaire immediately, for reply by February 15. That, he felt, would straighten out the situation; moreover, since the firms themselves in most cases did not know the Exchange's schedule for mailing out the forms, there would be nothing particular in the early arrival of his questionnaire to arouse Whitney's suspicion that *he* was under suspicion.

Thus a false scent had set the dogs on the true trail. Whitney got his questionnaire. On February 15, the due date for its return, he requested a week's extension, which was granted. He filed his return on February 21; a quick check of it was made by the comptroller of the Exchange that same evening. Whitney's return, although necessarily far more detailed than his Thanksgiving Day accounting for his brother, nevertheless similarly contained omissions that had the force of falsifications; even so, the comptroller's preliminary analysis indicated that the firm's capital position fell far short of the requirements of the Business Conduct Committee. So the next step, routine in such cases, was taken: on February 23 a staff accountant of the Exchange was sent to the Whitney offices at 15 Broad Street to make an audit of the books.

Again, the books themselves were falsified—but insufficiently. Realizing this, Whitney on February 24 called on Davis at his apartment uptown to plead for more time. He knew, he said, that his capital fell short of requirements, that his assets were injudiciously concentrated in certain specific securities, and so on. But, he explained, he was actively negotiating for a loan of about $700,000 that would enable him to correct all deficiencies; he very much disliked the prospect of having an even partially unfavorable report on his reputable firm go into the Exchange records; and in view of all this, might not the accountant now in his offices be withdrawn, to return in a few weeks when everything would be to rights?

The reply of the man who had once thought Whitney a pain in the neck, and later grown fond of him, was that it seemed to him advisable that the accountant be permitted to continue his work in the normal way.

By February 28—five days after he had begun his digging in Whitney's office books—the Exchange accountant had extensive but not conclusive evidence of misappropriation of customers' securities. On March 1 Davis told Gay of the findings so far. The following evening, at the Metropolitan Club, Gay, Davis, Simmons, and the Stock Exchange lawyers met with Whitney's personal lawyer, L. Randolph Mason, to hash the whole thing over. Delicately, they warned Mason that there appeared to be serious doubt as to whether his client's books truly reflected his financial situation. They would be in touch. The day after that—Thursday—Whitney made a second unsuccessful attempt to influence Davis to call off his dogs. On Friday the dogs found the corpse. The Exchange comptroller reported to his superiors that he had now established positive proof that Richard Whitney was an embezzler and that his firm was insolvent.

On Saturday morning, March 5, the comptroller confronted Whitney in person with the evidence he had uncovered. Whitney, as the comptroller put it later, gave a "tacit admission" that he had misused customers' securities. This was a feint; Whitney had not given up yet. That afternoon he spent two hours in Gay's office playing his last card. Readily admitting misconduct, he asked for special consideration—specifically, that the Exchange quietly allow him to sell his membership, then drop charges against him. On what grounds? Gay wanted to know—and then Whitney made his play. "After all, I'm Richard Whitney," he said. "I mean the Stock Exchange to millions of people." Therefore what affected him affected the Stock Exchange—and Wall Street. His exposure as a bankrupt was now inevitable, but his exposure as an embezzler—it would make a mockery of the trust on which all stock trading is based; it would be a triumph for the reformist forces in Washington; it would be a bonanza beyond the wildest dreams of the SEC. . . .

This was a telling point, and Whitney emphasized it; in the course of the two-hour session he brought the same argument up over and over again. "I wouldn't say that Mr. Whitney was pleading," Gay recounted later. "He assumed more of a reasoning attitude, as if he were discussing somebody else than himself." Indeed he was: the White Knight was discussing the thief. It is possible to imagine that Charley Gay was sorely tempted. He had the deep conservatism of the self-made—had grown up admiring the Wall Street Old Guardsmen with their easy languorous charm, and had spent his life working like a peon to try to become one of them; now he was surely no more anxious than Whitney himself that Whitney should bring the Old Guard and its era crashing down with him. If Whitney were allowed to resign quietly with the announcement that he was going to retire from the bond business and take up some other line of work, there was at least a good chance that nothing would ever come to light about his defalcations and that, after a brief flurry of scandal, the whole thing would blow over and things would be back where they had been before. If, on the other hand . . .

But Gay was also a passionately honest and conscientious man. His horrified conscience triumphed over his desire to preserve the world he had accepted and admired so long. Adamantly, over and over again, he told Whitney that the drawing up of charges and specifications against him would proceed, and that they, along with the evidence, would be presented to the Business Conduct Committee on Monday morning as planned.

III

Through the two months preceding that Saturday afternoon, Whitney, fighting for his life and perhaps his way of life, had indulged in one last binge of cash-raising efforts, the details of which add some bizarre footnotes to his story and indeed to the history of borrowing. Turndowns on loan requests were getting to be commonplace now, and he was learning to accept them without batting an eye. "How about George?" people would ask him, bluntly, when he came to them for money. "My brother is out of town, and if he were here I wouldn't be coming to you," he would reply loftily. "Well, I am very sorry . . ." he would hear again and again, and would simply turn on his heel and leave. In January the long-suffering, long-awestruck Paul Adler turned him down; unable to face the idol he saw toppling before him, Adler scrawled on a piece of Stock Exchange notepaper: "Dick, I am sorry, but we have decided that we are not willing to make any loans to anyone at this time, and I deeply regret to say so. Sincerely, Paul." In mid-February he walked up to John H. McMannus, a floor specialist far outside his normal social orbit, and asked for $100,000. McMannus, after a stunned pause, offered to make the loan provided Whitney's note be endorsed by George. Whitney offered instead his wife's endorsement—"She's worth half a million dollars," he confided without shame. McMannus said he never accepted a woman's endorsement on a note. Whitney nodded. "Don't say anything about this," he remarked casually as he turned away. McMannus said later that the episode had been one of the most surprising events of his business life: "I thought he was the essence of everything fine in the world. I was so shocked I couldn't think clearly." If he had thought clearly, McMannus realized only afterward, he would have known that he didn't have the $100,000 to loan anyway.

Late in February Whitney asked Sidney Weinberg, by this time a partner at Goldman, Sachs and well on his way to becoming the "Mr. Wall Street" of the early postwar years, for $50,000. The only trouble, or one trouble, was that Whitney seems to have thought the gentleman's name was Weinstein.

But simultaneous, and more astonishing, were several spectacular successes. In mid-February Whitney asked Alexander B. Gale, an Exchange member, for the usual amount—$100,000. Gale said he could lend only $75,000, and immediately sent along a check for that amount. Whitney, however, brazenly sent back his note for $100,000. Thus made to feel like a piker, Gale sent along the additional $25,000 to round out the note. At about the same time Whitney approached one Walter T. Rosen for the usual amount— as usual, without offering collateral. Rosen handed over the money along with a charming and flattering little speech: "I have always been much impressed by the attitude of the elder Mr. Morgan, who held the view that the personal integrity of the borrower was of far greater value than his collateral." "Mr. Morgan was entirely right," the Morgan broker graciously allowed as he took his check.

Whitney's two last borrowings were memorable for their own reasons. On March 1, four days before his Saturday showdown with Gay, he approached two partners of Brown Brothers, Harriman & Company, Knight Woolley and W. Averell Harriman—the latter not yet launched on his diplomatic career—for the usual amount. Unlike the elder Mr. Morgan, although members of an equally distinguished and aristocratic firm, Woolley and Harriman wanted collateral. Whitney promised to have the collateral delivered within a few days, and got his loan on the spot; somehow the collateral never arrived. That same day Whitney borrowed $25,000 from an old and none too hale friend of his, a man who has spanned our turbulent story—Colonel John W. Prentiss, the tactful mediator in the 1920 dispute between Allan Ryan and the Stock Exchange. Eighteen days later, Colonel Prentiss, unrepaid. would be dead.

And late in January Whitney had made one last, grand embezzle-ment—his grandest. On the twenty-sixth, without explanation, he ordered the cashier of his firm, Robert J. Rosenthal, to turn over to him a batch of securities belonging to various customers of the firm, among them the estate of his father-in-law, and having a value of about $800,000. Two days later he took these securities to the Public National Bank and, representing them as his own, pledged them as collateral for a loan of no less than $280,000.

Let us sum up in broad strokes, for the astonishing record, Whitney's true financial condition as of the first week of March, 1938. Over the preceding four months he had negotiated, all told, 111 loans aggregating $27,361,500; of this, more than $25 million had been in more or less soundly secured borrowings from commer-cial banks, constantly turned over as he made new loans to repay those that came due. Apart from this, he owed, entirely unsecured, $2,897,000 to George Whitney, $474,000 to J. P. Morgan & Com-pany, and about an even million dollars to others. He owed borrowed stocks worth about $390,000. Quite apart, then, from the sums he "owed" to the customers from whom he had embezzled, he had managed to accumulate on the strength of nothing, or almost nothing, more than his character and good name net borrowings well in excess of five million dollars.

In those last days he was walking up to men he didn't know on the Exchange floor and asking them in tones casual to the point of indifference to lend him his standard sum—$100,000. He also did one thing suggesting that madness or something like it was over-taking him at last. On Tuesday of the frantic week that ended with his Saturday-afternoon confrontation, he went to Ben Smith. He made no lame effort to ingratiate himself. Rather, he announced brusquely that he "wanted to get this over quickly"—as if, say, his mission were to administer a justified rebuke to an inferior. Then he said that he wanted to borrow $250,000 "on my face." Smith's reply was, in the circumstances, not startling, and can scarcely be described as ruder than the occasion called for. "I remarked he was

261

putting a pretty high value on his face," Smith recounted later. "So he told me that was his story and his back was to the wall and he had to have $250,000. I told him he had a lot of nerve to ask me for $250,000 when he didn't even bid me the time of day. I told him I frankly didn't like him—that I wouldn't loan him a dime." Whitney nodded; that was that.

Of course. But why had he done it? What had he expected from Ben Smith but a harsh rebuff? Was this the ritual of capitulation, the beaten wolf intentionally baring his neck to the teeth of his conqueror? It could not have been; as we know, on that Tuesday Whitney was by no means ready to capitulate. The remaining assumption must be that he was as insensitive in the matter of slights received as he had so long been in that of slights delivered; that he regarded this upstart so little as to be immune to his bad opinion, and had made the approach simply because it could cost him nothing; that, as Smith said, he had a lot of nerve, a rather awesome lot, and the nerve at least had not failed.

IV

Francis Bartow, J. P. Morgan's "Stock Exchange man," was the firm's responsible partner in the absence of Lamont, who had followed his trip South with one abroad, and George Whitney, who early in 1938 had returned to the South to resume a long convalescence from his 1937 illness. Let Bartow tell, with a fine dramatic flair, what happened Saturday night after Whitney's last-ditch attempt to persuade Gay to drop charges:

"On the afternoon of March 5, I was playing bridge with some friends at the Links Club in New York and I was called to the telephone by Richard Whitney. He said he wanted to see me as soon as possible. I explained where I was and inquired where he was and he said at his office. I suggested that he stop by and see me where I was. He said he would.

"Some time later he appeared and we sat down together to talk. As we did so, he drew from his pocket a large folded piece of paper which he proceeded to open. He said, 'I am in a jam.' I said, 'Wait a minute, is your idea in talking to me now to borrow money?' He said, 'Yes.' 'Well,' I said, 'in all frankness I will not agree to that.' I think in my mind at the moment I was a little impatient with him because I assumed he must have known that I had talked with Randolph Mason about his affairs and the promised audit report and other information had not been given to me. He said, 'Well, on Monday at ten-thirty my affairs are coming up for examination before the Business Conduct Committee.' I said, 'Now, wait a minute, stop right there. I am not the proper person for you to talk to. My advice is that you go and get Randolph Mason and tell him.'

"He folded his papers up and left me. I resumed my game with my friends. I think as he left me I said to him, 'I expect to be here some time longer, if you should want me.'

"Quite a considerable time later, word was brought to me that Richard Whitney would like to speak to me in the floor below. As soon as I was free I went there. He and Randolph Mason were together. He said, 'Frank, we have been talking this over and I want to know if you have any suggestions to offer.'

"I said, 'I have already told you that I have no suggestions to offer.'

" 'Well,' he said, 'when my affairs come up for review before the Business Conduct Committee on Monday, it is conceivable some embarrassing questions will arise.'

"I said, 'What do you mean, embarrassing?'

" 'Well,' he said, 'for example, the New York Yacht Club have securities with me and I have taken those securities and I have pledged them in loans.'

"I said, 'How much does the New York Yacht Club owe you?'

"He said, 'They don't owe me anything.'

"I said, 'Do you mean that you have taken a client's securities and pledged them in loans and taken the proceeds of that and placed it in your business when they did not owe you anything?'

"He said, 'Yes, I do.'

"I said, 'That is serious.'

"He said, 'It is criminal.'

"I asked, 'Are there any other cases where this had occurred?'

"He said, 'Yes, two; the Sheldon estate of which I am an executor, and Mrs. Baird.'

"I said, 'Dick, now this is such an entirely different nature than the matter that you originally discussed with me that I will not discuss it with you any further. And I want now to go to the telephone and call my counsel.' "

Does it seem rather odd that a man, on hearing a friend and business associate confess that he has been engaged in criminal activities, should react simply by saying that he is going to call his lawyer? It does, but it should not; remember that, in a time when Wall Street was still very much on the public griddle, Whitney was the most publicized man in Wall Street and Morgan's the most publicized firm, and that private knowledge of a crime on the part of a Morgan partner raised the possibility of the Morgan firm's being considered an accessory. Bartow called the Morgan lawyer—no lesser lawyer than the former Presidential candidate John W. Davis—and made an appointment to see him that evening at his home at Glen Cove, Long Island. Then he went back to Whitney and Mason. The three of them had a hasty supper together at the Links, and just before or during the meal Whitney said to Bartow, "I would like to explain this to you. I have a loan of $280,000 at the Public National Bank. In that loan are all of the securities taken improperly from the accounts in my office—the Yacht Club, Sheldon, and Baird. If I could borrow $280,000 and pay that loan off, it would enable me to restore all of those improperly used securities and when I went before the Business Conduct Committee on Monday morning I could state truthfully that there were no irregularities in my office."

Bartow gave no immediate answer. A prudent man, he was going to wait for advice of counsel. Immediately after dinner he and Mason left Whitney at the Links and took the hour's drive to Glen Cove to see John W. Davis. Davis, after hearing the story, replied without hesitation that no one could or should do anything to help Whitney now—"Anyone who did would run the risk of taking actions that would be misconstrued," as Davis put it euphemistically.

"All right, Mr. Davis," said Bartow. "I accept your advice and counsel on that. I am glad I came to you." One other question: would it be proper to call Gay, and ask him for a one-day or perhaps even two-day delay in the meeting of the Business Conduct Committee that would consider the Whitney case?

Davis gave it as his opinion that there was no reason not to do that.

So back to New York hurried Bartow and Mason, this time for a midnight meeting, arranged on the spur of the moment, with Gay at the Metropolitan Club. They found Gay there with a Stock Exchange lawyer, who, on hearing Bartow's request, replied most emphatically that under no circumstances would there be a single minute's delay in the scheduled Monday-morning meeting. That seemed to be that. Bartow and Mason went back to the Links, where they gave a glum Dick Whitney their grim news.

On Sunday there was more frantic scrambling. Bartow takes up the story again:

"Quite early, I called my partner, Mr. Anderson, and at the same time called my partner, Charles Dickey, in his home in Philadelphia, and in a general way told them of the events of the day before and asked if they would meet me at my house in New York at two-thirty that afternoon, and they agreed. I then called my senior partner, Mr. J. P. Morgan, at his house at Glen Cove, and made an appointment with him for twelve o'clock. I then called Mr. Randolph Mason and told him of a meeting that was to be that afternoon at my house and asked if he would come. I also asked—if it were possible, I would like to have Mr. Rodewald there, as I wished to learn from him firsthand how long, in his opinion, it would take to make an audit.

"Mr. Mason said he would come and, if possible, arrange for Mr. Rodewald to be there, too.

"I then motored to Glen Cove. I went to Mr. Morgan's house, where I told him of the events of the night before, and my advice from John W. Davis, and the conclusions that Mr. Davis had reached. Mr. Morgan was naturally shocked beyond measure and gave it as his judgment, which was mine, that there was no course for us to follow except to abide by the advice that we had received from counsel."

(But in view of what he already knew, can J. P. Morgan have really been all that shocked? Or did the old gentleman put on a show for the benefit of his junior partner?)

"I then left and returned to my house in town. Sunday afternoon Mr. Anderson and Mr. Dickey arrived and we sat down and I told them what I had learned in as great detail as I recalled. I then telephoned Mr. Sunderland, who is Mr. John W. Davis' partner, and asked him if he would come to my house. He did. About that time Mr. Mason arrived. Some while after that Mr. Rodewald arrived. I asked Mr. Rodewald how long, in his judgment, he thought it would take for high-class accountants to make a proper audit. He was vague and to me disappointing because he gave the impression it would take a great deal longer than I presumed it would take. . . .

"When Mr. Sunderland arrived, I told him what I had done, and what I planned. I asked him if he thought it was a proper and right thing for me to do and he said, 'Under no circumstances can you or anyone else from J. P. Morgan & Company go into the office of Richard Whitney & Company to find out anything.'

"I then told Mr. Rodewald that the reason for his being called was over with, and we did not need him any more and I presumed he was busy, and he left to go about his business. A little later . . . one by one I expressed my regret at calling [Anderson, Dickey, and Mason] from their homes in the country, and they went back to where they had come from, I presume. . . .

"Late in the afternoon I determined that the time had come when I must call my partner, George Whitney, on the telephone, and advise him of everything that I knew. Accordingly I put in a call to get him on the telephone in Florida, which I did. As guardedly as I could, yet as fully as I could, I told him of my knowledge. . . .

"Mr. Whitney said, 'My God!' "

"My God" indeed: there was apparently little else George Whitney could say, and nothing more he could do.

So on Monday the wheels of Stock Exchange justice turned. That morning, right on schedule, the Business Conduct Committee met, heard the evidence, and voted unanimously to present forthwith the charges against Whitney and the two of his partners who held Exchange memberships, Edwin D. Morgan, Jr. and Henry D.

Mygatt, to the Governing Committee for action. Early in the afternoon the Governing Committee considered the charges and voted unanimously that they be served on the three member partners, that the accused be notified that they would have the customary ten days to prepare their answers, and that a hearing on the charges be held at the end of the ten-day period, on March 17. The charges were served on Whitney, Morgan, and Mygatt the same day. That evening, by telephone, Gay notified the SEC in Washington of the affair.

Meanwhile, no public announcement had yet been made and there had rather astonishingly been no leaks to the press; and Whitney's remaining allies, most of them now thinking chiefly of the public disaster for Wall Street that his exposure would be, were continuing with sinking hearts their furious efforts to find some way out. Early Monday morning George Whitney called Bartow back from Florida. He was very much disturbed about not being in New York, he said; shouldn't he come at once? Bartow urged him not to, reminding him that he was still not entirely recovered from his illness, and pointing out that there was nothing he could do anyway. Later that morning, grasping at straws, Bartow—after again getting clearance from John W. Davis—called on Roland Redmond, the Stock Exchange lawyer who was perhaps Whitney's closest friend. "Is there anything that anybody can humanly do in this thing that you know of?" Bartow asked. Redmond replied, "Absolutely not. I don't know of a solitary thing." Poor Redmond was obviously in distress; to him, as Exchange lawyer, fell the duty of drawing up the charges against his friend—a duty he had performed at his office the previous afternoon, with tears actually streaming down his face.

"We parted," Bartow recounted later. "In the afternoon of that day, Randolph Mason called me on the phone and said that he would like to see me that evening. He would probably be late, and would I wait at my house until he came, and I said I would. And that evening he did come, and I am not quite clear now why he came, because there did not seem to me any purpose in it, because the only thing he told me now was that he had been engaged all afternoon and evening on papers dealing with the proposed bankruptcy proceedings of Richard Whitney & Company the next day— and after a very brief talk he left." But in retrospect it is clear enough why Mason came to Bartow's house—he wanted to have a wake.

V

John Wesley Hanes, with mixed emotions, became the SEC's liaison man in the Whitney case. Chairman Douglas on Monday night, right after hearing the news from Gay, picked Hanes for the assignment on the spot and called him shortly before midnight, asking him to take it on.

Hanes took the night train to New York, sleeping little and brooding much en route. "My first and principal concern was the extent of public participation in this failure," he said later. "We were unable to find out the extent of the public interest [in Washington]. I came to New York to find out if I could get any more facts than we had at Washington." Some insisted later that he had had another major concern. Far from lusting for the Morgan broker's scalp, Hanes was indubitably as worried as his idolized friends, the men at No. 23 themselves, for the good name of Wall Street at large and J. P. Morgan & Company in particular, and there was talk in Wall Street early that morning—circulated, it is true, by the die-hard remnants of the Whitney Old Guard—that Hanes was coming to New York with the specific mission of recommending on behalf of the SEC that public announcement of the disaster be postponed while final efforts were made to negotiate some kind of accommodation. Whatever his intentions may have been—and he later denied that they were these—Hanes found, on his arrival in Wall Street at nine forty-five, only fifteen minutes before Stock Exchange opening time, that events were wholly beyond reversal. The place, he found, was seething with rumors about Whitney that were, if possible, even worse than the facts; from the point of view of Wall Street's public image, no announcement would be the worst possible course. Hanes accordingly recommended to the Stock Exchange authorities that they go ahead with the announcement as planned. In any case, by that time it was already inexorably in the works. Some three-quarters of an hour earlier, at nine o'clock sharp, the Business Conduct Committee had convened with Howland Davis presiding; on the carpet before it were Mason as Whitney's representative and two of Whitney's partners. Davis had opened the meeting by saying, "Gentlemen, I think the thing the committee is most interested in is whether between now and ten o'clock we have to do something with regard to the plans of Richard Whitney & Company to do business today."

Mason had said, "We don't know all the figures. . . . I am obliged to say . . . that the firm is insolvent."

The chairman then asked Kingsley Rodewald, Whitney's partner—a bewildered man who, like all Whitney's partners, had for years been kept entirely in the dark as to Whitney's defalcations and even as to the desperate financial plight of the firm—whether he had anything to say. Rodewald replied that he had not.

"Can your firm meet its obligations?" the chairman had inquired.

"No, sir," Rodewald had replied.

So the failure was formalized, ipse dixit; now the Exchange under its own rules had no choice. At ten-five, just after the start of the day's trading, Gay mounted the rostrum overlooking the floor; the secretary rang the gong that suspends trading; the hum on the floor faded into dead silence; and Gay read an announcement of the suspension of Whitney & Company for insolvency. Immediately thereafter the Exchange released a statement that did not fail to make clear that wrongdoing was involved in the holocaust:

> In the course of an examination of the affairs of Richard Whitney & Company, the Committee on Business Conduct discovered on March 1, 1938, evidence of conduct apparently contrary to just and equitable principles of trade, and on Monday, March 7, 1938, at 1:30 P.M., presented to a special meeting of the Governing Committee charges and specifications. Hearing on the charges was set for March 17, 1938. This morning the firm of Richard Whitney & Company advised the Exchange that it was unable to meet its obligations and its suspension for insolvency was announced from the rostrum of the Exchange shortly after 10:00 A.M.

With the fall of its champion, the fall of the Old Guard was accomplished.

Chapter Twelve

Denouement

I

It was, of course, an instant national sensation. "LINK WHITNEY TO MISSING BONDS," the New York *Daily News* screamed on its front page. On Tuesday, March 8, the day of the Stock Exchange's first announcement, Whitney and his partners filed bankruptcy papers; the New York State and County authorities, caught wholly by surprise, rushed to prepare indictments; and Whitney testified before a hastily convened hearing of the SEC. Here he was candid, self-possessed, almost offhand; to a questioner who asked him something that seemed to him not to make sense, he showed that he was determined to remain casual and in character by answering out of the language of the hunt: "Your question doesn't gee and haw, Commissioner."

Next day he did the thing that minimum decency required of him—exonerated his innocent partners. In the first place, as Cochran of Morgan's had pointed out years before, they were hardly real partners at all. Apart from Edwin Morgan, an amiable hunting companion and fellow member of Porcellian, they belonged to neither Whitney's social class nor presumed financial class, and had no financial investment in the firm—"office-boy" partners, Cochran had said, partners of convenience rather than of shared responsibility. One of them, indeed, had started with the firm as an office boy, and the wife of another, a former telephone clerk on the Curb Exchange, insisted even now that he was in fact and in law not a partner at all but an employee. In the second place, Whitney had long since elaborately set up a special "control account" for the express purpose of concealing from them his defalcations and the true state of the firm's finances; knowledge of the control account was confined to Whitney's accountant and his private secretary, both of whom understood well enough that their jobs depended on their silence.

In a statement issued through his newly engaged criminal attorney—Charles H. Tuttle, former Republican candidate for Governor of New York—Whitney said, "I want to say emphatically that the difficulties in which my firm has become involved are the result of actions as to which I alone have responsibility and in which none of my partners, none of my business associates or connections and, in fact, no one but myself has or had any responsibility or participation. . . . I fully realize that certain of my actions have been wrong. I am determined to meet the consequences. . . . I am, therefore, putting myself at the disposal of the Attorney General of the State, who is now investigating, and shall be ready to give him a full statement."

On Thursday the tenth New York County District Attorney Thomas E. Dewey beat the state to the indictment, citing the 1932, 1937, and January, 1938, misappropriations from the Sheldon estate in his true bill. While Bowery derelicts stood around watching with bewilderment or glee, Whitney was booked at the Elizabeth Street police station by a sergeant who said, "Mr. Whitney, I'm sorry to see you in this trouble and I wish you luck." "Thank you," replied Whitney, and the two men shook hands—the sergeant with the abashed and delighted air of one unexpectedly hobnobbing with celebrity. Then in a ten-minute proceeding in General Sessions Court, after the clerk had called Whitney to the bar, he stood silent and motionless, his hands clasped behind his back, his head slightly bowed, his face quite expressionless, and his gold Porcellian pig hanging prominently from the watch chain across the vest of his dark-blue suit, while the indictment was read and he was released on ten thousand dollars' bail. Then he posed willingly for photographers, but asked them to spare his wife.

The next day—while the Nazis were seizing Austria and the voices prophesying war were rising—he was haled into court again, this time by the State Attorney General on complaint of the Commodore of the New York Yacht Club, who spoke harshly indeed of his faithless treasurer. This time it was at the Criminal Courts Building, and this time the bail was $25,000; but again there was the cool, stoic prisoner, again the impassive stance, again the flaunted Porcellian emblem. After accepting a bail bond, Magistrate Thomas A. Aurelio ventured to comment ingratiatingly, almost humbly, "My little experience in life has been that it's a whole lot easier to make money than to hold on to it, even in hard times. I guess that applies to all of us." The judge waited for some reply; Whitney remained icily silent. He could still wear the pig, and he could still administer a snub.

II

Meanwhile there were repercussions everywhere. Old New York society, so long so closely involved with the downtown Old Guard, and now already weakened by hybridization with the newer café society, sensed a death blow. Nancy Randolph wrote in the *Daily News:* "Not in our time, in our fathers' time nor in our grandfathers' time has there been such a social debacle. . . . He had no need to overreach himself for power, for money, or for social position. He had them all!" Or so society had thought!

Wall Street at all levels was shocked into temporary catatonia—not only the big men who had liked and trusted Whitney, but the little men who had hated and trusted and, in a way, counted on him. The stock market scarcely even dropped in reaction to the terrible revelation; in truth, most of the brokers spent much of that day at the Luncheon Club bar discussing it.

In Whitney's clubs there was strange, glum silence. Open discussion of the tragedy would be in poor taste. But how could one discuss anything else?

The day of the revelation or soon afterward, Harry Simmons said, "I have had a terrific shock over this thing—I am so stunned over it, and it is so beyond my comprehension . . . that Richard Whitney could do any of these things—absolutely impossible." Duke Wellington said simply that it had "never occurred to him" that Whitney might do such a thing. Roland Redmond said, "I had more confidence, I think, in his personal integrity than in that of almost anyone else that I know." Whitney's old friend of both town and country, Roger D. Mellick, said, "There couldn't have been a more straightforward person, to my knowledge." Those beneath Whitney socially again and again echoed John McMannus' stunned avowal of having thought of him as the essence of everything fine in the world. Even Whitney's own cashier, Robert Rosenthal, who apparently would have had to be remarkably blind not to see what was going on under his nose, said emotionally, "I can't believe it. I think I am in a fog; I honestly do, because I never would question Mr. Whitney. He is one man I would never question—one man I would take an arm off, if he wanted it he could have it. That is what I thought of the gentleman." Of course, these statements were self-serving. Moreover, in light of the fact that most of these men were stuck with bad loans to Whitney, they take on a somewhat comical aspect. But for all that, can anyone mistake the note of pathetic, heartbroken sincerity in them?

By March 17, the previously designated date, the Stock Exchange Governing Committee had recovered sufficiently to hold its hearing and—with Whitney absent and offering no defense—unanimously expel him from the Exchange, while letting off his unfortunate partners Morgan and Mygatt with three-year suspensions.

And the country at large, sick of depression and thirsty for the blood of millionaires, was having such a field day as not even the Pecora hearings had afforded. As the *Nation* said, "Wall Street could hardly have been more embarrassed if J. P. Morgan had been caught helping himself from the collection plate at the Cathedral of St. John the Divine." The Whitney exposure was the stuff of myth, yet was true—a happening so satisfying to the deeper and less admirable human drives, envy and aggression and desire for revenge, as to be beyond the contrivance of imagination; a work of muckraking fiction containing an invented episode like the Whitney case, had one been published before March, 1938, would surely have been dismissed as too fanciful and propagandistic. (Only a single detail marred the perfection of the allegory—that Whitney had not stolen from the poor or even from the "public," but only from people and institutions of the plutocracy.) As if the whole affair were not already sufficiently to the mass taste, there was even a woman involved, and just the right sort of woman—no drab secretary or cliché showgirl, but a rich, handsome, well-born, fox-hunting widow, as haughtily patrician as Whitney himself; the United States Attorney's office did not neglect to inform the press that it had questioned her as to what she knew of Whitney's finances. The United States Attorney apparently got little from the lady; she resolutely refused to receive the press, and managed, after a brief flurry, to vanish from public view.

Gloating, then, the country quickly became ashamed of its gloating. Hardly more than a week after the first shock of revelation, newspaper commentary began to emphasize Whitney's personal tragedy, to take on a subdued tone of "Let the poor man pay his penalty in decent silence." President Roosevelt, that sensitive barometer of the public temper, caught it this time, and made no political capital of Whitney's disgrace. An old Grottie like Whitney as well as the scourge of economic royalists, Roosevelt never once alluded to it.

Gloating was so easy—and the man was behaving so well!

Indeed he was. He was hewing rigidly to the code of his class. It is almost possible to say that he had never deviated from it. That code, the code of old families and good prep schools and gentlemen's clubs and Old Guard Wall Street, was equivocal on the matters of ruthless acquisitiveness and even on certain forms of stealing—many of the class's members owed their membership to practices not far removed from stealing—but was explicit and inflexible on the matter of conduct when caught. There were even moments when it seemed as if Whitney had, by some psychological quirk, concocted the whole baroque drama to give himself the chance to play its last act. Pleading guilty to the State charge on March 14, he read a seven-hundred-word *mea culpa* expanding on the previous one. He read it in a firm, clear voice—almost with a certain joy. Sentencing was set for April 11; during the four-week interim, free on bail, as a routine matter he was examined by the court's psychiatric clinic and by its probation officer. Together with his personal bankruptcy petition, which was filed March 25, the subsequent reports of the clinic and the probation officer show Whitney's state of mind and demeanor as he passed what he knew well enough were the last days of his life as it had been.

The psychiatric clinic found his reactions to be "urbane and sportsmanlike," his intelligence rating in the top one percent of the population; in sum, no shadow or trace of mental incompetence or disorder.

The bankruptcy petition showed his town and country houses and his life insurance all mortgaged to the hilt, but his prized New Jersey livestock—"seven hundred laying hens and chickens, the outstanding herd of Ayrshire cattle in this country, twenty thoroughbred Berkshire pigs, twenty horses of fair breeding stock which turns into excellent hunters"—still free and clear. It also showed that he still lived at a cost of over five thousand dollars per month, maintaining in both town and country his full staff of house servants and, in the country, his outside staff of twelve—the herdsmen, the grooms, the jockey. And it showed that he, of all men, was still as always a prime sucker for get-rich-quick schemes, a quaint votary at the obsolete American shrine of the better mousetrap, the apocalyptic, ever-opening frontier that would solve all problems and make everything all right: his current business interests, he revealed for the first time in the petition, included not only all that unwanted applejack and cider but also patent rights to a process for spraying metal to repair rust, and a patented air-pressure bearing that "is almost revolutionary in its possibilities."

The probation officer was more fulsome than the psychiatric clinic. He found Whitney faultlessly groomed, self-composed, precise of speech; also "not without humor" and "alive to some of the ironical aspects of his difficulties." The report went on:

> Contributing factors in his delinquency are pride, obstinacy, unshakable belief in his own financial judgment, and a gambling instinct. . . . Egotistical to a marked degree, it was apparently inconceivable that he, a figure of national prominence in financial circles and one whose judgment in economic matters was considered that of an expert, should prove a personal failure. . . . Courage he possesses

in an unusual degree. He also possesses a certain gentlemanly code
of honor. . . . Combined with this he has a sustaining savoir-faire
and a Spartan-like spirit of fortitude, which enables him to maintain unflinchingly his self-composure in the face of his present
humiliating predicament.

Waxing unexpectedly literary, the probation officer summed up:
"Pride and a Micawber-like capacity for borrowing are the keynote
qualities of his inner character." Did Whitney, we may wonder,
spending his last free days sequestered at home on East Seventy-
third Street, sheltered from the curious press and public by his
servants and his family, take down a dusty old calfbound copy of
David Copperfield, its pages perhaps previously uncut, to find out
what his alleged prototype had been like?

At nine o'clock on April 11, the day of his sentencing, he left 115
East Seventy-third Street, escorted to the door by his liveried butler,
who bowed ceremoniously low. The mob of onlookers in the street
loved it. He was alone except for his lawyer, Tuttle; his wife and
brother had wanted to come to court with him, knowing that their
presence there would certainly have its effect on the suddenly
sentimental public and perhaps on the judge, too; but Whitney had
refused them. The crowd on East Seventy-third Street gradually
dispersed. But all that day limousines drew up at intervals to No.
115 to deliver flowers to Mrs. Whitney, as if for a funeral.

In court this time Whitney showed signs of strain at last. His face
was haggard and his hands unmistakably twitched as he heard
District Attorney Dewey's demand for a "substantial and punitive"
sentence. Tuttle answered with a long, florid plea for mercy,
emphasizing that Whitney had "neither avoided the law nor chosen
the coward's course of flight from the country. . . . He still has
character. . . . He has faced his friends, which perhaps is the
hardest task of all." But Judge Owen W. Bohan seemed unim-
pressed; he preceded sentencing with a harsh tongue-lashing in
which he said to Whitney, "Your acts have been deliberate and
intentional and were committed with an unusually full opportunity
for understanding their effect upon others and the consequences to
yourself." Once, when he called Whitney a "public betrayer," the

276

prisoner flushed scarlet. The sentence was five to ten years at Sing Sing, and an injunction against Whitney forbidding him ever again to deal in securities in New York State.

More curious crowds watched as Whitney was taken by an officer from the Criminal Courts Building to the Tombs. Through his overnight stay there he was constantly watched by guards to forestall any attempt at suicide; he made none. The next morning, handcuffed to two petty racketeers, he went by police van to Grand Central Station for the train trip up the Hudson. A crowd estimated at five thousand jammed the station waiting room to give him a send-off, but the police ducked them by driving the van into the baggage room and by-passing the waiting room. At the gate to Sing Sing there was another crowd that couldn't be dodged. Whitney, fully composed again, looked in his black coat and bowler almost as if he were ready at any moment to ask one of his handcuff mates or a jailer to let him have a hundred for a week, simply out of force of habit; but he went through the gates refusing to say a word.

That very day, April 12, happened to be the birthday of a teenage godson of his, the son of one of his old friends and Wall Street associates. For years Whitney had punctiliously honored the occasion with a present that arrived on the dot: a gold piece until 1933, when possession of gold coins had become illegal, and thereafter a check. On this particular April 12 the young man got his check as usual. With it was a note from Whitney's secretary, saying that she was sending it along in his absence, and adding that the godfather wanted to say that, in the circumstances, he regretted there would be no more checks on future birthdays.

Next day Harvard announced Whitney's resignation from the Board of Overseers' Visiting Committee to the Department of Economics.

III

Where, now, were the envied, hated, and slyly idolized Wall Street plungers of the wild gone days?

One of them, the one with the greatest capacity for growth and change, lived now in a different world. He was Ambassador to the Court of St. James's, in London, and would go on finally to achieve heights of glory and horror beyond the scope possible to things recorded on ticker tape.

We have seen what had become of the former public enemy Ben Smith—he had become a pillar of Wall Street respectability. But others were less fortunate.

Michael J. Meehan of the shipboard brokerage offices and the famous Radio pools, for example, had fallen on evil days. He had not changed with the times. One of his friends later attributed his downfall to "an honest failure to realize that the New Deal in respect to Wall Street had made fundamental changes in its modes of business." At any rate, he went on manipulating stocks after passage of the Securities Exchange Act, and the SEC caught him. During the week of May 15, 1935, using all the old shell-game methods at which he was so adept, he moved the price of Bellanca Aircraft from 2½ to almost twice that figure; between June 10 and early autumn, he held it at around 5 while he and his colleagues in the pool quietly disposed of the hundreds of thousands of shares they had acquired in the spring. It was almost a year later, in the summer of 1936, before Meehan learned that the SEC was actively and vigorously investigating him. He abruptly disappeared. Four months later, in November, 1936, he surfaced again in Bloomingdale, the posh private hospital for the well-to-do insane in Westchester County, New York. "He's not under restraint; he's been sick for about a year and has given no attention to business during that period," a partner in his still-flourishing brokerage firm reported. Those who saw Meehan at Bloomingdale, however, did not find him conducting himself like a sick man, far less one broken in mind or spirit. Rather, they found him his old self, ebullient, generous with friends, strutting the grounds, puffing on cigars, and shouting greetings with all his old cockiness and élan.

In June, 1937, Meehan left Bloomingdale. The SEC was all but at the gate to greet him. That August it charged him with violation of the Securities Exchange Act in the Bellanca matter and ordered his expulsion from all national stock exchanges. So ended the Wall

Street career of the man who, some say, did more than any other to bring together the stock market and the public.

We do not know whether Meehan at Bloomingdale was a subject for irony or pity, a shrewdly scheming malingerer or a man truly broken on the wheel of changing times. What we do know is that when he would die it would be in his own bed and with an intact fortune to pass along. If he did not change with the times, he contrived to carry something of the past with him.

Jesse Livermore, bleakest of the money machines of the old Wall Street, was destined for the bleakest end. Still rich after the crash, and far richer after a series of coups in the bear market of 1930, he plunged gratuitously, superfluously, all-out, the wrong way in 1931 and, as so many times before, went in a few days from regal riches to debt. But the day of the trading game was past. He could not make another million; it was all he could do to keep going. He published a book explaining his stock-market techniques—a tip-off that they were no longer working for him. Still, reaching sixty as the decade went on, he remained "eerily young-looking, his hair still blond, his complexion unlined." Thus in 1938 the exterior of the onetime boy plunger who had made Pierpont Morgan take notice in 1907. But two years later, one November afternoon in 1940, he would walk from his office in the Squibb Building to the nearby Sherry-Netherland Hotel, take a table by himself in the bar, slowly drink two cocktails, go to the ground-floor men's room, and there kill himself by shooting a bullet into his brain.

Livermore left behind, besides an estate publicly announced as being "less than $10,000," a contrite and affectionate note to his wife—"tired of fighting," "couldn't carry on any longer," "my life has been a failure"—that suggests some sort of final inner triumph, some last-minute conversion to humanity. Next day the *Times* wrote his epitaph in an editorial:

> What good he did, what harm he did, what his life meant to himself and to others—such questions are for novelists. . . . His passion drove him on. . . . He lived in a time when the speculating he did came to seem like that of boys pitching pennies. . . . He left no clouds of glory behind him, nor any miasma of human misery that he had himself created. . . . The "Street" in which he operated is not what it used to be. His death punctuated the end of an era.

IV

The Fortinbras of 1938 Wall Street, the man of clean limb and forthright character who came in to pick up the pieces after the general holocaust, was William McChesney Martin, Jr., the startlingly young St. Louis broker who had first joined the Stock Exchange board of governors in the same election in which Richard Whitney had been denied its presidency.

The exposure of Whitney deprived the Old Guard not only of its champion but of its last intangible resource, its morale. Gallantry was made a mockery; the SEC had Wall Street over a barrel; resistance collapsed, and the long struggle was over. The very week of the exposure, the Governing Committee hastily passed a rule requiring every member firm to make available on request to any customer a statement of the firm's financial condition. On May 9 the first election under a new set of rules providing for more democratic procedures was held; the slate elected virtually constituted a new management, since only thirteen of the new forty-man board of governors were survivors of the old one, while the other twenty-seven—not just a majority, but an overwhelming one—were avowed liberals. The nominating committee that had selected the new slate had forthrightly stated that it considered its duty to be "to take another forward step in applying the principles set forth in the Conway committee report."

The new chairman, replacing Gay, was Martin. Still only thirty-one, he was already a remarkable man, a precursor of the even more remarkable man he would later become. A graduate of Yale, a son of the governor of the Federal Reserve Bank of St. Louis, he was a serious-looking bachelor who wore owlish round spectacles, never smoked or drank, lived soberly in bachelor quarters at the Yale Club of New York, served as a trustee of the liberal-intellectual New School for Social Research, and regularly attended evening classes in economics and politics at Columbia. He liked to think things out for himself in his own way. On evenings when he had no Columbia classes he would go to a room he kept at the Astor, in Times Square, apparently just for thinking; after a few hours' cogitation there he would repair to Sardi's, just down the block on Forty-fourth Street, where he would invariably order a cup of hot chocolate and was therefore known to proprietor, waiters, and other customers as "Mr. Chocolate." Then at midnight he would place a long-distance call to St. Louis, to discuss whatever he was thinking about that evening with his father.

A far cry from Dick Whitney, or even Charley Gay!

In office, Martin and his board moved quickly. A week after his election the Exchange adopted a new constitution embodying the reforms proposed by the Conway committee and, in effect, converting it in one stroke from a private club to an essentially public institution. The next question was who would be the key man in the new setup, the independent, paid president with broad executive powers. During May various alternatives were considered by the governors—a business executive, a political figure, a prominent Stock Exchange member. Midway in the month they tended to conclude that they already had their man in young Bill Martin; they made him interim president as well as chairman. Next day, for his inaugural in the new job, the press was admitted to the Governors' Room for the first time in history. On June 30 Martin was formally elected the first paid president of the Stock Exchange at an annual salary of $48,000, and he announced that he would immediately comply with the constitutional requirements for the presidency by selling his interest in his brokerage firm and his seat on the Exchange.

About that time, Chairman Douglas of the SEC said, "The day of the crackdown on Wall Street is over. The prosperity of the Stock Exchange is not incompatible with the national welfare."

The Wall Street–Washington war was indeed over, with Washington and its liberal friends in Wall Street the winners. The reformed Stock Exchange was not perfect, as many subsequent events would amply show, but it at last had a structure appropriate to its function in a democratic society. Still—as perhaps in all triumphs of progress and virtue—something had been lost, some essence of kindliness and high-mindedness that the Old Guard, unlikely as it had often seemed, had harbored under its fierce exterior. Howland Davis, the gentle, high-minded man who had been the key figure in bringing Whitney to justice, put it this way many years later: "The Exchange before the reform *was* a private club, no question about it. But for the most part, the men who were running it—men like Warren Nash, Allen Lindley, Gayer Dominick—were decent men. They were trying to run a responsible Exchange. They were trying to run a decent club. And they were men you could sit down and talk to. Afterward, I don't know, it all got so impersonal."

The best, or at least the quintessence, of what was disappearing from Wall Street and perhaps from the country was embodied in Thomas Lamont. Sixty-seven now, he was still at the height of his career—still the brains of Morgan's, still the man Lundberg had rashly characterized as the most powerful in the Western world, although he knew as well as anyone that his power, like that of his firm, had ebbed. Yet the firm was still set apart. "Morally and intellectually Morgan's stands head and shoulders above the rest of the Street," wrote Bell of the *Times,* perhaps the most astute daily financial reporter of those years. As for Lamont, the man who had come to stand for Morgan's, he was personally not awe-inspiring; rather, he was a short, slender, gray-haired, slightly stooped, aging gentleman, charming, urbane, unfailingly polite, never brusque with anyone: very much the "serene and sturdy son" that his mother, the poor upriver parson's wife, had once prayed for on her porch in Claverack facing the blue-green Catskills. A passionate Italophile, Lamont used a lovely antique Italian refectory table as his office desk, and—curious quirk!—even in 1938 kept an autographed photograph of his old friend Mussolini hanging prominently on his office wall.

Late in April the SEC, investigating the Whitney case and eagerly sniffing for evidence of collusion in high places, called the Morgan partners to Washington to testify. In the hearing room waiting their turn, they were sad and grim rather than defiant as in 1933. And sitting with the partners, making a point of being seen sitting with them, was a most unlikely figure—a key member of the very body that had called them on the carpet, a commissioner of the SEC. He was, of course, John Wesley Hanes, whose heart and mind had been torn so long between the old gentlemanly ideal that he found incarnate in Morgan's and the liberal reform on Wall Street that his practical intelligence told him was essential. Now at last he was able to do something for the men he idolized above all others: to show them his devotion by risking being called a traitor. "I was widely criticized for sitting with them at the hearings," Hanes recalled years later. "But I was thoroughly sympathetic with the heartbreak they felt, and, damn it, I stayed right with Mr. Lamont and helped him all I could."

It came out soon enough how two of the Morgan partners, Morgan and Lamont, had learned from George Whitney before the end of 1937 something of Richard Whitney's misdeeds. That George Whitney had kept the secret was understandable to the most inexorable SEC questioner—after all, the man's brother. But what of the others? Why, with all the moral and intellectual superiority they stood for, had J. P. Morgan and Thomas Lamont not spoken up?

Morgan's testimony was brief, laconic, resigned, almost dreamy. Almost all the while the old man sat with his eyes closed as if to protect himself from the ugly facts—a betrayed and abdicated monarch like King Lear. His interrogator, the SEC's senior attorney Gerhard Gesell, had not the heart to press him much.

So it came to Lamont. He took the witness chair, and Gesell, well prepared and implacable, relentlessly drew out the details of how George Whitney had come to Lamont on the Tuesday before Thanksgiving, how George Whitney had explained his brother's dilemma in connection with the Gratuity Fund assets, and how Lamont had instantly agreed to lend George Whitney the million dollars that both men believed would bail George's brother out and cover up the defalcation. Then Gesell came to the crux—the moral implications of Lamont's action and his subsequent silence; and Lamont, in a series of replies, revealed what the SEC later called "a stubborn indifference to the public responsibility"; and he also caught, perhaps for the last time in American public life, all the style, the charm and the hardness, the warmth and the ice, that were Morgan's and the Old Guard:

> Q. Did you consider your responsibilities as a citizen toward anyone or your responsibilities as a member of a Stock Exchange firm toward anyone, or did you consider only your responsibilities toward Mr. George Whitney?

A. Well, Mr. Gesell . . . my partner described the need of his brother. He thought it was a perfectly isolated thing. He never dreamed that anything like that could happen again nor did I, and he said he was going to see that the business was liquidated. Well, that was enough for me. . . .

Q. Did you feel that you had any obligations to advise anyone connected with the government of the Exchange about the matters which Mr. George Whitney brought to your attention?

A. No, Mr. Gesell; I did not!

Q. Did you feel you had any obligation to go to anybody—to any public authorities and acquaint them with the facts?

A. No . . .

Q. What did the district attorney's office know about this thing— what did any prosecuting agency know about this thing?

A. Are you addressing a question to me?

Q. Yes.

A. They did not know anything as far as I am concerned, but would you expect me, Mr. Gesell, to say to Mr. George Whitney, "Yes, George, I will help you out to cure this default, which you believe is a perfectly isolated thing, but I must trot down to the district attorney's office and denounce your brother forthwith"? Did you expect me to say that? . . .

Q. You did not conceive that you had any obligations as a citizen to report these facts to the prosecuting officials or any obligation as a member of the Exchange to report the facts to the Stock Exchange?

A. Why, no, Mr. Gesell, I did not. I did not.

Q. Let us suppose the Mayor of New York had improperly used the relief funds, Mr. Lamont, and it came to your attention. Would you assume that the relief board had ample opportunity to find out about this and not go and tell anybody about it?

A. That is a theoretical question, Mr. Gesell. It really does not interest me, if you please. . . .

284

Later in his testimony Lamont said, "I had the utmost confidence in Richard Whitney," and Gesell was quick to pick him up:

Q. You had absolute confidence in Mr. Richard Whitney after this event [the pre-Thanksgiving conference] occurred?

A. After this event occurred. The news of what happened in early March came to me when I was abroad as the greatest shock in the world.

Q. Even though you had known on the 23rd of November, 1937, that Richard Whitney had stolen approximately a million dollars' worth of securities?

A. Mr. Gesell, I don't think I ever put it in . . . the term which you put it now. Do you see what I mean? I did not use—

Q. You thought it was something unwise or improper?

A. No, sir.

Q. You knew it was illegal and unlawful?

A. Sure; but you used the word stealing. It never occurred to me that Richard Whitney was a thief. What occurred to me was that he had gotten into a terrible jam, had made improper and unlawful use of securities; that his brother was proposing to try to make good his default. That is what occurred to me, and even then, as I say, my confidence in him was such that when the story came out, when I was abroad, it gave me the most tremendous shock in the world. It made me ill almost that all that time he could have been deceiving his brother, deceiving his partners, deceiving his wife and community. Well, it was just—it is inconceivable.

Q. Well, you must have been more or less unwilling to face the facts of November 1937, Mr. Lamont?

A. (No response.)

Q. Isn't that the answer to it: you were just unwilling to believe even after what you heard what Mr. George Whitney told you?

A. Well, I don't agree with you, Mr. Gesell. With all due respect, I have to say as I said before, that if I had been a lawyer or if I had retained a lawyer, I might possibly have adopted a somewhat different course, but I don't know that I should have, but I am

285

not a lawyer and I did not consult a lawyer and I moved as my heart dictated.

So Thomas Lamont, the greatest man in our story, to whom it never occurred that Richard Whitney was a thief; to whom the later revelations came as a terrible shock not on account of their public effect but because his partner's brother had deceived his brother, his partners, and his wife; who kept Mussolini on his wall even after the Ethiopian rape because he was an old friend; who moved, as he said, as his heart dictated.

V

At Sing Sing the prison barker called, "All men who came Thursday, Friday, Saturday, Monday, or Tuesday and Mr. Whitney please step out of their cells!" "Mr. Whitney" had a cell exactly like those assigned to other prisoners, but there was no stopping his fellow convicts, as well as his guards, from lifting their caps to him and asking for his autograph. He took no undue advantage of this deference. His code, where it called upon him to snub as brutally as possible those who showed pretensions above their proper class, conversely required graciousness to those who did not. For Sing Sing life, it was by no means a bad code. First assigned to mop-and-broom duty, Whitney performed it with dispatch and dignity, and was within two months assigned to teaching in the prison school; soon he was playing first base on the prison school baseball team, and it is recorded that in a game on June 25, 1938, between the school and another Sing Sing detachment he lined out two solid base hits in three times at bat and fielded flawlessly.

In May the once-sacred Stock Exchange Post No. 2, where Whitney had bid "205 for Steel" on Black Thursday, and which had been on display in the office lobby of Richard Whitney & Company since 1930, was put on the auction block along with his other office effects; it brought five dollars.

What remains to be said about the man who helped pull down a way of life with him? That his almost incredibly loyal brother

286

George eventually made good every penny he had borrowed or stolen. That his Distilled Liquors Corporation quietly went bankrupt not long after he did. That at Sing Sing he continued to be a "model prisoner," eventually coming to function as a kind of host to new arrivals, handing out cartons of cigarettes to them as they entered, and earning parole in the earliest month when he was eligible—August, 1941. That, his town house and his country estate having long since been sold in mortgage foreclosures, he then went to stay for a period with relatives on Cape Cod, not far from where the *Arabella* had once landed with his ancestors. That his life thereafter, details of which are no part of this chronicle—except that his wife, Gertrude Sheldon Whitney, stuck with him always—was quiet and law-abiding and even apparently productive; that a young lady at a dinner party in 1968, the year he turned eighty, was startled to hear the "twinkly old man" she sat next to introduced by his name. That with his background, education, and connections it would certainly appear that, had he wished, he could have been rich enough even for his extravagant purposes without making waves of any sort; that what happened to him instead may perhaps draw attention to something George Santayana wrote in 1931 about American life: "Despite preachers and professors of sundry finer moralities . . . we are invited to share an industrious, cordial, sporting existence, self-imposed and self-rewarding."

But in the summer of 1938 Whitney was visited at Sing Sing by his old mentor and admirer, heartbroken but staunch in his loyalty, the American Dr. Arnold, the Reverend Endicott Peabody, headmaster of Groton, who had attended both Presidential inaugurals of his other famous former charge, Franklin Roosevelt. On those occasions he had offered Roosevelt the benefit of his continuing prayers and advice, and the President, thanking him, had remarked on how much he relied for strength in meeting his terrible responsibilities on the memories of his school days. Now, in this less happy reunion with another old boy, Peabody again offered his services, asking the old boy whether there was anything he could do to help him.

"Yes," Whitney said. "I need a left-handed first baseman's mitt!"

ACKNOWLEDGMENTS

Among the many persons who gave me help of one sort or another in connection with this book, I should like to express my particular thanks to Arnold Bernhard, Henry Billings, Philip Claflin, Howland S. Davis, John Diebold, Lewis Galantière, Perry E. Hall, John W. Hanes, Eliot Janeway, Elizabeth Janeway, Henry S. Morgan, E. A. Pierce, Jeffrey Potter, and Thomas O. Waage.

Sources

CHAPTER ONE: OVERTURE: THE OUTRAGE

I

Sidney Sutherland, "The Mystery of the Wall Street Explosion," *Liberty,* April 26, 1930.

Edmund Gilligan, "The Wall Street Explosion Mystery," *The American Mercury,* September 1938.

New York Times, New York World, New York Sun, and *New York Herald,* September 1920.

II

Alexander Dana Noyes, *The War Period of American Finance, 1908–1925* (New York, 1926).

George Soule, *Prosperity Decade: From War to Depression, 1917–1929* (New York, 1947).

Robert Sobel, *The Big Board* (New York, 1965).

III–VII

Robert K. Murray, *Red Scare: A Study in National Hysteria, 1919–20* (Minneapolis, 1955).

"Wall Street's Bomb Mystery," *Literary Digest,* October 2, 1920.

See also references under Section 1.

CHAPTER TWO: TICKER TYRANNY

I

Barnie F. Winkelman, *Ten Years of Wall Street* (Philadelphia, 1932).
Matthew Josephson, *The Robber Barons* (New York, 1934).
Gustavus Myers, *History of the Great American Fortunes* (revised edition, New York, 1936).
New York Times, September 6, 1925.

II–V

They Told Barron: The Notes of the Late Clarence W. Barron, edited and arranged by Arthur Pound and Samuel Taylor Morse (New York, 1930).
New York Times, 1920; also November 24, 1928, December 1, 1928, and November 27, 1940.
New York *World,* 1920.
McClure's magazine: Automobile Yearbook 1920.
Motor magazine, 1919–20.

CHAPTER THREE: THE ALMOST ARISTOCRACY

I

Winkelman, *Ten Years of Wall Street.*
Soule, *Prosperity Decade.*
Frederick Lewis Allen, *Only Yesterday* (New York, 1931).

II

Frederick Lewis Allen, *The Great Pierpont Morgan* (New York, 1949).
Edwin P. Hoyt, Jr., *The House of Morgan* (New York, 1966).
Harold Nicolson, *Diaries and Letters, 1930–1939,* edited by Nigel Nicolson (New York, 1966).
Frederick Lewis Allen, *The Lords of Creation* (New York, 1935).
Josephson, *The Robber Barons.*
Thomas W. Lamont, *Henry P. Davison: The Record of a Useful Life* (New York, 1933).
Harold Nicolson, *Dwight Morrow* (New York, 1935).
Ferdinand Lundberg, *America's 60 Families* (New York, 1938).
Thomas W. Lamont, *My Boyhood in a Parsonage* (New York, 1946).
Current Biography, 1940, article on Thomas W. Lamont (New York, 1940).

III

Joseph Wechsberg, *The Merchant Bankers* (Boston, 1966).
Stephen Birmingham, *"Our Crowd": The Great Jewish Families of New York* (New York, 1967).
Sobel, *The Big Board.*
Allen, *The Lords of Creation.*
In the District Court of the United States for the Southern District of New York, Civil Action No. 43–757: Opinion of Harold R. Medina, C.J. (1953).
Dictionary of American Biography, article on Otto H. Kahn, Vol. XXI, Supp. 1 (New York, 1944).

IV

Birmingham, *"Our Crowd."*
Sobel, *The Big Board.*
E. Digby Baltzell, *The Protestant Establishment* (New York, 1964).
Heywood Broun and George Britt, *Christians Only* (New York, 1931).
Nicolson, *Dwight Morrow.*

V

Allen, *The Lords of Creation.*
James P. Warburg, *The Long Road Home: The Autobiography of a Maverick* (New York, 1964).

VI

Frank Parker Stockbridge, "The Problem of the Downtown Church," *Saturday Evening Post,* March 31, 1928.

CHAPTER FOUR: SO NEAR THE APES

I

Elias Canetti, *Crowds and Power* (New York, 1966).
Joseph Stagg Lawrence, *Wall Street and Washington* (Princeton, 1929).
John T. Flynn, *Security Speculation* (New York, 1934).
Soule, *Prosperity Decade.*

II

Flynn, *Security Speculation.*
Allen, *The Lords of Creation.*
Stock Exchange Practices: Report of the Committee on Banking and Currency pursuant to Senate Resolution 84, 72nd Congress, and Senate

Resolutions 56 and 97, 73rd Congress: Report No. 1455, Senate, 73rd Congress, 2nd Session, 1934.

Winkelman, *Ten Years of Wall Street.*

William Z. Ripley, *Main Street and Wall Street* (Boston, 1927).

Alexander Dana Noyes, *The Market Place* (Boston, 1938).

III–IV

Dana L. Thomas, *The Plungers and the Peacocks* (New York, 1967).

Earl Sparling, *Mystery Men of Wall Street* (New York, 1930).

Sobel, *The Big Board.*

Edwin Lefèvre, *Reminiscences of a Stock Market Operator* (New York, 1931).

Josephson, "Sell 'em Ben," *The New Yorker,* May 14–21, 1932.

Richard J. Whalen, *The Founding Father* (New York, 1964).

V

Claud Cockburn, *In Time of Trouble* (New York, 1956).

J. M. Keynes, *Essays in Persuasion* (paperbound, New York, 1963).

CHAPTER FIVE: THINGS FALL APART

I

New York Times and *Wall Street Journal,* August 1926.

II

John Moody, "The New Era in Wall Street," *Atlantic Monthly,* August 1928.

Allen, *Only Yesterday.*

Lester V. Chandler, *Benjamin Strong, Central Banker* (Washington, 1958).

Literary Digest, May 12, 1928.

III

Lawrence, *Wall Street and Washington.*

Arthur M. Schlesinger, Jr., *The Crisis of the Old Order* (Boston, 1957).

J. K. Galbraith, *The Great Crash, 1929* (Boston, 1961).

Chandler, *Benjamin Strong.*

IV–V

Allen, *Only Yesterday.*

———, *The Lords of Creation.*

Stock Exchange Practices.

Galbraith, *The Great Crash.*

VI–VII

Matthew Josephson, *Infidel in the Temple* (New York, 1967).

Sobel, *The Big Board.*

Noyes, *The Market Place.*

Allen, *Only Yesterday.*

Cockburn, *In Time of Trouble.*

Alec Rackowe, *All the Millionaires* (New York, 1967).

Graphic Stocks 1924–1935 (F. W. Stephens, distributor, New York, 1949).

New York Times, August–September–October, 1929.

CHAPTER SIX: ENTER THE WHITE KNIGHT

I

Trinity Church Parish Year Book and Registry, 1930.

II

Cockburn, *In Time of Trouble.*

Schlesinger, *The Crisis of the Old Order.*

Allen, *Only Yesterday.*

Josephson, *Infidel in the Temple.*

Edwin Lefèvre, "The Little Fellow in Wall Street," *Saturday Evening Post,* January 4, 1930.

———, "The Bigger They Are," *Saturday Evening Post,* January 11, 1930.

Hoyt, *The House of Morgan.*

Winkelman, *Ten Years of Wall Street.*

Galbraith, *The Great Crash.*

Thomas, *The Plungers and the Peacocks.*

Sparling, *Mystery Men of Wall Street.*

III

Whalen, *The Founding Father.*

Josephson, *Infidel in the Temple.*

Warburg, *The Long Road Home.*

IV

Allen, *Only Yesterday.*

Josephson, "Groton, Harvard, Wall Street," *The New Yorker,* April 2, 1932.

Richard Whitney, "The Work of the Stock Exchange in the Panic of 1929," speech to the Boston Association of Stock Exchange Firms, June 10, 1930.

V

Caroline Bird, *The Invisible Scar* (New York, 1966).
Edward Angly, *Oh Yeah!* (New York, 1931).
Broadus Mitchell, *Depression Decade, 1929–1941* (New York, 1964).
Herbert Hoover, *The Memoirs of Herbert Hoover: The Great Depression 1929–1941* (New York, 1952).

VI

Securities and Exchange Commission in the Matter of Richard Whitney, Edwin D. Morgan, Jr., F. Kingsley Rodewald, Henry D. Mygatt, Daniel G. Condon, John J. McManus, and Estate of John A. Hayes, individually and as partners doing business as Richard Whitney & Company; pursuant to Section 21 (A) of the Securities Exchange Act of 1934 (three volumes: Washington, 1938).

VII

Mitchell, *Depression Decade.*
Flynn, *Security Speculation.*
Sobel, *The Big Board.*
Hoover, *The Great Depression.*
Flynn, "Bearing Down on Short Selling," *Collier's,* April 16, 1932.
S. J. Woolf, "The Man Behind the Ticker," *World's Work,* March 31, 1932.
"Whitney's Defense of Wall Street," *Literary Digest,* April 23, 1932.
Stock Exchange Practices.

VIII

William E. Leuchtenberg, *Franklin D. Roosevelt and the New Deal, 1932–1940* (New York, 1963).
Mitchell, *Depression Decade.*
Bird, *The Invisible Scar.*
Hoover, *The Great Depression.*
Stock Exchange Practices.

CHAPTER SEVEN: GOLD STANDARD ON THE BOOZE

I–III

Raymond Moley, *After Seven Years* (New York, 1939).
Arthur M. Schlesinger, Jr., *The Coming of the New Deal* (Boston, 1959).

Hoover, *The Great Depression.*
Herbert Feis, *1933: Characters in Crisis* (Boston, 1966).
James P. Warburg, *The Money Muddle* (New York, 1934).
————, *The Long Road Home.*
Leuchtenberg, *Franklin D. Roosevelt and the New Deal.*
Mitchell, *Depression Decade.*

IV

Newsweek, November 25, 1933.
Literary Digest, December 9, 1933.
Warburg, *The Money Muddle.*
————, *The Long Road Home.*
Charles O. Hardy, *The Warren-Pearson Price Theory* (Washington, 1935).
G. F. Warren and Frank A. Pearson, *Prices* (New York, 1933).
Josephson, *The Robber Barons.*
John M. Blum, *From the Diaries of Henry Morgenthau, Jr.* (Boston, 1959).
New York Times, May 25–26, 1938.

V–VII

Schlesinger, *The Coming of the New Deal.*
Feis, *1933: Characters in Crisis.*
Hoover, *The Great Depression.*
Warburg, *The Money Muddle.*
Leuchtenberg, *Franklin D. Roosevelt and the New Deal.*
Noyes, *The Market Place.*
Papers of George Harrison, the Columbia University Library, New York.

CHAPTER EIGHT: ORDEAL IN WASHINGTON

I

New York Times, June 2–3, 1933, and June 1, 1963.

II

Ferdinand Pecora, *Wall Street Under Oath* (New York, 1939).
Stock Exchange Practices.
Hoyt, *The House of Morgan.*
George Harrison papers, March 28, 1933.
T. L. Stokes, *Chip off My Shoulder* (Princeton, 1940).
Leuchtenberg, *Franklin D. Roosevelt and the New Deal.*

III–IV

Flynn, *Security Speculation.*
Pecora, *Wall Street Under Oath.*
Stock Exchange Practices.

V–VI

Joseph Alsop and Robert Kintner, "The Battle of the Market Place," *Saturday Evening Post,* June 11 and June 25, 1938.
Stock Exchange Practices.
Schlesinger, *The Coming of the New Deal.*
"Wall Street's Raid on the New Deal," *Today,* April 21, 1934.
John T. Flynn, "The Marines Land on Wall Street," *Harper's,* July 1934.
Josephson, *Infidel in the Temple.*

VII

S.E.C. in the Matter of Richard Whitney, esp. Vol. I, pp. 10, 60–63, 72–76.
Time, March 21, 1938.

CHAPTER NINE: THE WHITE KNIGHT UNHORSED

I

Hoyt, *The House of Morgan.*
Robert Bendiner, *Just Around the Corner* (New York, 1967).
John Brooks, *The Seven Fat Years* (New York, 1958).
New York Times, May 19, 1936.

II

Schlesinger, *The Coming of the New Deal.*
New York Times, October 1934 and September 25, 1953.
Whalen, *The Founding Father.*

III

Frederick Rudolph, "The American Liberty League, 1934–40," *American Historical Review,* October 1950.
George Wolfskill, *The Revolt of the Conservative* (Boston, 1962).
Marquis W. Childs, "They Hate Roosevelt," *Harper's,* May 1936.
David C. Coyle, *Ordeal of the Presidency* (Washington, 1960).
Baltzell, *The Protestant Establishment.*
Lundberg, *America's 60 Families.*
James P. Warburg, *Hell Bent for Election* (New York, 1935).
———, *The Money Muddle.*
———, *The Long Road Home.*

IV–V

Alsop and Kintner, "The Battle of the Market Place."
Rudolph L. Weissman, *The New Wall Street* (New York, 1939).
New York Times, 1935.

CHAPTER TEN: RISING ACTION

S.E.C. in the Matter of Richard Whitney.
Alsop and Kintner, "The Battle of the Market Place."

CHAPTER ELEVEN: CATASTROPHE

S.E.C. in the Matter of Richard Whitney.

CHAPTER TWELVE: DENOUEMENT

I–II

S.E.C. in the Matter of Richard Whitney.
New York *Daily News*, March 10 and 12, 1938.
Time, March 21, 1938.
New York Times, 1938.

III

Thomas, *The Plungers and the Peacocks*.
Weissman, *The New Wall Street*.
New York Times, August 3, 1937, November 29–30 and December 6, 1940.

IV

Elliott V. Bell, "The Decline of the Money Barons" (in *We Saw It Happen*, edited by Hanson W. Baldwin and Shepard Stone, New York, 1938).
S.E.C. in the Matter of Richard Whitney.

V

Newsweek, May 16, 1938.
George Santayana, *The Genteel Tradition at Bay* (New York, 1931).

Index